Critical acclaim for
JOHN L. SMITH

"John Smith lies when he says this book is about Vegas. This wonderful collection of his columns are essays of the universal populace, a series of glances at the people around us, the ones we see and don't see, the famous and the unknown, who compose our cities. Smith gets into their hearts and into their souls. He writes about stunt nun Jenny Malcolm, about the Great G.L. Vitto's voice of midnight, about ex-boxer Gary Bates whose gift of blood saves lives, about the violent death of mobster Herb Blitzstein, and about the ultimate godfather Frank Sinatra, who, for a moment, finds peace in anonymity. The book is a glorious mix of winners and losers and of gentle introspections. When we aren't watching Redd Foxx become a bitter old man, we're hearing about a boy, some ants, and a bike at Christmas, and about an old friend on the streets struggling to regain the part of him that was once real. You don't have to be from Vegas to love John Smith's writing. These are essays for all seasons. I love every one of them."

> —Al Martinez, columnist for the *Los Angeles Times* and author of *The Last City Room*, a 1999 release by St. Martin's Press

"Smith gives you a fascinating look behind the hype, neon, and glitz of Vegas to the real heart of this crazy city and its colorful, wacky people."

> —Dennis McCarthy, columnist for the *Los Angeles Daily News*

"An old pro fighter by the name of Eddie Simms died in Las Vegas last October. John L. Smith, columnist for the *Review-Journal*, wrote an obituary...Readers of Smith's column could see the old man reminiscing of the time he took a punch from Joe Louis. Smith let us smell the smoky arenas of the 1930s. We could hear Simms playing his accordion for old friends. Here was a writer at work."

> —James J. Kilpatrick, "The Writer's Art"

On the Boulevard

On the Boulevard

The Best of John L. Smith

Huntington Press Publishing
Las Vegas, Nevada

On the Boulevard—The Best of John L. Smith

Published by
    Huntington Press
    3687 South Procyon Avenue
    Las Vegas, Nevada 89103
    phone: (702) 252-0655
    email: books@huntingtonpress.com

Copyright © 1999, Las Vegas Review-Journal

ISBN 0-929712-69-2

Cover Photos: Jason Cox, Jim Laurie
Cover Design: Jason Cox
Interior Design/Production: Bethany Coffey

For my sweet sisters, Cathy, Christy, Margaret, and Marie.
And, as ever, for my best girls, Tricia and Amelia.

Acknowledgments

No newspaper writer is successful without plenty of competent editing. Fortunately, at the *Las Vegas Review-Journal* I am surrounded by real professionals who spruce up my prose, catch deadline errors, design pages, repair the computers, and generally ensure that the newspaper comes out every morning. To them I owe many thanks. They include Dan Behringer, Darin Bunch, Annette Caramia, Glenn Cook, Tom Dye, Mary Greeley, Greg Haas, Don Ham, Bruce Huff, Rose Hutchinson, Mary Hynes, Karl Kistner, David Lanson, Joe Lowell, Debra McGuire, Steve Moore, Dennis Rudner, Greg Ryan, Joan Tammariello, Roy Vanett, Lindsey Whitlock, Ched Whitney, Eileen Woods, Mike Wrzesinski, and Charles Zobell. Photographers Jim Laurie and Jeff Scheid provided invaluable assistance on this book's cover. Thanks always to editor in chief Tom Mitchell and publisher Sherman Frederick for their encouragement.

At Huntington Press, I am grateful to Deke Castleman, Bethany Coffey, Anthony Curtis, and Lynne Loomis for their attention to this manuscript. The rest of the gang endures my inquiries and idiosyncrasies without complaint. Thanks to Michele Bardsley, Len Cipkins, Jason Cox, Jodi Dewey, Jacqueline Joniec, Jim Karl, and Deanna O'Connell.

Finally, I am thankful for a loving and supportive family. To my wife, Patricia, and daughter, Amelia, who endure my long hours and many moods. Together, we will dance down the boulevard of time.

Contents

Boomtown Blues

Beefs With Bureaucrats

Sporting Life

Crime and Punishment

You Are My Sunshine

Introduction

The back bar at Binion's Horseshoe was crowded the night I fell in love with column writing. I drank a 50-cent beer and listened to the hustlers work the tourists and the crapshooters lament busted dice rolls when an old man took the stool next to me. He unfolded a copy of the street edition of the newspaper and, to my delight, turned right to my story.

In the early 1980s, I ran the sports department of the *Las Vegas Sun* during the final years of publisher Hank Greenspun's life. As a young sports editor, I supervised a staff of nine, wrote five columns a week, covered the minor-league baseball team, and nursed a mean little ulcer. By the time my shift ended, I invariably found myself at one of several late-night watering holes in a city with more bars than stoplights. One night at Frankie's Bar, the next night the Philly Pub, then over to the Tap House, and downtown to Binion's. Sitting next to the old man, I stole glances over his shoulder and watched him as he read my words.

Suddenly, the old man laughed. That was a relief, since I'd written what I believed to be a humor column. A few moments later, he laughed again, and I was hooked. It was then I understood the potential of deadline writing, the incredible rush of knowing that, if I did my job right, some stranger could be found laughing to himself in a smoky bar early the next morning. I saw first-hand that the words really did mean something to someone; they really could entertain, enlighten, and inform. To this day I have no recollection of the subject matter of that story, but I can still hear the old man's laughter above the din of boozy voices.

"Like that column?" I asked, fit to burst with pride of authorship.

"Funny stuff," the old man mumbled.

"I wrote it," I stammered.

"Yeah right, kid," the old man said. "Whatever you say."

After a few years I gravitated from the sports department of the *Sun* to the news pages of the *Las Vegas Review-Journal*, where in 1986 I began writing a daily column. Since then, I've generated more than 2,000 columns on topics ranging from ballet to organized crime. Along the way, I've met the famous, the infamous, and the near-anonymous. All things considered, I prefer the dinosaur mobsters to the corporate casino bosses, the Thunderbird drinkers to the Dom Perignon sippers, the blackjack dealers to the puffed-up politicians. I'll take the angels in the alley over the thieves in the temple any day.

Newspaper stories aren't meant to live. Purple prose and breathless leads fade quickly, just as today's celebrity is tomorrow's table waiter. If the tales of daily events were meant to endure, you couldn't buy the whole package for 50 cents— including coupons, comics, baseball scores, and, of course, columns. I am reminded of that fact every time I see a page of newsprint blowing down the street.

But once in a while a column simply refuses to lie down and yellow. Against the odds, the piece of deadline writing manages to escape and accomplish something that sets it apart from the countless other stories that see print. Somehow, it's remembered by readers.

As a newspaperman, I can think of no greater compliment than to have some of my daily journalism reprinted. As I think of it, there can be no greater conceit than to presume readers will want to pay good money to retrace the steps of a trip they've already taken. I've always been satisfied enough to think that my work is syndicated on bar walls and refrigerator doors throughout Nevada.

But here it is, more than 100 pieces culled from 1990 to 1998. I have attempted to do what all Las Vegas writers do—capture the odd but indefatigable spirit of one of the world's toughest and most intriguing cities. If my stories fall short, I know I'm not alone, for Las Vegas buries its history and, like a showgirl discussing her age, rarely reveals the truth.

While reviewing the selections for this collection, it occurred to me that many of the most interesting Las Vegans I've known have died in recent years. From fight trainer Johnny Tocco and trumpeter Chico Alvarez to illegal bookmakers Marty Kane and

Joey Boston, Las Vegas has been home to some of America's most colorful characters. I am proud to say their voices echo throughout these pages. It is to those characters, and to you readers, that I dedicate this book.

I hope you laugh in all the right places.

.

Everyday
People

'Flying Nun' stunt double lands on her feet in Las Vegas

April 10, 1994

Visitors may think they know what makes Las Vegas a place apart, but it's not the Dali-on-steroids architecture or the endless sea of $2 steaks.

It's the people.

Every color and kind, thrown together like pigments in a Jackson Pollack painting, all seeking a slice of secular salvation in America's last great boomtown. They save this city's neon soul.

Over the years I have met gangsters and governors, chiselers and champions in this maddening metropolis in the making.

If memory serves, Jenny Malcomb is my first stunt nun.

Yes, stunt nun.

What a town.

Malcomb's work history reads like a script from "Saturday Night Live" when it was funny or "Monty Python's Flying Circus" any time: She has been a stunt sister to the stars, a Disneyland dancer, a psychedelic babe in a go-go cage, a backup singer to Steely Dan, a leading member of an almost successful pop ensemble.

In short, a bit player in a world that only rewards big stars.

Today Malcomb sells wholesale goods at Valley Foods, but her story is no teary lament of a fame that faded. Fact is, Malcomb embodies the best of Las Vegas. But I'm getting ahead of myself.

In the late 1960s, Malcomb was an azure-eyed California girl with blonde pigtails and little interest in the hustle of Hollywood. She loved singing and dancing and only auditioned for the movie *Harlow* as a favor to a girlfriend.

Fate was kind. She won a place in the crowd, joined the union, and eventually wound up on the set of "The Flying Nun."

Sally Field was the star, but one bit part remained.

Stunt nun.

Malcomb had little experience but even less fear. She faked it.

"I said, 'Do I do aerial work? Of course I do aerial work,' " she says, laughing. "He said, 'Show up Monday morning.' I showed up. They fit me into a leather harness. I signed a six-year contract and never looked back."

Or down, for that matter.

Malcomb sailed over land and sea as the stunt double for Field. The situation comedy featured Field as Sister Bertrille, who spent her days doing the Lord's work with just enough time left over to fly her way into trouble.

Trouble was Malcomb's business. With the harness in place, she was outfitted in a nun's habit and was suspended up to 100 feet in the air by hair-thin piano wire. Rigged to a construction crane, she was cast over the bay like a large fishing lure. It was enough to make a California girl recite the rosary, but Malcomb wasn't scared.

"I guess I was too young to realize that what I was doing was dangerous," she says. "I was a carefree kid. What did I know? Off I went, flying over Marina Del Rey."

Sister Bertrille was a frequent flier. After Field was finished with the close-ups, Malcomb winged into action wearing her habit and cornet. In one scene, she was perched on the pinnacle of a sailboat mast 60 feet up. She soared over a church steeple, and swooped inches from the breaking waves.

The fact that she came away without breaking bones is just short of a miracle.

It was not her only role. She wore considerably less clothing in episodes of "Mannix," "Mission Impossible," and "Run for Your Life." She was a dancer, remember, and those male-dominated shows rarely made it through a week without setting a scene in a funky nightclub featuring go-go girls behind bars.

"I was in a lot of cages," she says.

She won other parts and for a while had steady work. When the work went away, she reached a crossroads. Malcomb had her dreams, but she also had two children, no husband, and no income.

Sound familiar?

It's the neon story.

A dozen years ago fate brought her to Las Vegas, where go-go jobs are plentiful, but the nuns perform their own stunts. She sang awhile with *Legends in Concert* at the Imperial Palace, but gravitated toward steady work. After flying for a living, she landed on her feet, remarried, and took a job selling food to restaurants and resorts.

It's not as glamorous as Hollywood, but then stunt-nun jobs don't come along all the time.

As I said, Jenny Malcomb embodies what is right about Las Vegas. It's a second-chance town in a long-shot world.

Despite its reputation, this is a place to call home for go-go girls and sisters of every habit. ◆

Wild days fade, but streaking pinup girl remains a bombshell

July 16, 1995

Liz Renay's rose garden is mature and dotted with red, yellow, and pink blooms. Red tiles lead to her front door.

In the driveway, a dark red Karman Ghia has seen better days, but still could turn heads in traffic. Its license-plate frame reads, "Lucky Liz of Las Vegas."

The owner of the house is a big blonde who gushes as she greets you at the door, then ushers you into the dining room. Her lips are redder than any rose in the garden. Her lavender eye shadow matches her satin blouse and casual ensemble.

She painted the self-portrait that hangs in the living room. It's a nude, as are bright oil paintings in the house, but on this day Liz Renay has her clothes on.

There was a time when that fact alone would have made headlines. Lord knows she made plenty of news by removing her clothes.

This, ladies and gentlemen, is the face and figure that launched a thousand fantasies for divisions of soldiers, scores of movie actors, and myriad mob lieutenants from New York to Hollywood. Time was, Liz Renay walked the street accompanied by an orchestra of wolf whistles. She was a voluptuous vixen who resembled Marilyn Monroe—only, well, more so. Lucky Liz could stop traffic, clocks, and hearts.

The flesh being fickle and fated, the life of a pinup girl is fleeting. Party favors and pretty faces fade. In a life packed with experiences that line the walls of her home, and thus far have filled five books, including a national bestseller, Liz Renay transcends the stereotypes.

As a fashion model, she posed and preened for the biggest names in New York. As a 52nd Street stripper, she became acquainted with the underworld while in her underwear.

The Palomino Club in North Las Vegas was one of her favorite venues. She became known for her spangles and beads and occasional bullwhips.

"I met a husband at the Palomino Club," she says, laughing lightly. She had seven husbands altogether. Most of her relationships faded faster than the bouquets she received after her nightly bump-and-grind routine.

"It was very naughty, but I had a tremendous act."

You bet, Ms. Renay.

As an actress with more than 50 movie and television credits, she was known more for her cleavage than her character development. With titles such as *Refinements in Love, Date with Death, The Thrill-Killers,* and *Spies-a-Go-Go,* her movies were far more popular at the Friday-night drive-in than on Academy Awards night. Those wishing to see her in action might catch her in a leading role in John Waters' cult feature *Desperate Living.*

She is quick to mention that she never did pornography. Here's how popular she once was: In the few X-rated flicks she did appear in, she was allowed to keep her clothes on.

Not that she was shy. She once attracted 5,000 frothing fanatics by streaking at high noon at Hollywood and Vine.

"It was like the Santa Claus Lane parade," she says, acknowledging that she neglected to don a red suit and black boots.

The nude sprint generated national headlines and didn't hurt her career.

Neither did the bestseller, *My Face for the World to See* or her latest literary offering, *My First 2,000 Men.*

That last title is just a figure of speech, by the way. Besides, ladies don't keep count. She says, "I was in my heyday in World War II. I was having a ball, going out with every branch of the service."

She also carried on with screen stars Burt Lancaster and Glenn Ford and mob characters Tony "Cappy" Coppola and Mickey Cohen.

Her relationship with Cohen earned her a stack of gun-moll notoriety and a three-year stretch at Terminal Island for perjury.

Alas, in her life, Liz Renay has shown an aptitude for many things, but not for lying.

"There was no way I was going to say anything bad about Mickey," she says. "Since I wasn't telling the truth, I ended up telling some lies. I thought Mickey had a great deal of charm."

That and the fact that she would have been murdered for ratting on the Los Angeles mobster.

At 69 years old, the lady of the house no longer removes her clothes professionally. She busies herself with songwriting, portrait painting, and writing.

In an age in America when sex sells everything, but somehow isn't very sexy, Liz Renay remains a bona fide bombshell. ◆

Real magic of Las Vegas is making money disappear

September 17, 1995

Looy Simonoff rolls two pieces of a Carrow's napkin into paper balls the size of walnuts, then proceeds to make one vanish before your very eyes.

There it is, the essence of Las Vegas captured in a Maryland Parkway coffee shop. It is the magic of the city, illustrated by a prestidigitating mathematician.

With his deep voice, white beard, floppy hat, and cane, Simonoff strikes you as a cross between a desert prospector and a journeyman wizard. In a way, he is both.

The act of misdirection, the numerical sleight of hand that confuses what is known with what may be believed, is at the heart of what makes Las Vegas a special place. That's the real Las Vegas, the genuine gambling town, not the metropolis that pretends to be a theme park.

This city was built on the dark magic of chance and the incredible ability of the human brain to fool itself into finding a pattern where none exists.

How many of you have strained to remember a long series of dice rolls or sweated while attempting to will the appearance of a fifth spade to complete a royal flush?

Simonoff understands the feeling. He knows it defies logic and has no basis in reality, but there it is.

Despite 27 years as a mathematics professor at UNLV, and the vast majority of his 67 years on the planet spent learning the intricacies of magic tricks, Simonoff still catches himself wishing for the right cards and numbers to appear at the precise moment.

"I know it's fallacious, but I still get the superstitious feeling," he says. "It's the feeling that the laws of nature are suddenly suspended. It's the same feeling that magic gives."

Before lunch arrives, Simonoff removes a deck of cards from a pocket. He asks you to shuffle and pick a card without disclosing its identity, then return it to the stack. (You picked the eight of hearts.)

"In magic, you can fool anybody who is sufficiently intelligent," Simonoff says, smiling as he sizes up the audience of one. He reshuffles, manipulates the deck, and continues his patter. "In magic, you prove things that are false."

In time, the eight of hearts finds its way to the top of the deck. Baffled by the trick, you are forced to take Simonoff's remark as a compliment.

In Las Vegas, the real trick comes in ensuring that the falseness remains fun. That is proving increasingly difficult as casinos across the nation find themselves riddled by scandal and Congress warms up to the ideas of regulation and taxation.

That's the irony at work: The Vegasization of America might turn out to be bad for Las Vegas, just as overexposure cheapens a trick and embarrasses the magician.

Although traditional sleight-of-hand tricks and up-close magic are not ideally suited for big showrooms, Simonoff agrees that the art of playful deception is an essential part of the Las Vegas mystique. It is to be respected and protected.

To that end, Simonoff teaches a weekly magic course through the continuing education program at UNLV. "You'll learn enough to make people think you're good," he says of the class. "And in magic, that may be the same as being good."

After lunch, there is time for one more trick.

By now, Simonoff's audience has grown to three tables of gawking diners.

Another magical card moves through the deck and somehow finds its way back to the right place in the pile. The baffled eaters smile.

Obviously, they are very intelligent, too.

Even the most secular societies search for feats that defy logic and natural law. Magic dazzles us that way.

At its best, so does Las Vegas.

"The magician Randy likes to say, 'I'll now show you a miracle of a semi-religious nature,'" Simonoff says, laughing. "People resent having magic explained to them. They don't want to know how it happens. They want to suspend their belief."

He is talking about sleight of hand, but as he speaks, you are picturing a whole mysterious city. ◆

Lyricist discovers old popularity through hit stage show

April 30, 1995

A little bit south of North Las Vegas, Sunny Skylar greets you at the door of his immaculate mobile home.

Here in the last great last-chance town in the country, he is snappily dressed in a gray sweater and orange sports shirt, and possesses more energy than a big band's brass section. Here is a man with a song in his heart—hundreds of songs, in fact.

Here is a man who was made for Las Vegas.

In a moment, you can't help moving in Sunny Skylar time. That's a step slow for the jitterbug, perhaps, but too quick for a fox trot. You hustle to keep up the way he hustled for years before forcing his way into the New York record industry.

Born Selig Shaftel a world ago on the edge of Broadway's Tin Pan Alley, the 81-year-old Sunny is a lyricist whose songs have sold millions of records. He has a wall full of memories— his words have been sung by stars ranging from Frank Sinatra to the Ray Charles Singers—but more news clips than greenbacks.

So why is Sunny Skylar smiling?

He's back in the swing after his 1946 hit "Gotta Be This Or That" was chosen as part of the repertoire of *Forever Plaid*, a pre-rock 'n' roll '50s tribute that has been a hit from Broadway to Las Vegas Boulevard. The show now plays at the Flamingo Hilton.

The song sold more than 600,000 records when it was recorded by Benny Goodman, but it didn't rain pennies from heaven on Sunny. He made only a few cents per platter.

After years of receiving nothing but the usual bills in his mailbox, Sunny is receiving royalty checks again. It's $60 here, $150 there: Receiving the checks is like having an old friend suddenly remember, after more than 40 years, that he owes you a few bucks. Thanks to *Forever Plaid*, in a sense Sunny has been rediscovered.

"It's unbelievable, really," he says during the tour of his

personal wall of fame. "The money is good, and it's great to have it played again. The old people love the show. You should have seen that room."

It took some time, but then Skylar is used to waiting. He worked for years sprucing up other writers' rhymes as a Tin Pan Alley song doctor before landing his first hit in 1939 with "Just a Little Bit South of North Carolina." Guy Lombardo made it a smash.

But it was a little farther south that Sunny became a sensation when he wrote the English lyrics to "Amor, Amor, Amor." Latin audiences loved it, loved it, loved it in 1941, and it sold more than 2 million copies for an assortment of artists. Soon enough, Skylar was living in a spiffy apartment at 100 Central Park South.

He never tried to give his lyrics deep meaning, but then again no one ever accused the popular listening public of craving heavy poetry. He excelled in the Broken Romance school of writing and obtained an advanced degree in Destination Songs. It wasn't Mozart, but it was easier to sing.

By 1944, the *New York Times* recognized Skylar as one of the pillars of Tin Pan Alley, which boasted more than 1,500 songwriters even during the war. Each year the writers pitched 50,000 songs; about 2,000 were picked up. Skylar was mentioned in the same breath with Irving Berlin, Cole Porter, George M. Cohan, and Richard Rogers. It was world-famous company, but then Sunny was a hot commodity. Almost everything he wrote became a hit performed by a major entertainer.

"Besame Mucho," "It's All Over Now," "Atlanta, G.A.," and "It Must Be Jelly Cause Jam Don't Shake Like That" made him a popular fixture in recording studios and nightclubs.

Although "Gotta Be This Or That" makes him smile, Sunny gets blue when he thinks of "Amor." It's not his wife, Jackie; she's the greatest.

It's the song, which Sunny says was filched, albeit legally, by Julio Iglesias for a hit in the mid-1980s. Sunny didn't see a peso from what remains one of the most popular songs ever recorded south of the border.

"'Amor,' that was my baby for fifty years," he says. "If he was any kind of gentleman, he would have said, 'I'm sorry,' and made it right."

When that didn't happen, Sunny Skylar figured he had seen his last royalty check and had met the last entertainer who was hungry to perform one of his tunes. There was a time the top crooners in the country were eager to listen to his latest ditty.

Skylar's last hit came in 1960 with "Love Me With All Your Heart." More than three decades passed, and he moved to Las Vegas more than a decade ago.

Then along came *Forever Plaid* and his old friend, "Gotta Be This Or That."

In the last great last-chance town, anything is possible.

Even a sunny ending for a man named Sunny Skylar. ◆

Sinatra wished he was a stranger in the night 40 years ago

May 27, 1998

It was a few days after Christmas in 1958, and Sonny King couldn't get over the cold snap that had swept through Las Vegas. But the weather was not half as chilly as the reception he was receiving from the Reverend John Ryan.

The subject was the christening of King's daughter, Antoinette, who had been born on Christmas day. King and his wife, Nancy, had chosen the baby's godparents and were anxious to welcome the child officially into the Catholic Church. Sonny and his wife were members of St. Anne's, and they naturally approached Father Ryan with the news that the godmother would be Dorothy Entratter, wife of Strip casino man Jack Entratter. And the godfather?

King's pal, Francis Albert Sinatra.

When the words were spoken, the usually affable Father Ryan lost his smile. He shook his head. Sinatra wouldn't do at all.

"Mr. Sinatra's considered an undesirable in the eyes of the Church," Father Ryan said.

"Undesirable?" King asked, astonished. "But he's my friend, father. If he's undesirable, what does that make me?"

"Mr. King, I think you're a fine fellow, but you're also considered an undesirable," the priest said.

With that, Sonny and Nancy King and Dorothy Entratter and Frank Sinatra set out to find a priest who would christen little Antoinette. Sinatra might have been too notorious for the Church, but on his worst day he was good enough for Sonny King.

Sonny was singing and managing at the Copacabana in New York in 1948 when he first met Sinatra. They were introduced at Lindy's and became friends over a cup of coffee. It was that simple. Their friendship lasted 50 years and was interrupted by Sinatra's death last week. Sonny figures his friend, Frank, is scouting new showrooms for them to work, but Sinatra's passing reminded King of Antoinette's christening—and the controversy the Chairman of the Board was capable of generating.

When Nancy King went into labor, Sinatra was at Sonny's side all night.

"I stayed up with you," Sinatra said after the baby was born. "I think I deserve to be the godfather."

Mention godfather in the same sentence as Sinatra and most people think of something other than the blue-eyed saloon singer who was struck silent by the beauty of a newborn baby. But King's friend Frank was full of surprises.

Father Ryan was out of the question, but surely another priest in Las Vegas would do the job. Try as King might, the answer was consistent. He even tried a nondenominational church, but that failed, too.

"I'd already been to three churches and all around town," King recalls. "By the third church I didn't care whether it was Catholic or what, I just wanted my daughter to be christened. I said, 'Let's ride around,' and saw Frank was getting madder and madder. If anything, Frank's eyes got bluer the madder he got."

Driving around Las Vegas on the coldest day of the year, the travelers found themselves downtown. King pulled up outside St. Bridget's Catholic Church. Inside, they were met by a young priest, who knew plenty about christening but, thankfully, not a damn thing about popular music.

The priest started the paperwork. Then came the moment of truth: The godmother was Jewish; the godfather was a notorious ladies man.

As he filled out the certificate, the priest asked, "What is the godfather's name?"

King responded, "Francis Albert Sinatra."

Sinatra quipped, "Hey, I know my own name."

The priest asked, "How do you spell Francis, with an 'I-S' or an 'E-S'?"

Sinatra responded, "I-S. E-S is feminine."

The priest didn't know Frank Sinatra from Frankenstein, and the christening went off without a hitch. On the way out, Sinatra, anonymous for the first time in many years, smiled and tipped the priest $1,000.

Over the years, Las Vegas warmed up considerably to Sinatra. Today, he's the subject of the sort of remembrance and adulation usually reserved for the greatest presidents. He had far more impact on the lives of Americans than all but a few leaders of the free world.

From the pulpit of the local church to center stage at the MGM Grand, Southern Nevada celebrates Sinatra's incredible life this week. The tribute features parties and performances, Barbara Sinatra's memorabilia exhibit, and the Frank Sinatra Celebrity Golf Classic golf tournament.

Sonny King is warmed by his own memories of Sinatra, a godfather for all seasons. ◆

Chico Alvarez plays the sweetest music life has to offer

December 16, 1990

If you are fortunate, truly blessed, over the years you will meet a few people who transcend the dreary din of everyday existence.

They are not so much human beings as rare birds, colorful and sweet-voiced and all too fleeting.

Trumpet player Chico Alvarez is one of those rare birds.

After a music career spanning five decades, Alvarez is happiest when playing his horn in the Friday night shadows at Pogo's Tavern. Pogo's is a small and delightful dive on Decatur and has featured jazz weekly for two decades, nearly half that time with Alvarez as its leader.

Sometimes the joint jumps with revelers from wall to wall. Other times, the band members outnumber the barflies. At all times, it is unpretentious but professional.

Chico blows his horn the way loose-limbed Jackie Robinson ran the base paths. He is at once effortless and athletic, improvisational and inspired.

Until the recent spread of abdominal cancer nearly killed him, he led the band with an energy that masked his 70 years. Despite undergoing painful chemotherapy, the gentle Alvarez recently took time to reflect on his life and music.

Throughout the 1940s, he was a standout player with the Stan Kenton big band. Soon after Kenton's jumping original sound was broadcast on the radio, Alvarez had his own international fan club and received sacks of mail. Not bad for a California boy who grew up playing the violin and hadn't considered the trumpet until age 16.

"I guess I just had the soul for it, the feel for it," he said.

The days when young jazz fans asked for his autograph at the stage door of New York's Paramount Theatre are decades in the past, but he still laughs at the memory.

"I received dozens of letters from Latin American countries because of my name," Alvarez said, smiling and not looking terribly Latin. "Our band was offbeat. It didn't swing worth a damn, but it had something the people liked. And all of a sudden, at 21, I'm in New York like a real hick from the country."

The Kenton years were prosperous, and Alvarez performed on 30 albums. But the costly big bands were musical dinosaurs, and by the mid-1950s Alvarez found himself headed toward Las Vegas.

He is one of the players who helped make the Strip music scene famous in the 1950s and '60s, the city's Golden Age. With the Rat Pack sharing headlines with slick-dressing Chicago mobsters, those years were heavenly for a good player. An adequate musician could earn a living, and a great player was in constant demand. While top musicians in Chicago and New York struggled to find steady work, the lounges and showrooms of Las Vegas clamored for competent help.

Those glory days began to fade about the time Elvis started shaking his hips on the Strip. Changes in technology, musical taste, and business philosophy have turned most of the once-marginal lounges into keno parlors and barge-long buffets.

After retiring as an officer from the musicians union, Alvarez quickly grew bored with a life without jazz. In time, he found his way to Pogo's.

Today, he refuses to dwell on his illness. Though painful, it is only a small part of a much larger life.

"I am one of the luckiest men who ever lived. I've got so many lovely friends," Alvarez said. "I've been so healthy all my life until this thing hit me. I really haven't suffered until two months ago."

Since then, he has lost more than 30 pounds to the cancer and his hair to chemotherapy. While the cancer was steadily killing him, the treatment nearly did the trick quickly.

Of late, he has rallied. Though a physical shadow of himself, enough vitality has returned to give him not only hope but energy to pick up his trumpet.

"I'd love to have some strength," he said a few weeks ago. "I'd love to be at Pogo's playing my horn."

Last week, with Pogo's packed, the band played on, led by

one deliciously familiar sound.

Wearing a floppy hat to keep his bald head warm, leaning back and smiling, Alvarez returned to the small stage. He had enough energy for a few songs, and he could think of no better place to spend it.

"I'm not frightened, really. I've had a real good life," he had said. "I thank God for my years at Pogo's. It's been heaven for a guy like me."

When Chico Alvarez plays, it's heaven for the rest of us, too. ◆

Elvis may be dead, but impersonator keeps his spirit alive

August 17, 1997

His name is Charles David, but tonight he is the King of Las Vegas Boulevard.

It's a tough crowd. The only chicks swooning around here have had too much to drink. The King sings "Love Me Tender," but there isn't much affection in the eyes of the intoxicated tourists and swing-shift street people who inhabit the Holy Cow! Brewery at Sahara and the Strip on Friday night.

The boozy frat boys are more interested in collecting outcall entertainment fliers than in listening to the rock 'n' roll preaching of a disciple of Sin City saint, Elvis Aaron Presley.

A CAT bus pulls up to its stop, drowning out the music coming from the King's portable amplifier. The bus exhales exhaust and passengers, then resumes its run. A portly streetwalker, strutting south and balancing on four-inch clogs, hesitates long enough to listen to the one about the Heartbreak Hotel before going about her business.

In a moment, the King's hip swivels and picks up the tempo. He's caught in a trap and can't walk out. Because he loves you too much, baby. In his crimson jump suit and jet-black hair, from across the street he could be the King, or at least kin.

The real King, of course, died 20 years ago Saturday. We are left with images and street-corner Elvi paying tribute to the Man from Tupelo, Mississippi. Men like Charles David.

Now 37, he wasn't old enough to vote when Elvis died. David was born in Gary, Indiana, and raised with relatives who adored the real King. He got attention by imitating Elvis and never got over it.

"When I heard him sing, I liked it right from the get-go," he says. "I started doing Elvis just right after my tenth birthday. I was a little Elvis."

That was more than 26 years ago. He does approximately 300 performances per year, of late at the Holy Cow! and the Las Vegas Club. That's a lot of "Jailhouse Rock" and "Blue Suede Shoes" for even the most devout believer. But not for Charles David.

"It's really a true passion," he says. "Elvis, in a respect, gave me a life when I really didn't have one. Elvis was a very prominent figure, a very loving figure, something I really adored."

And so it just happened. He dyed his hair, made his own outfits, and worked on his vocal stylings. Today, he augments his income by making costumes for other Elvis impersonators. In that regard, he's the King's tailor.

Now, about that moniker. David is quick to point out that Elvis was sensitive about being called the King.

"We know him today as the King, but he had a strong belief, and I've got to give respect to that," David says. "He was not the King. He was an entertainer. He used to say, 'There's only one King and that's Jesus Christ.' Those were Elvis' very own words.

"We are all the King's men. However, none of us should ever forget that, musically, there is only one King, and that's Elvis."

Charles David doesn't feel even a little strange dressing up night after night like a dead rock singer. Despite the all-pervading presence of the Big E in his life, he swears he hasn't lost his sense of reality.

"I'm no different at home than I am on stage," he says. "I

don't have a problem. Elvis was Elvis and I'm Charles. I'm always Charles David even when I'm on stage. Out in public, sometimes people look at me and see what they want to see. They don't see what really is."

Could it be the hair, sideburns, clothes, and drawl?

Maybe.

But, frankly, I like the Elvis impersonator phenomenon, and not because I was a huge fan of the man who made the words "You ain't nothin' but a hound dog" famous.

Elvis is a sign of the longing human beings have to believe in something that never dies or fades away. We search for permanence and find it in the oddest places.

In a way, Elvis is more alive today than he was two decades ago, when his fast living finally caught up to him. By dying when he did and not exposing us to the "I can't carry a tune or remember the lyrics" stage old entertainers go through, Elvis lives on in the memories of millions. He holds a place in the pantheon of popular culture and, by modern American standards, that's as close to immortal as it gets.

"He was only a human being, probably one of the most human beings we've ever known," David says with reverence. "He's only human, but undoubtedly he's the greatest entertainer that the entire universe has ever known."

And a universe is a big place.

Charles David is just proud to be standing in for the King on one corner of it. ◆

Justice serves the people at popular downtown saloon

March 26, 1993

Those who lament that justice no longer serves working people never have set foot in the Bunkhouse Saloon downtown.

At the Bunkhouse, justice, or at least a justice of the peace, serves cold beer and occasionally knocks out a helluva tune. On Friday night, increasing numbers of downtown's hired hands mosey down to 11th Street to tilt a few longnecks.

Customers are courted in style by part-owner Jim Bixler, who hangs up his judge's robe at quitting time at Justice Court and spends the next few hours as a member of the Bunkhouse Bar Association. This may be the only place in town you can give orders to a judge without being held in contempt.

Although local attorneys are commonly sighted making semicoherent motions, the saloon is an unpretentious club adorned with rodeo memorabilia and photos of Hollywood wranglers.

It has Bixler's personality and sense of humor all over it.

Raised on a Nebraska ranch in the heart of the Sioux war grounds, Bixler grew up on horseback. The cowboy lifestyle fit him like an old pair of boots. He even rode bucking horses until the landings became harder than his head.

These days, the rodeo saddles of Bixler and his father hang from the walls of the Bunkhouse.

"A lot of the paraphernalia is home-grown," Bixler, 45, says. "We've got personal stuff all around. The photos we ordered out of Hollywood."

Pictures of Clint Eastwood, Roy Rogers, Benny Binion, and Gabby Hayes add a funky touch to the place and distinguish it from red-neck and urban cowboy bars. The joint is better suited to Rexall rangers than bona fide buckaroos.

Bixler bounced around the saloon business in college and was bucked out of a few Las Vegas lounges after passing the state bar. Drinking in gin joints is a lot easier than earning a living off them. The part-time bartender became a lawyer, then a judge.

About 18 months ago, he teamed up with attorneys Stew Bell and Tom Burns and opened the Bunkhouse. Because all three have day jobs, turning a profit was not a first priority.

But, so far, their mixological experiment is working.

"It's just a neighborhood kind of place. We've tried to market to the downtown crowd," Bixler says. "People who think it's easy to make money in this business are absolutely wrong. The whole challenge has been to see if we can take a place not generally thought of as being in a great location and turn it into something that's fun and attractive and beat the experts.

"We want to show them we're not just dumb attorneys, show them we can do something right outside the field of the law."

Allowing rookie Justice of the Peace Debbie Lippis to sit in on live music nights qualifies as one of those right moves. A former college voice major whose father was a concert violinist, Lippis brings the crowd to life by belting out country and jazz standards.

On a recent Friday, with sax-playing district attorney's office investigator Mike Gamboa's jazz combo backing her, Lippis toured the country with renderings of "Chicago," "Kansas City," and "New York, New York." A set by Lippis qualifies listeners for frequent flier mileage. As long as it's not Mayberry R.F.D., she'll dedicate a song to your hometown, too.

Lippis, 44, replaced a judge who, by coincidence, was bounced out of office for hanging out in too many bars. She's partial to club soda and standards.

"Singing is the best hobby in the whole world," she says. "If I had my choice, I would sing all the time."

Sounds great, but what would the prosecutors say?

Set a few blocks from downtown's neon hustle in a neighborhood more seedy than scenic, the Bunkhouse probably won't ever rival the town's trendiest taverns. But it sure beats most of the smoky slot swamps and homogenized sports bars that have popped up like warts all over the city.

It's refreshing to see justice serve the people for a change. ◆

Harry Korie can do it all, but he just can't win

September 3, 1992

It was the morning after the '92 primary. Harry Korie was packing his bags and taking his political show off the roadside one hand-painted sign at a time.

Sure, he was disappointed after collecting 651 votes (23.6 percent) in the Democratic primary in Assembly District 2. Harry placed second to Mike Perrah, who garnered 1,581 votes (57.5 percent), and the loss surprised him.

Which may surprise some voters, who tend to mistake his political forays with the follies of the '62 Mets.

Reporters often refer to Harry as a perennial candidate, but biennial is more accurate. He ran for county recorder in 1982, assembly in '84, '86, '88, '90, and this year. He also ran for justice of the peace in Henderson and Las Vegas.

He didn't win, but it would be wrong to lump Mr. Harry Korie in with all those political fringe players. He's not just out to grab a slice of celebrity. He really would like to win, go to Carson City, and make his vote count.

Problem is, he keeps coming in second. After numerous valiant efforts and a small forest of hand-stenciled signs, Harry Korie has yet to win a race.

And, at 85, he may not have many primaries left.

But he hasn't lost hope.

That's because inside Harry Korie beats the heart of a vaudeville hoofer.

You can almost see him there in the footlights, a straw hat in one hand, working the crowd as he soft-shoes across the stage. He gives them a one-liner, takes a pratfall, and comes back smiling.

You name it, he'll play it.

Just ask him.

That's why he was bewildered at his non-success. Again.

"There was an awful mix-up in that damn race," Korie said. "I'm well-known out here. I'm very well-known and very nice to people."

So nice, in fact, that he refused to criticize his opponents.

They seemed like nice fellows, he said; the guy who won probably will make a good legislator.

But, he said, Harry Korie would have done a good job, too. He has been hustling and scuffling since getting his first break as a shoeshine boy on a Philadelphia sidewalk. A famous cowboy actor named Jack Hoxie noticed him and hired him as a personal valet and took him to New York.

That's where Harry received his first big break in show business. He was a chorus-line singer, until it was discovered that he couldn't sing much. He landed a few jobs, one or two on Broadway, but his vocal chords betrayed him.

That didn't deter Harry.

In the 1920s, he toured the country as part of an adagio dance team. He also worked in vaudeville and burlesque shows. On stage when he could score a job, backstage when he couldn't.

Eventually, he landed at MGM and Columbia studios as a director's assistant. He had good ideas for shows, still does. One was to be called, "Where Are They Today?"

These days, Harry spends much of his time downtown at the courts. He has friends there and once was a justice court hearing master.

But that's small potatoes compared to singing on Broadway in the '20s, managing Miss Colombia in a beauty pageant, selling Florida real estate, and working as a Hollywood PR man.

He runs for office because he likes to, because being an assemblyman wouldn't be the hardest job he's had in 85 years. After all, he can act a little, sing a little, dance a little.

That's more than most of them can say. But they enjoy advantages Harry does not. Like a few thousand in campaign contributions, radio ads, and professionally painted signs.

"I make my own. I didn't have the money to go around buying them," he said. "I hardly spend any money at all. But I've got the most beautiful signs you'd ever want to see."

Compared to some littering the roadside, they're downright dignified.

Before folding his one-man campaign, he confided, "I've got more experience than a youngster. I think I have a much more colorful background than any candidate."

Of that there is no doubt.

So, another primary came and went and Harry Korie didn't win.

He'll collect his signs, store them safely, maybe peek at a few of his press clippings, and wait for the next political opportunity. Just don't expect Harry Korie to stop trying.

He has been many things, but never a quitter. ◆

Willpower gets 85-year-old cowboy through life's wild ride

November 29, 1990

These days, 85-year-old Turk Greenough's daily routine doesn't get much wilder than a little bingo down at Jerry's Nugget.

Considering the road he took more than six decades ago, the long-time Southern Nevadan has earned a rest. There was a time his life was the most exciting imaginable.

Greenough was a rodeo legend, a champion saddle-bronc rider who thrilled cowboy-crazy fans from Calgary to Sydney. He rode in the last of the Wild West shows, which rumbled across America before fading with the popularity of moving pictures. He was a trick rider and a stuntman in Hollywood and played everything from treacherous Arabs to white-hatted rangers. He also married fabled fan-dancer Sally Rand, who tickled the nation's fancy with her alluring routines in the years before World War II.

Capturing Greenough's life in a brief story is like trying to catch a river in a water glass, but independent film producer Michael Amundsen has made an admirable attempt with *Take Willy With Ya*, a documentary on Turk and the rest of the riding Greenough family. The film, narrated by Hollywood cowboy star Rex Allen, represents a homecoming of sorts for Amundsen, a Rancho High and UCLA graduate whose credits range from small films to such projects as *Witness* and *The Color Purple*. Turk was a bronc-riding prince during what became known as the Golden Age of Rodeo. From 1926 to 1948, he won championships at Calgary, Cheyenne, Pendleton, New York and Boston. The name Greenough was synonymous with rodeo, and today the family is featured in the sport's hall of fame in Colorado Springs, Colorado.

To hear Turk tell it, he barely knew which end of the horse to feed. In a recent interview between trips to a bingo parlor, the soft-spoken Greenough downplayed his successes with, "Well, I guess I was pretty good. I wasn't one of the real top ones, but I held my own."

Yes, and Babe Ruth could hit a little, too.

Born on a homestead six miles outside Red Lodge, Montana, Turk grew up riding and taming his own horses. By the time he was old enough to vote, Greenough was thrilling crowds from the back of a bronc.

Turk is only part of the incredible story. With family patriarch Ben dishing out tough discipline and sage advice, the rodeoing Greenoughs included champion bronc and bull riders Alice, Marge, and Bill. Alice and Marge were major celebrities in the days before rodeo rules limited women to barrel racing or the grandstands.

They rode the meanest bucking horses in the country. While it was hardly an activity most young girls aspired to, Alice and Marge were Greenoughs and that meant a life on horseback. In those days, women's liberation meant an equal opportunity to get tossed by a wild-eyed bronc.

So imagine Alice's delight at being treated to tea with the Queen of England and being treated like a queen herself in rodeo-mad Australia. It is just one of many amazing experiences recounted in *Take Willy With Ya*, which borrows its title from father Ben's message to his children to take their willpower wherever they traveled.

Turk's will gained him entrée into high society in New York and Hollywood, which was smitten with his clean living and plain speaking. His company was sought by movie stars such as John Wayne and heavyweight champs the caliber of Jack Dempsey.

Life has settled considerably for Turk since his early years. He has spent the past four decades in Southern Nevada and currently lives in North Las Vegas. He occasionally returns to Red Lodge to visit family and friends and reminisce about the days when the name Greenough conjured romantic images of the Wild West in hearts across the nation.

Turk still rides horses when the occasion arises, but these days he no doubt appreciates the comfort of a cooperative animal. After all, even rodeo's greats can't ride the broncs forever.

"I'm just as old as Las Vegas," he said recently. "I've seen a lot of it, from horse-and-buggy days to the man on the moon."

Bronc rides last ten seconds or less. Turk Greenough's wild ride has lasted more than 85 years, and that's a record no cowboy is likely to match. ◆

His eatery closes and Poppa doesn't have a brand-new bag

July 15, 1998

It was nearly noon, but for once I had no trouble getting a seat at Poppa Gar's. The place was all but empty.

The venerable restaurant was as silent as the taxidermic big game and the photos of stuffed politicians that hang from its walls. The elk and deer were mute. The buffalo stared even more vacantly than usual. A mallard lay on the counter as if it were just shotgunned from the sky, or had only moments before died of a broken heart.

There was no hiss of bacon frying, no eggs over easy, and no O'Briens sliding my way. No rustling of newspapers, no construction-crew laughter. No small-potatoes politicians acting like Boss Tweed, no genuine movers and shakers dining incognito.

Only the sunlight seeping through window blinds disturbed the dark. Poppa Gar's was in mourning, and so was I. The missing regulars surely realized the pain they were feeling wasn't heartburn, but I was especially distressed.

Without Poppa Gar's, where would I meet someone for a sunrise interview? Where would I grab a sandwich and a column note on a slow news day?

You just don't meet the same class of crook at McDonald's, man. Poppa Gar's had it all. Any eatery that serves meals made from the same animals that peer longingly from their home on the wall qualifies as a restaurant of distinction.

When Poppa's place closed last week after 34 years, at first I thought the AMA had taken its anti-cholesterol campaign too far. I had to see for myself.

There in the shadows, accompanied by a cane and that stuffed mallard, was Garland Miner. Poppa Gar to you and me.

He looked like a lonely guy with nothing but time on his hands. It wasn't always that way. For decades Poppa and his wife and partner, Alma, ran the restaurant from before dawn until long after dark. But Poppa is 91 now, and Alma is 82. Although he still came to work eight hours a day, and Alma hustled behind the counter and cash register as late as this spring, they had more than earned a break.

Poppa began cooking as a six-year-old boy after his folks took sick. Growing up in Ronda in the Blue Ridge Mountains of North Carolina, he kept his five brothers and sisters fed, and gravitated toward the restaurant racket. He worked in a soda fountain, opened diners in upstate New York, then moved to Las Vegas in 1939. He had the Roundup Drive-In, operated Bob Baskin's restaurant, then in 1965 opened Poppa Gar's on West Oakey Boulevard.

It immediately became a safe harbor and morning briefing place for politicians and police officials of every stripe. Wiseguys and newspaper reporters mixed with contractors, casino men, and overdressed attorneys.

For many years, Poppa would special order exotic game

for his more discriminating customers. With wild boar, rattle-snake, and even calf testicles available, this was not the average burger joint.

Poppa Gar was proof that neither hanging out with minor-league politicians and cynical lawmen, nor ingesting a steady diet of eggs, sausage, biscuits, and gravy was necessarily fatal.

But it took a sense of humor to eat there. I loved taking vegetarians to Poppa's for a salad in the zoo room. Nothing like having a moose staring at your bowl of greens to test your appetite.

Another favorite pastime was studying the photo gallery and counting all the politicians who had gone from sitting at Poppa Gar's to squatting in the penitentiary. If the restaurant's back booth could talk, half the city would be indicted. The other half would be living in Belize.

Poppa himself liked politicians. For that matter, he liked most everyone who came through his doors and greeted regulars by name.

Over the years, he played host to Burt Reynolds during the shooting of *Heat* and was excited when Sig Rogich brought in President Bush and 19 of his friends and Secret Service agents for a bite to eat.

But as he sat there in the shadows, I couldn't help but wonder what he will do now that his namesake has shut its doors. Competition from corporate restaurants has grown steep, and not everyone eats bacon and eggs for breakfast any more.

"It's been a wonderful life, to tell you the truth," Poppa said. "Now I don't know what to do with myself.

"I can sleep later in the morning now, but I just can't do it. I've been coming in here for 34 years. I'm more at home here, meeting people and talking to them."

The feeling was mutual. From paupers to presidents, everyone was at home at Poppa Gar's. ◆

Diner's owner eschews big time for his family of customers

August 6, 1995

It seemed like just another morning at the Huntridge Drug Restaurant.

As Bill Fong stood in his apron and prepared another meal at his lunch counter's grill, the handsome married couple at the counter wrestled with an age-old Vegas question:

Walk away a few bucks ahead, or risk it all for a piece of the neon-lighted big time.

Had the intense young man and wife bothered to ask the cook for advice, he would have told them to save their money and instead concentrate on the little things that give a life meaning. Things like family, friends, and work.

But then, Bill Fong wasn't the star of the Hollywood hit *Indecent Proposal*.

He was merely a bit player. Bill, and his tiny restaurant.

In a world filled with corporate barons and billion-dollar buyouts, you won't find Fong's name on anyone's board of directors. He is not a newsmaker or Hollywood celebrity. He is one of life's bit players.

Bill Fong cooks chow mein for a living.

And eggs over easy. And hot turkey sandwiches.

At 68, he has simple tastes. With his wife, Doris, at his side, he works seven days a week at the lunch counter. They greet customers by name. On Sunday, the Fongs close the restaurant early to attend evening church services. In her precious spare time away from the lunch counter, Doris takes piano and violin lessons.

That's the way it has been for Bill since he left Hong Kong and traveled to Las Vegas 45 years ago. When the communists rose to power in China, no place was safe for the son of a politician.

Bill went to work for his uncle at Wing's Cafe near where the California Hotel now stands. From there, Wing's moved to Sixth and Fremont.

Two decades ago, Bill and Doris opened the Shanghai Tea Room inside the Mayfair Drug Store at Fremont and 15th. Bill's chow mein and hamburgers were so popular that locals called it the Chinese Drug Store. The Fongs moved to the fountain and lunch grill inside the Huntridge Drug Store in 1987.

Bill and Doris have served chow mein to the biggest businessmen in Las Vegas and still count many as regular customers. They had plenty of chances to move out of downtown, or at least to open a place inside a casino.

Instead, they stayed. They were in business to earn a living, not a fortune.

"We like it small," Bill says. "No overhead. No bosses. Just family. They (casino operators) ask me a few times, but I don't like it. Too many bosses."

The three Fong children were raised at the cafe. They did their homework at the empty tables and chatted daily with the regulars. As they grew, they waited on the customers. Today, elder daughter, Teuyling Stafford, or "2-E" for short, works in the family business.

The clientele at the restaurant is mostly older, but customers often bring their children and grandchildren to watch Bill grill his chow mein. And in part because the Fongs make them feel special by remembering their first names.

"There's just something about it," Doris says. "Basically, this is our social life. Each day you get to see your customers. It's like family."

The other day, an elderly stranger ambled into the restaurant and was stunned at the sight of Bill standing behind the grill. It was the way the old man had remembered Las Vegas 40 years ago at Wing's Cafe.

In no time he struck up a conversation with an equally experienced customer, and the two reminisced about Las Vegas in the decades before the Strip.

"They congregate here and they like to talk about the past years," Doris says.

Despite all the changes, Bill Fong likes Las Vegas. But he prefers to cook where he is most comfortable. He is satisfied with his small piece of the American Dream.

"Las Vegas was real small," he recalls. "Hardly anybody here. No one dreamed it would get this big. A lot of old-timers didn't buy property. It was all desert. Who'd want to come here?"

Then he laughs.

Bill Fong came all the way from Hong Kong.

On most mornings at the Huntridge Drug Restaurant you won't find a Hollywood production crew or a couple of handsome movie stars.

The regulars know that their favorite cook doesn't need footlights or film credits to shine.

But who was that married couple with Bill Fong, anyway? ◆

Las Vegas mixologist met them all during life behind bars

December 18, 1994

Benny Siegel was a gentleman, and Virginia Hill was a lady. Jack Benny was a big tipper, and Howard Hughes was as eccentric as you might imagine.

It was the fabulous '40s, and Las Vegas was a different place. It had guys and dolls, gunsels and molls, and not nearly so many people who fretted about their image. Sin City had a nice ring to it, and Hollywood's elite was hooked on the action. For a while it seemed like half the neon-mad world was paying a visit to Ralph Koehn.

Koehn, a Las Vegas historian and philosopher, remembers it all as if it were last week and not half a lifetime ago. Koehn holds a Ph.D. in mixology with a specialty in observing the human condition.

Often, an inebriated condition.

Koehn is a senior member of Southern Nevada's bartending fraternity. Alcohol aficionados wish they had hooch as aged as the stuff he has spilled. Koehn has been serving whiskey since your old granddad was in short pants and gin was shipped by night in five-gallon cans or clandestinely concocted in cast-iron bathtubs.

From the perils of Prohibition to the Disneyfication of Las Vegas, Koehn has survived 60 years serving scotch and soda to strangers. He could probably use a double, but he doesn't drink anymore.

At 86, a stroke forced him into retirement earlier this year. Although he has earned a rest and has no immediate plans to return to work, Koehn has recovered everything but his leg strength.

"I just love people," he says. "I'd like to go back to work now if I could. After 60-odd years, I miss the people."

Koehn first stepped behind a bar in 1929 during Prohibition in the Northern Minnesota burg of Bemidji. The selection was limited, but the clientele wasn't exactly finicky.

"Back then, you didn't ask what they wanted. They asked you what you had," Koehn says. "And they drank it. We had good bootleg whiskey then. Even when we didn't, the lumberjacks didn't care. With the lumberjacks in Northern Minnesota, if it was drinkable, they'd take it."

From the Cocoanut Grove in Minneapolis to the Del Tahquitz in Palm Springs, Koehn worked his way west. He knocked around with Patsy Cline and Martha Raye in Palm Springs; one of them sang "Crazy" but both got wild-eyed when they were drinking. He counts them among his many friends.

When the El Rancho Vegas opened in 1941, he poured the first drink. At the Last Frontier in early 1946, Koehn encountered Siegel and his favorite squeeze, Virginia Hill. The happy, hell-raising couple lived in the hotel's third-floor penthouse during the construction of the Flamingo.

Although Siegel probably wouldn't last long in today's corporate casino culture, Koehn liked his style. Back then no one expected a gangster casino boss to be a sober saint. Sure Siegel killed people, as many as a dozen before he rolled lead snake eyes at the hands of a syndicate hitman, but Koehn figures most of the infamous Bugsy's victims must have had it coming.

"They were real pleasant to wait on. They were never out of line or anything," he says. "He was good with working people. They weren't the biggest tippers, but they treated you nice."

For generosity, few of Koehn's customers could match Jack Benny. Although many of Benny's fans believed he was the ultimate cheapskate, the comedian toked like a champ.

"Everybody'd rather wait on Jack Benny because he always took real good care of everybody."

There were plenty of laughs and forays to different clubs with the celebrities he served. He drank with the Mills Brothers at the North Las Vegas Elks Lodge back when black entertainers could sing in Strip showrooms but weren't allowed to sleep in the hotel, eat in the gourmet room, or imbibe in the lounge.

It was at the Last Frontier that Koehn got to know Howard Hughes. The idea that the quirky industrialist would go half-mad in his older years would not have been a difficult call even in 1946.

Hughes drank daiquiris, but he wouldn't trust his favorite bartender to mix the cocktail.

"You had to put all the mixings in front of him," Koehn remembers. "Somebody must have mickeyed him some time. He was real fussy about his drink. I had to hand shake it. He wouldn't let me use a blender. But he had to pour it."

Koehn opened plenty of clubs and casinos—the El Rancho, Thunderbird, Showboat, Landmark, and Maxim among them—then settled back at the Showboat, where he mixed drinks for special parties until a few months ago.

"I just thank God for all the good years he gave me," he says. "The people were the greatest. You never know who you'll meet."

Somewhere along the line, the dapper guys and luscious dolls slipped off their perches and strolled back into the neon-lit night.

In a quiet moment, Ralph Koehn can still hear their laughter through the ages. ◆

Honest cabdriver treated more than fair by grateful fare

February 16, 1997

David Hacker heard the words and winced.

"Take me to Bally's," his fare drawled, sliding into the back seat of Hacker's Yellow Cab around midnight.

Bally's was a nice enough place. It's just that he had made the pickup at the Mirage, and a trip that short meant chump change on his Tuesday-night meter.

"It's a three-dollar-and-fifty-cent ride, and I hope I get the five," Hacker explained.

The driver managed a smile as he deposited the gambler, received the $5 he expected, and headed to his apartment near the Strip to take a break before turning in his cab at 1 a.m. The 10-hour run was over, and Hacker was counting coins.

Then it happened.

As Hacker checked the back seat of the cab, he found a wallet belonging to Lance Dykes of Georgia. Tuesday nights would never be the same.

Inside were three $5,000 packs of $100 bills in casino wrappers, a sports-betting slip worth another $10,000, and enough gold credit cards to buy out the Fashion Show Mall.

The common cabdriver found himself faced with a $25,000 question: Would he report the wallet, or quietly keep the money?

No one would know but the gambler and the driver.

To appreciate David Hacker's dilemma, you need to know a little about the man. He was born in Cleveland 45 years ago and raised by his single mother, a waitress, in the heart of a poor, ethnic neighborhood near East 116th Street and Buckeye Road. From there, you needed a tank of gas and a map to find the light of day.

"We had nothing," he said. "It was just me and my mom."

He moved to Las Vegas nine years ago for the chance to turn nothing into something and wound up driving a cab. It was a living. He liked people and, give or take a tip, most drivers make around $30,000 a year.

That night, Hacker held a year's pay in his perspiring hands. Before he had time to think, he called Yellow's night dispatcher and reported the wallet and raced to Bally's.

He found Dykes at the roulette wheel and showed him the wallet. He hadn't known it was missing.

"I don't believe it," Dykes said. "I can't believe you did this. I can't believe anyone would do something like this."

Dykes peeled off 20 $100 bills and handed them to Hacker.

"Take the rest of the week off," the high roller told him. "You're my guest."

Thus began David Hacker's week as a wealthy man.

On Wednesday night, the cabby ate lobster tails in an expansive suite.

"It was the first time for me," he admitted later. "I'd never eaten lobster before."

Dykes raved about his newfound friend, surely one of the last honest men in Las Vegas. When they gambled, the high roller found his good luck charm in the cabby named Hacker. Dykes won $40,000 and handed over $2,000 more to the driver.

On Thursday, Hacker brought along his Cleveland pal Bob Kadunc, and the trio went shopping at Bally's. About $1,000 later, Hacker and Kadunc looked like billboards for the resort with their $250 jackets and $80 shirts. They gambled a little more and ate a stack of lobster tails.

"I acquired a taste for lobster pretty quickly," Hacker said.

On Friday night, Hacker and his girlfriend were treated to another gourmet meal and front-row seats at the Engelbert Humperdinck show.

By the time Saturday rolled around, Hacker's head was spinning. He joined Dykes in the sports book to place a few bets before the Georgia businessman's flight home. Dykes won again and swore to keep in touch with his good luck charm. Hacker drove Dykes to McCarran and received a $500 check, about a week's pay for the cabby.

And then the spell was broken. His benefactor was gone, and some would argue Hacker was a common cabdriver once more.

Except, there's nothing common about an honest man.

"I was sick four years ago with very bad stomach problems," Hacker said. "I made a little pact that if God got me out of that, I would return whatever I found in the cab. God and a good doctor got me out of it, and today I feel great. I feel even better doing this. I think God made me find the wallet to test me."

He passed the test.

"Going back to work, this is not going to be easy," he said. "Last week I was eating lobster tails. This week it's back to Burger King. Really, though, I could care less if it happened again. I've been to the mountain. To be able to order whatever you want. To be able to buy whatever you want. I mean, how many times in your life are you ever going to be able to do that?"

David Hacker's week as a high roller is over now, but he is as rich in character as any man in town. ◆

UPDATE: The honest cabby column was reprinted in the August 1997 issue of *Reader's Digest.*

Lack of shoes started one man walking the road to cheating

September 3, 1995

It started with shoes.

Not the kind that hold playing cards and the promise of fortune. The kind a poor boy longs for.

That's what Bill Land remembers most from his Kentucky childhood. Shoes, and hunger.

If you follow the gambling industry, then you probably know that William Gene Land ended up in Las Vegas with a rap sheet and a reputation as one of the biggest cheaters in the history of cards and dice. He is a member of Nevada's slender Black Book of gambling industry ne'er-do-wells. He is barred from entering a casino; Gaming Control Board investigators would prefer he refrain from even looking at one.

At 60, Land is known as a guy who can corrupt a game quicker than you can shuffle up and deal. His two felony convictions don't begin to explain the scope of his skill or guile. They also don't fully explain his motivation, or how he arrived at this strange destination.

By some estimates, he has stolen millions on either side of the table. Imagine that. Millions of dollars.

But there was a time Bill Land would have given anything for a pair of shoes and something more than oatmeal to eat.

Land's father was a Kentucky coal miner who was an organizer for labor legend John L. Lewis. His father died of black lung at age 42, leaving 13 children and a wife who worked in an industrial laundry to keep her brood from starving.

Shoes were to be worn only on Sundays. After the family moved to Cincinnati, Bill Land quickly noticed that all the other students had shoes and clean clothes at school. He was ridiculed by the teacher and the other kids. When the urge to be like everyone else grew too great, and he smuggled his shoes to school, his mother whipped him.

Those days are gone, but the memory remains.

"I can still remember the teacher saying, 'I smell feet. I smell feet,'" Land says over coffee at the Country Inn. He wears tennis shorts, a casual shirt, and a touch of gold around the neck. "In Kentucky, we were all poor. But in Cincinnati, all the other kids had shoes. I hung my head. The next day I snuck my shoes out. My mother came down to school that day and spanked me in front of everyone. She didn't do it out of meanness. She knew that if I wore my shoes out I wouldn't have any more.

"I said right then, 'Whatever I have to do to get that, I'll do it.'"

At seven, after moving to Newport, Kentucky, he hustled customers for local brothels for a quarter a play. As a shoeshine boy, he met the gamblers who possessed enough money to afford to have others polish their oxfords. As a cab driver, his whorehouse finder's fee increased to 40 percent.

As a dealer at Moe Dalitz' Beverly Club in Newport, Land overpaid his relatives and stole a little each day. When he moved to Las Vegas around 1960, he thought he had died and gone to heaven.

He dealt and worked the floor at the Frontier, Sands, Aladdin, Tropicana, as well as casinos in Laughlin and throughout the Caribbean. He stole from most of them. By then it was in his blood. He wore stylish clothes and jewelry, gambled away most of his loot, and drank away the rest.

Then came the first conviction in 1984 and the Black Book entry in September 1988. In 1994, he was convicted of heading a cheating ring that separated more than $1 million from a Lummi Indian reservation casino in northwestern Washington.

"These people need some help," Land says. "They have no idea what can happen to them. They're thinking, 'How can I be getting cheated?' I'm making a million a month. They definitely need somebody to show them. Because there's a lot of guys out there like me."

After spending a short time in prison for the Indian caper, today Land is under house arrest in Las Vegas. He says he is retired. He also no longer confuses the city with heaven, nor does he blame it for his impoverished upbringing or for his station in life.

If he carries a message, perhaps it is only this: No man can predict how his life will turn out. You walk along in new shoes or in bare feet, make a few choices, and one day wind up a million hard miles from home. Some of his old blackjack buddies are casino executives now; he is on the outside looking in.

He laughs at the irony and remembers Kentucky.

"I was always hungry," Bill Land says, briefly feeling the ache of youth. "It seemed like everybody I knew was never hungry. Just me." ◆

UPDATE: At last check, Bill Land was staying out of the casinos and trouble.

Photographer's scrape with hoodlum leaves indelible image

December 15, 1991

It was near Christmas three decades ago and *Las Vegas Sun* photographer Frank Maggio had just returned from a three-day fishing trip to Lake Mead.

The award-winning former Associated Press White House cameraman smelled like a month-dead carp as he dropped by the newspaper to pick up his mail. Reporter Alan Jarlson collared him and announced the feds had just captured notorious Chicago gangster Marshall Caifano.

Maggio grabbed his Pontiac-sized Speed Graphic camera and went to work.

Running the streets under the alias Johnny Marshall, Caifano was the mob's Las Vegas enforcer. An ex-boxer with an arrest record stretching from the Strip to Rush Street, the Chicago hood had a maniacal stare and a ferocious reputation for violence. His mere presence in a casino struck fear into the mob's front men.

A suspect in several murders, Caifano hit the FBI's 10 most-wanted list in 1961. When the feds finally caught up to him, dapper Johnny Marshall was hiding out at the mobbed-up Desert Inn.

Caifano, the first hood placed in Nevada's infamous Black Book of notorious characters banned from casinos, was arguably the most feared gangster in America. It would be a decade before he would breathe free air again.

Lucky for him.

If he had stayed out of prison, he might have gotten hurt.

In December 1961, as federal agents escorted Caifano through the plush hotel, Jarlson and Maggio arrived in the lobby. Maggio set his camera and fired a flash.

Caifano wasn't in the mood to say cheese. The mobster broke loose and punched the camera half way to Las Vegas Boulevard.

"When you hit a Speed Graphic with your fist you're taking

a chance on cutting your hand up," the unassuming Maggio said during a recent visit to his photo store. "All I know is the camera went flying and it put me in position."

In position for the best shot of his career, a dandy right cross that landed flush on Caifano's notorious mug.

The punch knocked the toughest hoodlum in the country all the way to La La Land.

"I'm not a fighter," Maggio said. "It was just natural reflexes."

Sure, Tiger.

Likely story.

With Caifano taking a carpet nap in the Desert Inn lobby, chaos ensued. The feds picked up the nodding hit man. Security guards grabbed Maggio, who stunk like bait and resembled a transient.

His career flashed before him.

What had he done?

According to local legend, Caifano had killed people for less.

Maggio eventually was released, Caifano was escorted to the friendly confines of the local slammer, and the *Sun* bannered the story. Jarlson painted Maggio as a camera-toting Marciano.

Although Maggio looked over his shoulder for weeks afterward, Caifano never retaliated. Perhaps he knew better than to mess with Tiger Maggio.

Or, maybe the bad guy took the punch as an omen.

The consummate mob hard case eventually served nine years on extortion charges. Thanks to a 1980 racketeering conviction, he grew old in prison.

Maggio went on to become Hacienda matron Judy Bailey's personal photographer and confidant and spent 15 years as the Union Plaza's director of promotions.

From Harry Truman to Mario Lanza, from pugilists to pimps, Maggio has captured on film some of the most famous people of the 20th century. He has occasionally paid for standing close to the action. He has had 14 cameras smashed by unwilling subjects and has absorbed three broken noses and a $2 1/2$-inch skull fracture by others seeking to remain out of focus.

But he has always gotten the picture.

At 73, Maggio runs his One-Hour Photo Lab on Decatur Boulevard and quietly fights cancer that has stolen one of his kidneys.

At 80, Caifano was released from federal prison last week after being declared no longer a threat to society.

But the memory of Maggio's first and last boxing match with one of Murder Inc.'s top executives lingers.

Call it the Revenge of the Shutterbug.

He said, "If I had used my head, I wouldn't have done it."

But Tiger Maggio took his shot, and the rest is Las Vegas history. ◆

UPDATE: Frank Maggio died in 1996.

Salvagers of surplus are junking their longtime business

January 14, 1996

The day he bought Boulder City in 1954, Phil Wilensky figured he was in the salvage business for the long haul.

He didn't purchase the whole dam town, actually, just a few dozen truckloads of it. The mountain of auctioned government surplus fortified Phil's fledgling salvage business with piles of plumbing, electrical fixtures, machinery, streetlights, and their lampshades.

Not that there was a long line forming to buy those shades. But when Main Street Station's builders needed old-style street lampshades nearly 40 years later, you'll never guess where they found them.

"There's a buyer for everything," Wilensky says.

When Mr. Phil's Salvage says everything, he means it. That includes the kitchen sink. And the toilet, tub, shower, and vanity.

And camp stoves, pot belly stoves, and hot plates.

And Army boots, snowshoes, horseshoes, and tennis shoes. And copper cow bells, World War I cavalry feedbags, walking plows, safari helmets, pipes, parachutes, cribs, and coffins.

Literally, from the cradle to the grave.

Everything. Well, almost.

"We had saddles and horseshoes, but no livestock," store manager Jerry Church says. After 25 years, he knows his way blindfolded around the Sears & Roebuck of surplus. "We never did keep anything that would eat or spoil."

That's probably a good thing. If something went foul at Phil's, it might be hard to find.

Until recently, Phil's Salvage was a staggering tangle of goods and gadgets. Today, it is a shadow of its super-stuffed self.

Phil's Salvage, the maintenance man's Macy's, is closing after 42 years. The hearts of project-hardened handymen throughout the valley surely are sinking at the news.

Where will they get their pipes threaded? Where will they find a replacement for their bent thingamajig?

The city has seen enormous change since Phil and Norma Wilensky teamed up with David and Gertrude Katzman to create a kingdom of castoffs. In fact, Phil and Dave made the store's first office out of ammo boxes.

"Wilensky and Katzman," 70-year-old Phil says with pride. "That was a name good enough to be a law firm."

Wilensky is a compact man who wears a camouflage hat and peers through thick spectacles. His common uniform is accented by rainbow suspenders.

With his negotiating skills, Phil could have been a lawyer.

But his father, Max Wilensky, was a professional junk man who worked the streets of Minneapolis in a horse-drawn cart. He bought and sold newspapers, bones, hides, batteries, anything. It was door-to-door capitalism, and Phil was hooked.

"A horse thief, what else does he know?" he asks, smiling. "I didn't know anything else."

Like his father before him, Phil possesses the rare gift of

being able to see the value in everyday things.

Where others saw rubbish, Phil saw Rembrandts. Where lesser men looked upon 5,000 toilet tank lids and laughed, Phil was flush with anticipation.   .

After all, quality toilet fixtures are hard to find.

Ask anyone with a leaky loo.

"We were one of the first, I believe, to get bathroom vanities." Phil says. "We did very very well."

"We were the first ones to have plastic pipes," Church says knowingly.

"In the early years, we sold a lot of clothesline poles," Norma recalls. "We sold hundreds of pairs a week. Today, nobody knows what clothesline poles are."

In the early days, Dave and Phil delivered telegrams to augment their income. Gradually, their business gained a reputation for having any item you could name, even if you couldn't name it.

"Half the time they would come in and not know what they needed," Phil says. "They came in for a thingamajig and would try to describe it to us. After a while, we got busy and we had them bring in the old part."

Most of the time, they left satisfied.

When a plane full of passengers went down outside Las Vegas, officials looked for metal coffins and found them at Phil's.

The store even has attracted tourists.

"Canada, Mexico, South America, they came here on vacation and they saw things they couldn't get back in their own country," Church says. "They would buy it here and ship it back home."

Down at Phil's Salvage, the motto always was, "Prices born here, raised elsewhere."

Now that Las Vegas has outgrown Phil and his amazing store, who will help us appreciate the value of everyday things? ◆

Chaplain Joe tries to weld souls as well as scrap metal

January 20, 1994

Chaplain Joe Prange has a way of turning heaps of scrap into useful things.

He uses five decades of experience, a flawless faith, and a fair amount of fire. Chaplain Joe is a welder and die-maker by trade, a Christian soldier by calling, and he's as comfortable talking about Jesus and the hereafter as he is about blow torches and power drills.

On this day, Chaplain Joe has his work cut out for him.

He is constructing a trailer out of discarded iron using a few tools. He hadn't planned to go into the trailer-building business, but then he hadn't anticipated having his rig and most of his tools stolen in separate burglaries late last year. He knows the Lord moves in mysterious ways, but he's still trying to figure out this one.

He adjusts his thick specs, screws up his bill-less cap, and tugs at his rope suspenders. His new guard dog, a grinning uncoordinated golden retriever mix, spills its kibble nearby.

Chaplain Joe's God in Me Ministry may not be much to look at, but his faith is unflappable.

"We got to learn to treat each other decent," he says, leaving the sun-lit yard and entering his spartan office near Pecos Road. "Our world is decaying into immorality."

The 72-year-old, who once owned a Boulder Highway shop called Joe's Ornamental Iron, already is talking about his favorite subject.

For those unfamiliar with his ministry, an explanation is in order. For the past 11 years, he has spread the good word from the Good Book to down-and-outers all over Southern Nevada. He has volunteered to help teach them the welding trade and he has donated most of his retirement toward creating prayer groups and neighborhood halfway houses. Although he has a few helpers these days, he's done most of it by himself.

Along the way, he's helped salvage some of the city's human refuse.

Two weeks before the new year, thieves cut the locks off his yard gate, pilfered his mobile welding shop, and made off with his hammers and drills, nuts and bolts. On December 27, they stole the trailer.

He is bewildered, but not bitter.

"A lot of these people have bitterness in their lives. They become bitter," Chaplain Joe says, inadvertently explaining the transgression. "We've got to get the bitterness out."

For his part, he works to keep open his group home on Hassle Street. This week, the ministry has 41 clients. They are people who have shown an interest in rising up from the asphalt, gaining employment, and making the transition back into society. He gives them shelter, food, a telephone to call about jobs, and transportation to work sites.

Although he knows many, perhaps most, will fail, this simple welder is proud of all of them.

"We hug them," he says. "They say to us, 'Nobody ever hugged us before.'"

Chaplain Joe's ministry is in transition. He has picked up a couple of assistants, and they want to expand the simple operation into a full-service homeless help center complete with sophisticated networking and public grants. They already claim a growing number of success stories.

With my cynical nature, I am suspicious of anyone in the professional homeless business. But Chaplain Joe likes the idea of expanding the ministry.

When he isn't dreaming of the Promised Land, he has another dream.

Chaplain Joe foresees a day when churches throughout the valley will open halfway houses for down-and-outers. The neighborhood centers not only would provide food and shelter, but counseling and job leads as well.

As likely, such a move would create a flurry of lawsuits from outraged homeowners. At many churches, the heathen unwashed do not rank as a high priority. That's the real world.

But that's what makes Chaplain Joe different. He's just a

welder, but he cares about the things that bond people.

He's lost plenty, but not hope.

"It's just letting them know there's hope," Chaplain Joe says. "Without hope, what do you got to live for?"

They stole his physical tools, not his spiritual ones. ◆

Widow eases death's darkness by adding some light to one life

August 2, 1998

The late summer thunderstorm uprooted trees across the valley, and Carmella Chris was concerned about the big elms that shaded her George's grave. That's how she found herself at Woodlawn Cemetery on the darkest afternoon of 1997.

The weather reflected her very soul. Since the death of her husband the month before, grief had consumed her spirit like a dark wave. Losing George after 21 years of marriage was like losing the sunlight.

The rain came down in slanting sheets as she neared the gates of the cemetery.

Then she saw him.

He was an old black man, bent over and shuffling down the boulevard against the rain. He shivered violently. His matted hair and tattered clothes were soaked and his boots were no more than rags.

She shook off the image and tended to her husband's grave. Upon exiting the cemetery, she saw the old man again.

As broken as she felt, here was a man who was infinitely worse off. The streets in that area are riddled with such people, but she found herself focused on one person.

She drove home, picked out a coat and sweater that had belonged to her husband, stopped off at a KFC, and bought a small lunch box. When she found him again, she dropped the clothing and food, signaling that it was meant for him.

And so began Carmella Chris' strange relationship with the old transient. She did not know his name, but people on the street called him Shuffles. More biting wits referred to him as the Question Mark for the shape his spine made as he walked. He patrolled his neighborhood like a Sisyphean sentinel, rolling the rock of mental illness before him as he made his way from Las Vegas Boulevard North, up Foremaster Lane, and over to Main Street.

As the days passed, Chris made regular stops along the old man's route. She dropped off coffee and hot chocolate, soup and sandwiches. A slice of pot roast, a pair of shoes, a short-sleeved shirt, a pack of cigarettes. Little kindnesses that he acknowledged with a whispered "thank you" and a nod of the head.

When he wasn't walking, the old man slept under a railroad bridge near Ray's Auto Wrecking. She would find him there on days he was ill. She brought him food and a blanket.

As the months passed, she realized that by caring for a person less fortunate, she was able to raise herself out of the depression that accompanied the loss of her husband.

On July 4, she bought a pizza as a gift to the old man on Independence Day, but he was gone. When she returned the next day, street people told her he had been murdered. Shot in the back in the middle of the night after arguing with a stranger.

A few days later, Chris first learned the old man's name. He was Billy Ray Owens, and he was only 41 years old.

Owens was well known to Susie Taylor of Catholic Charities and John Farrell of the Community Health Center. They saw him grow old before his time. Owens was not a violent or argumentative man.

The Owens homicide, which is still under investigation, was noted in a three-paragraph news brief. Such brevity is common when the victim is a transient. His death was as marginalized as his life.

But he had come to mean something to Chris.

"I think he taught me to accept the loss of my husband," Chris, 59, says. "I felt so bad in my own loss. When I think back

I say to myself, there's so many things in life, but there's only one purpose in the world. Each and every one of us has one obligation, to love one another and maybe save one soul.

"Maybe it was my own mourning and grieving at the loss of my own husband. (Owens) always thanked me, was always so polite. He was always alone. He never talked to anyone.

"I'd ask, 'Is there something you'd like?' and he'd say, 'No, I just appreciate everything you've done for me.'"

Owens' obituary finally ran a week ago, a year to the day after George Chris' death.

On Monday, Carmella Chris went down to Bunker Brothers Mortuary and dropped off clean clothes for Billy Ray Owens one last time. His funeral was Tuesday and was attended by Chris and a few caseworkers.

"I didn't want him to be buried with no one there," Chris says.

Owens is buried in the Memory Gardens, not at Woodlawn as Chris would have preferred, but she has one more person to visit as she makes her rounds:

The husband who died, and the stranger who helped her return to the land of the living. ◆

UPDATE: The murder of Billy Ray Owens remains unsolved.

A royal act of charity outshines Windsor Park's decay

November 24, 1994

The roses in Fletcher Brown's front yard bloom red and pink even out of season. Like the woman who tends them, they appear oblivious to the chilly mornings and the daily decay at Windsor Park.

This beleaguered North Las Vegas neighborhood belies its regal namesake. On streets riddled with cracks from ground subsidence, Windsor Park's homes are sinking faster than England's own royal family.

But make no mistake. Windsor Park is not without its royalty. Her name is Fletcher Brown, and her roses are a Michale Street miracle.

Where her spring-green house once was flanked by other homes, it now stands alone between vacant lots. She has lived there 17 years and has watched other humble castles fall one by one. Across the street, a home has been reduced to its foundations. Plywood covers the windows of another place, condemned by authorities who live miles from Fletcher Brown's street. For some reason, her home continues to defy the odds.

Although the neighborhood is crumbling and outsiders never seem to do more than send letters, in truth she has little time to worry about such matters or even to think of her childhood spent in a Bahamian orphanage.

She is one small woman, and Kenny keeps her busy 18 hours a day. Kenny is a multiple-stroke victim. Entirely incapacitated, he must be fed and medicated every four hours. He must be hoisted from his bed with a hydraulic lift. He takes his formula through a tube implanted in his stomach. He must be bathed and changed by hand.

Their chance meeting is even more improbable than the story of the sinking neighborhood. A longtime volunteer, Fletcher had taken a friend to the county hospital. A nurse implored her to help temporarily with an indigent old man who had been abandoned at the hospital after suffering a stroke. "Take him for a few days," the nurse had begged. "Give him a little love and care." Against her better judgment, she relented. After all, it was only for a few days.

When she first saw Kenny, she immediately regretted her decision. He was a disheveled lump of a man sitting in a broken wheelchair out behind the emergency room. His gray hair flowed halfway down his back, and his gray beard was full. He had no shoes.

Also, he is white. Fletcher is black.

Kenny appeared to be somewhere between retirement age

and a century old. After returning him to her mostly black neighborhood, she gave the pathetic old duff a haircut and shave.

"He was a young man," she says, her voice full of disbelief even after the decade they have been together. "For some reason, I thought he was going to be a black man. When I came to pick him up, I was a little surprised. It took a little getting used to."

But there he was, filling up a bedroom in her small house, entirely dependent on her charity.

For some reason, she was reminded of her youth. Orphaned at birth, Fletcher had spent most of her childhood unwanted. When she dared to dream, she dreamed of having a mother and father and a family of her own. Where others might have been bitter and full of self-pity, Fletcher Brown was moved in other ways. She had been helped in coming to America and never forgot the blessing.

"My mother left me when I was born. I know how it feels to be alone and you need somebody," she says. "If you were brought up in that way, you'd know how it feels not to be wanted. Kenny keeps me active. He's happy and I'm happy."

In 1991, Kenny suffered another stroke. Without Fletcher, he would have been gone long ago.

"I know if he was in a rest home they'd probably sit him in the corner and forget about him," she says. "I guess if I've done this well in keeping him alive, I'm doing OK. If they'd taken him to the rest home, it would have broken my heart."

She is 67 years old and receives no stipend for the care she gives 18 hours a day, seven days a week.

On Sunday morning, Fletcher Brown takes her seat at St. James the Apostle Catholic Church on H Street and gives thanks to a God who enables her to appreciate the blessings in her life. She knows it is a long way from the Bahamas to Las Vegas.

Then she returns to Michale Street and Kenny.

"He keeps me doing something. I'm old, too, but he keeps me active," she says. "I love him. I know how it was."

Her home is an outpost filled with faith, a simple shrine dedicated to hope.

There is royalty at Windsor Park.
Her name is Fletcher Brown.
After 17 years, the roses in her front yard are still blooming.
Now you know why. ◆

Update: Fletcher and Kenny are still roommates.

Brown Bomber's daughter languishes in obscure isolation

November 24, 1991

The bust of the champ and the photos of the child are the first things you notice in Lauretta Holmes' modest apartment.

Although the clay likeness of the great Joe Louis is impressive, the pictures of young Janet Louis Barrow are enchanting. In large stills that would steal the Grinch's heart, the smiling child is a bathing beauty, a sparkling Christmas elf, and a little queen with a crown like an oversized halo.

The photographs are betrayed by the girl struggling in the pillowy chair beside you.

Her head tilted at an odd angle, her arms and legs uncomfortably splayed, each wheezing breath she takes is a struggle that would have tested her father, the late heavyweight champion of the world.

A victim of a near-drowning in her infancy, Janet is 15 but seems much younger. In her pink pajamas, she smiles as she hears her guardian's voice.

"I love you, Janet," Lauretta Holmes says. "I just love you so."

There are people you will meet who are so much better than you will ever be, who give so much more than you will ever give, that it awes you to be near them. Lauretta is one of those people.

A stroke left her legally blind eight years ago. Heart bypass surgery leaves her short of breath and on daily medication.

Laughingly inadequate government assistance pushes her to the edge of bankruptcy each month.

She long ago sold her nice things to care for the girl. Her apartment is sparsely furnished. She couldn't drive even if she owned a car; her eyesight is so poor she can barely dial a phone.

But she has Janet, and when Lauretta speaks the handicapped girl is transformed into the most special child in the world.

"She doesn't talk, but she can understand, and we communicate," Lauretta says as proud as any mother. "I just love Janet. She needed somebody and there was nobody. I just enjoy making her happy because she has so little."

So little, in fact, that a specially designed wheelchair that would ease the pain of her disfigurement, give her mobility, and allow her to attend a school for the handicapped is far out of reach.

"I don't want her to suffer more than she already has," Lauretta says. "It's too painful."

For now, the little queen is without a carriage.

In a city that has profited so much from the shadows of fighting men who have come in Louis' wake, the great boxer's adopted daughter languishes in obscure isolation. A generation ago, members of Las Vegas royalty with their street-tough pasts would have rushed to her aid. No child of the Brown Bomber's would have suffered as long as they were around.

But Las Vegas has changed.

At least Janet has Lauretta, a friend of the champ and his wife, Martha, for more than four decades. The parents are gone now. Janet has been under Lauretta's care for more than seven years.

The girl has cerebral palsy, severe curvature of the spine, and hip displacement. Her limbs have atrophied and without cushioning she experiences pain. She is fed through a tube attached to her stomach. Her constant care includes suctioning excess fluids from her lungs and throat. She must be lifted and carried from the bedroom to the living room.

"If she goes to bed at eight, I go to bed with her. If she goes to bed at four, I go to bed with her," Lauretta says, adding in a confidential whisper, "I don't hardly go to bed."

But she would not have it otherwise. The champ and his wife were her friends, the girl needs her, and any alternative is unthinkable.

The girl has been one guardian angel away from institutionalization for years. Lauretta is careful to mention the friends who give her strength, including Nettie Thomas, Erlene Bird, and Gene Kilroy. She speaks of them with pride.

As Lauretta reminisces about the little girl, she recalls the day Janet emerged from her three-month coma after falling into the pool at the family's Las Vegas home.

It was on Thanksgiving 1977 at Houston's Methodist Hospital. Joe Louis, a casino greeter at Caesars Palace in those days, had suffered an aneurysm and also was a patient at the hospital.

"Thanksgiving means an awful lot to me. It was the day we got Janet back. I knew she would be my baby," she says. "That was a welcomed day, that day."

Lauretta has no biological children. She has Janet.

"I have given up material things. Janet is more important to me," Lauretta says. "If there were other little children that I were able to take care of, I would."

Las Vegas has changed, but it is not without its royalty.

It still has a carriage-less little queen and a sightless angel who sees her timeless beauty. ◆

'Miracle Child' illustrates the true meaning of Christmas

December 25, 1991

Billy Young wondered what became of the little girl.

Driving a Mercy ambulance 14 years ago, Young and partner John Landaker had just finished taking a patient to Sunrise Hospital's emergency room when the fresh call came in. An infant drowning.

In those days, the mobile emergency medical technicians pulled staggering 24- and 48-hour shifts and answered up to three dozen calls between breaks. Sleep often had to wait for a day off.

There was nothing unique in their assignment.

The difference was the proximity.

"We cleared, then got the call," said Young, who now is a Metro lieutenant. "I turned my head, and we were just that close."

Frantic children waved at them as they pulled into the yard on Cherokee Lane. Another child was with the baby in the back yard by the pool.

"I just grabbed the child," he said. "She was so tiny. She wasn't breathing."

No heartbeat.

No vital signs.

The baby was gone.

After immediate attempts to resuscitate the infant, they transported her to the hospital. She was revived, but remained in a coma for several weeks before regaining consciousness. She emerged permanently changed.

"We could not have been there three minutes," Young said after describing the scene in meticulous detail. "That's what saved her was timing. We just happened to be in the right place at the right time."

Their action saved her life, but what kind of life was she left with?

It is a question Young often has asked.

The long-buried scene rushed back into Young's memory after he recently discovered the infant he helped revive is now a 15-year-old girl who suffers from severe cerebral palsy.

The girl, Janet Louis Barrow, is the adopted daughter of late heavyweight boxing champion Joe Louis. Janet is cared for by her long-time guardian Lauretta Holmes, who is legally blind.

The rescue was a mixed blessing, but a blessing just the same.

"We don't know how long Janet was in that pool," Holmes said. "But I've always said this is a miracle child."

Miracles are where you find them.

Janet's body is severely deformed. She cannot speak, but she manages to communicate with her guardian. Their relationship is pure proof miracles come disguised as tragedies, and blessings happen every day if we are wise enough to see them.

Besides all that, without Young's effort and Holmes' dedication, Janet would not know about Christmas.

"I get her all hopped up for Christmas," Holmes said. "I put her tree up just like she was a normal little girl. She understands. She knows it's Christmastime."

Janet no longer can digest normal holiday cuisine and must take sustenance through a tube attached to her stomach. But she participates where she can. Despite physical ailments that threaten her life, she is strong in spirit.

Holmes refuses to lose hope. Quite the contrary. Janet is hope.

"I don't give up on anything," Holmes said. "I just believe Janet will do better. I've been struggling and struggling and praying. My prayers are answered now."

From Henderson attorney John Marchiano to Veteran Boxing Association President Joey Curtis, many Southern Nevadans have come forward to ensure the girl's comfort.

After more than 14 years, Young has come to accept the things he cannot explain or change.

"You don't have the choice of making those decisions. There's no time to question if this is right or wrong," Young said. "If I could see into the future and see what a tough life the kid would have, see all the financial hardship, I don't know. You're not supposed to question that."

If he knew Janet, Holmes said, he would know why: "I'd like for him to see her. He'd never believe it."

The strength of one frail child is an awesome thing.

Young no longer need worry about what happened to that little girl.

Janet knows there is Christmas, and every day is a blessing. ◆

UPDATE: Janet continues to thrive under Lauretta Holmes' care.

Man defies dialysis odds with cigars, grandchildren's ballgames

July 5, 1998

As he hobbles to the door to greet a visitor, Walt Morton doesn't look like a marathon man.

Envision a tall, fat-free, health nut, and you have him pegged entirely wrong. Morton once was a stout muscular fellow, but his biceps have gone soft and his barrel chest has sagged to just above his belt line. His left arm is a mass of lumpy fistulas and discolored skin, and on many days his energy is sapped by noon.

But I swear he is a marathon man from the top of his head to the soles of his swollen feet. He is as much a long-distance runner as any athlete ever to hit the streets of Boston.

Morton, 67, has been on kidney dialysis for more than 20 years. His life's course has been more grueling than Heartbreak Hill. In a game that for most usually ends in a few seasons, where a person who lasts a decade is a genuine rarity, Morton has survived twice that long.

Hypertension caused Morton's kidneys to fail in early 1978, and the longtime Little League and American Legion coach reluctantly went on the dialysis machine that summer.

Not for himself, understand, for he swore he'd never spend his remaining days hooked to a machine watching his blood run the race of its life. He figured spending three hours every other day with a pair of needles jammed into his arm was no way to live. He did it for his wife Nadine, daughter Roxanne, and son Mark. His family loved him and wanted him to stick around. And so he decided to do just that.

"We are a very very close family," he says. "I refused dialysis in the beginning, but the three of them wouldn't allow me to not go on it."

Not that anyone expected him to have to worry about it for long. In the shape he was in, a nurse told him, Morton might last two years. He was put on a strict diet, told to keep close track of everything he consumed.

He soon discovered that the diet made him angrier than his

faulty kidneys and returned to his meat-and-potatoes ways. Although he did not drink alcohol, he continued to smoke his cigars.

In short, he was determined to enjoy life with his family.

Two years passed, then five more, and Walt Morton began to lose his friends from dialysis. New people took their places, then faded like old newsprint. Over the years, he has gone through dozens of friends and acquaintances. And every year his doctor, Neville Pokroy, shrugs and admits that he, too, is surprised at his patient's incredible run. Somehow, Morton's blood races differently than the rest.

Year after year, he has stayed loyal to the box that cleans his blood and keeps the fluids in his body from poisoning him. He bought two sets of clothes; between visits he gains 12 pounds of fluid. The alternative: Without dialysis, he'd die in a week.

But Morton's biggest fear is not death. It's needles.

"I would rather fight a lion or a tiger barehanded than get stuck, even after all these years," Morton says. "But I do it. I don't watch my diet. I smoke cigars. It works for me. It would probably work for no one else. I would never advise people to do what I do, but I feel I know my body better than anyone else."

He also knows that a positive attitude is essential.

He fights using his walker—"I can't walk with it and carry cigars, too"—and manages to work three days a week as a poultry salesman for City Pride. He misses coaching baseball, but he never misses his grandchildren's ballgames.

"I'm a very lucky guy," Morton says. "The average life expectancy is six to eight years, and basically no more than that. I've gotten to see my grandchildren come into the world. If I'd only lasted six years, I never would have gotten to know them."

Knowing that, it's easier to understand why he has never missed a session and keeps his considerable aches and pains to himself. His ritual rarely varies: On dialysis days, he calls Smith's, orders a honey-cured ham on rye with mustard and an American cheese on rye with Miracle Whip. He's rarely without his cigars and never far from a sports page.

Others might pity him, but from where he sits he's the luckiest man in Las Vegas. By being told he was not long for the world, Morton found a new passion for life.

And so he runs a marathon every other day, his blood racing like there's no tomorrow.

A machine cleans Walt Morton's blood, but his family keeps his heart beating. ◆

UPDATE: Walt Morton died in September 1998.

Sandy Valley man and friends relish the time he has left

March 20, 1994

You roll up State Route 161 in the late spring light and watch the dying day turn purple like a sun-baked bottle.

Road crows point the way past white crosses that mark the asphalt fatalities, beyond the silent cemetery, and over the hill to Goodsprings and the Pioneer Saloon.

The St. Patrick's Day wake is in progress, but the casket is empty.

The dearly departed laughs and drinks a Budweiser by the front door. His black T-shirt, accented by a floppy green bow, hangs on his fragile frame. Sandy Valley resident Chuck Frye is in some pain, but he isn't dead yet. He is 56.

He'll be gone soon enough, the doctor tells him. After four years, the prostate cancer has spread to his bones. He doesn't have many good times left, and attending his own wake sounded like a lot more fun than the alternative.

"Everybody in the valley was asking when the next party was. Well, this is the next party," Chuck says. "It's a reason for everyone to get together and have a good time. It's a joke. Who else would do one? Nobody in town's doing one.

"Any excuse for a party."

It's not the first excuse. Cancer's course is filled with pain and loss. A few months ago, a surgeon cut off Chuck's testicles in an attempt to slow the spread of the disease.

He isn't shy about discussing it. He knows he has little time for self-consciousness.

"I was castrated one day, and the next day we had a party," he says, laughing and delivering the one-liner: "And, it was my wife's birthday."

The wake is a chance for Chuck and his friends to laugh at death, and celebrate life, for awhile. Proceeds from the corned beef and cabbage dinner at Hank's Low Chaparral Cafe and the group's raffle at the Pioneer raise a few dollars toward the annual children's Easter egg hunt at the Sandy Valley Community Center.

"We just want to help the kids," he says. "They enjoy it."

With that, he moves through the shadowy barroom clatter greeting well-wishers as he goes.

The casket leans against a wall near the pool table. His pals made the casket out of plywood and did a fine job.

"Try making your own casket sometime," he says. "Now that's kinky."

Chuck poses inside the box as his neighbors and friends take snapshots of the only man they've ever met who had a good time at his own wake.

He remains a gentleman when the exotic dancer appears like a brunette apparition in a Kelly green G-string to sway and undulate to a rock 'n' roll beat. She moves around him on the wooden floor of the old saloon as if acting out an unnamed fertility ritual.

As the crowd reacts to Chuck's harmless antics, you remind yourself that even the brave fear death. Although many people would say life has forced Chuck Frye down a mean final road, in some ways he is fortunate. In blocking out our fear of the dark, most of us forget that life is finite and time is passing.

Chuck does not suffer from that delusion.

"I got a lot of pains, but I got a lot of pain pills," he says.

"What are you going to do, crawl in the corner and snivel? Forget that."

Later, the laughing mourners pile into cars and pickups and begin the procession past the Goodsprings graveyard and over the hill to Sandy Valley and a rendezvous with a corned beef and cabbage meal.

Had Chuck been a rich man, with access to the best treatment and costly medicine, things might be different. He might have more time.

But he's not a rich man. He's just a guy who spends his days crafting fancy belt buckles. His wife, Helen, makes change at a casino on the interstate. Together, they earn enough to get by in the desert community beyond the lights of Las Vegas.

Chuck has pain. Sometimes, plenty of it. But he knows where there is pain, there is life. It is a lesson some men never learn.

Despite the aches of the body and heart, the journey down life's highway is to be celebrated.

So while Chuck Frye lives, he laughs. The people who share his world laugh with him.

Any excuse for a party. ◆

Boomtown Blues

Big Springs another example of neglecting signs of past times

June 28, 1998

Close your eyes, and you can almost hear the stream flowing from Big Springs.

Open them, and you see that it is not a stream, but a river of traffic making that rushing noise. Automobiles rumble and roar barely 100 feet from what was once the source of water from which Las Vegas sprang.

To harried commuters, Big Springs is a patch of green on the breakneck trek from Desert Shores to downtown. Its fenced cottonwoods stand on property owned by the Las Vegas Valley Water District.

Save for some transients, it gets few visitors. The question is whether this 180-acre historical site, our last best reminder of Southern Nevada's beginnings, is important enough to save.

The question is being studied on the ground by archaeologists, biologists, and environmental planners. It is being considered at a political level by a variety of government entities. At stake is not only Big Springs, but dozens of homes on the opposite side of the expressway, which is overdue for widening.

Something's got to give.

In other communities, ones that do not deny their heritage, the question would have been answered generations ago. There would be a park at Big Springs. The buildings that once housed settlers and, later, well caretakers, would have been preserved. There would be a nature trail, and guides would educate visitors about the importance of the area throughout the centuries.

But Las Vegas is not like most cities. It denies, or simply neglects, its rich cultural heritage.

It has missed nearly every opportunity to preserve its cultural icons, architecturally important buildings, and historical sites. From the old ice house to the area surrounding the Mormon Fort, community leaders have done a shameful job of protecting our past.

Now comes Big Springs.

Make no mistake, there is treasure there. Not gold and silver, but the dramatic signs of civilization predating Columbus and even the first green-felt table and deck of cards.

Long before the spirit of Vegas Vic ruled the valley, Big Springs was an oasis for Indians. Tribes wintered there and prospered on the banks of deep artesian pools that roiled forth from the earth and created what later was called Las Vegas Creek. By desert standards, it was a raging river.

The water once flowed all the way to the Colorado River. After nearly a century of well-drilling, no water is visible on the surface. The older wells collapsed long ago, and the sites of the pools are now clodded pits surrounded by cottonwoods and mesquites.

Though much is taken, something abides.

If you seek proof of the area's cultural diversity, know that two prehistoric archaeological sites are there and that signs of Indian presence in the area have been dated to at least 1,500 years ago. From the Anasazi to the Southern Paiute, Indians relied on Big Springs for survival. The area was nominated for inclusion on the National Registry of Historical Places in 1978.

Today, the area is an unofficial wildlife refuge. Coyote and fox roam there. A keen eye might spot a rare desert pocket mouse or endangered loggerhead shrike.

As I toured the property recently, accompanied by environmental planner Kim Zukosky, archaeologist Greg Seymour, and public information coordinator J.C. Davis, I couldn't help but get the feeling that these intelligent well-meaning people were struggling in vain to save a place that already is as lost as the Anasazi who once drank from its waters.

It was a touch depressing. As a boy growing up not far from Big Springs, I sneaked over the fence and took an unofficial tour of the property. The buildings were rundown then, but they were standing. The structures were a reminder of a time when the lights in the valley were not so bright.

A few years later, a building burned. Another collapsed under the impact of a fallen tree limb and the heavier weight of neglect. Big Springs was going the way of so many other local historical places.

I still believe Big Springs is worth restoring, no matter how late in the day it seems. But I would not want to be the person charged with forcing out the homeowners on the opposite side of the expressway. They, too, have something worth preserving.

We have allowed our cultural heritage to slip through our fingers. It is a shame, but the question of Big Springs' future will not wait.

Our river of time flows from Big Springs.

The past is worth protecting, but time is now of the essence. ◆

Las Vegas desert water expert would like to turn off the growth

January 6, 1991

Think of gentle Jim Deacon as one man crying out in Southern Nevada's parched dusty wilderness.

The UNLV biology professor is probably best known as the champion of the Devil's Hole pupfish, the rare minnow-sized species found only in the remote desert pond.

Deacon, 56, surfaces almost everywhere the subject of water and the desert is discussed. With three decades of experience studying desert habitats for the university, it is hard to imagine a Las Vegas resident more keenly aware of the importance of water in arid lands.

What Deacon has to say no doubt will disturb developers, some public officials, and champions of the helter-skelter expansion everywhere. Given the sorry state of water usage in the valley, that's not such a bad thing.

"It seems to me fairly obvious that a majority of citizens think this place is growing too rapidly," Deacon said recently. "I think we're growing out of control. In effect, we're not paying the cost of growth.

"We're deferring all costs to the future."

That cost could be devastating.

"Nowhere is this more obvious than in the valley's current water crisis," he said.

The Las Vegas per capita water use is 360 gallons per day for everything from a cool drink to lawn maintenance. The number is far higher than the regional average and is deceiving because it does not account for the water used by many of Southern Nevada's more than 18 million annual visitors.

Other cities in arid climates consume far less. In Tucson, 160 gallons is the average. In Phoenix, it's 251. In North Las Vegas, it's 210.

With the valley's population rapidly growing, the Las Vegas Water District set out to find other major sources of water.

Last year, Clark County began seeking the rights to 865,000 acre-feet of state-owned water in Nye, Lincoln, and White Pine counties. The grand plan is to pump some of that water to Southern Nevada to avert what even generous experts believe will be a critical shortage before the end of the decade.

As no small aside, if approved, the project will cost hundreds of millions of dollars. Given the history of most government projects, the final cost could be billions.

"If local and state leaders show the courage necessary to stem growth," Deacon said, "that illogical billion-dollar project won't be needed.

"It's not even a difficult task using standard technology to cut our water consumption in half. We have enough water, if we ever apply standard efficiency, to support four times the population we have now."

Water district officials say a 25 percent savings would be outstanding, but 15 percent is a realistic goal.

Deacon asks, "Whose reality?"

Given the current pro-growth mindset, such figures probably are accurate, and that hits the heart of the problem. Merely fixing a drip or warning residents of impending doom if their neurotic lawn sprinklers aren't fixed isn't enough.

Tough sober ordinances must be passed, laws that force changes in business practices and public habits. Such changes will take a courage not commonly found on traditionally pro-growth governing bodies.

Thousands of apartments and homes can be retrofitted with water-efficient toilets and lawn systems. It has been done in other communities, though not in a boom town of Las Vegas' caliber.

"If developers are made to save the water on their previous projects that they plan to spend on future ones, then Southern Nevada's water consumption figure would be drastically reduced," Deacon said.

"While residential runoff is a chief culprit, water-main leaks account for much of the waste," he said. "Patching pipes can be costly, but the price is small when compared to the money needed to carve an aqueduct or lay a pipeline from Northern Nevada to a kitchen sink near you."

While installing a high-tech turbo toilet saves a couple gallons per flush, it isn't going to save the valley at the current rate of growth. But imagine how much water would be saved daily if every hotel room in Las Vegas were fitted with one.

"I would suggest we start looking at the demand side, rather than the supply side," Deacon said. "The technology exists for us to live more efficiently. We should encourage efficiency, not subsidize growth. It's simply wise for us to be efficient."

Unfortunately, in Southern Nevada, wisdom often has proved a far more precious commodity than water. ◆

Water cop just keeps sloshing along, against the tide

March 24, 1991

Steve Huffman, Clark County's water cop, patrols the streets like a territorial marshal from the Old West. He has a big job, pardner, but someone has to do it.

A Lone Ranger in a Ford Ranger, Huffman peers over the steering wheel and keeps his eyes on the gutters as the pickup starts and stops in midday traffic up Sahara Avenue toward the Lakes.

For the water cop, the Lakes is the Badlands of H_2O excess.

Despite the fact he works for the county and the Lakes is located in the city, most of his two dozen daily water-waste complaints come from the lush, pond-dotted, planned community.

"I can tell you right now where we're going to see the problem," Huffman says.

Most of the culprits are easy to catch. Foiling a faulty sprinkler and apprehending an overzealous water hose is not exactly like snaring Jesse James. A visit to a homeowner usually fixes the leak.

But not always.

As he turns left on Durango Road, the only water cop in town shakes his head. The sidewalk is soaked. The gutter is running strong. A wall-eyed sprinkler is supposed to be watering part of the Lakes' green belt. Instead, it is trying to grow asphalt.

"Here you have one of the best areas in Las Vegas to take a stroll, and you can't use the sidewalk without getting drenched," Huffman says with resignation.

The worst approaches.

As he turns right on Desert Inn Road, the pickup rolls through a fast-flowing creek. Ernest Hemingway would have written a short story about fishing here.

"It's about like a trout stream," he says. "It runs 24 hours a day."

While the water ends up in a detention basin seemingly built to collect the thousands of gallons of runoff, the source of the spill is not clearly known. Huffman travels a mile up Desert Inn, cuts through the subdivisions, and spots a half dozen tributaries. A busted green-belt sprinkler gushes hundreds of gallons. Runoff from water-logged lawns accounts for hundreds more.

Huffman takes a few notes.

The theory behind the water cop is logical. Residents consume the most water. Lawns consume most of the residential water. Much of that is wasted due to runoff and over-watering.

That's where the water cop steps in. The problem is that the county is large and the water cop is a Lone Ranger without even a Tonto to provide backup.

With the Las Vegas Valley Water District increasing its pressure on the public to conserve water, Huffman's job has become more important, and more difficult. While most residents are cooperative, a few don't want to hear about conservation until they see what they perceive as the big water dogs leashed.

"They look at me and say, 'Why don't you pick on Steve Wynn?'" Huffman says of the Mirage boss' watery resort. 'Have you seen all the golf courses in this town?'"

Being a water cop isn't easy. Huffman risks more than an earful of complaints and soggy shoes. He suffered three dog bites in 1990 and narrowly escaped a German shepherd attack earlier this year.

He also had a run-in with a karate expert at a kung fu clinic. Because the water cop is allergic to karate chops, he let the black belt keep his runoff.

The water cop has almost no real power to enforce local ordinances. Until he receives more clout, he will continue to plug away as the district's mobile reminder to residents to shut off spigots and replace busted sprinkler heads.

"It's everyone's problem. It's everyone's responsibility," he says. "We're spending our children's inheritance."

What about desert landscaping?

Huffman said it is a delightful idea, but too few people have embraced the cacti consciousness.

"I wish I could give you a good example," Huffman says. "Unfortunately, there aren't a lot around."

Despite warnings and the impending increase in monthly rates, conservation is on too few people's minds, he says. One guy wandering the valley in a pickup can't change an entire community's water philosophy.

After informing a woman that draining her pool into the gutter is against the rules, it's on to the Desert Shores community, where rumor has it the gutters are flowing like the Colorado.

One man standing against a tide of runoff, the water cop's work is never done. ◆

House that Bugsy built joining fallen Vegas landmarks

December 8, 1993

The Oregon Building's windows are as hollow as Ben Siegel's eyes.

I stand at the Flamingo Hilton outside crowded Lindy's Deli, staring across the empty pool area and into the construction site. The view is end-of-the-world empty.

If everything goes according to plan this week, the original Fabulous Flamingo, the house that Bugsy built, will go the way of all things in Las Vegas. Barring a mass protest, and so far I'm the only mope to whine about it, work crews will whack it into the history books before you can say, "Duck, Mr. Siegel."

Surrounded by polished corporate casino high-rises, the once-quaint Oregon Building is as ugly as an old shoe. Its paint is faded, its wrought iron railings are bent. Some of its windows are busted, a flaw bug-eyed Ben Siegel would have thrown a fit over.

I do my best to get misty over the demise of the four-story hotel with the built-in gun portals and the escape routes leading from the master suite to the underground garage and a get-away car. I want to pick a rose from the garden Benny dedicated to his sweet Virginia. Maybe recite a sonnet, or at least ask a few gray-haired tourists their recollection of the good old, bad old days.

I want to lament the demise of another Las Vegas historical landmark, no matter how notorious its origin.

But, you know, Siegel was a killer.

Hill was a glamorous tramp.

When the Flamingo opened a day after Christmas in 1946, it was a glitzy flop of a clip joint. It lost a small fortune, closed, then reopened in the spring a few weeks before Siegel took a one-way trip to Beverly Hills.

Siegel had big plans, but an even bigger overhead. His $1 million desert dream bungled its way into a $6 million death sentence. The unannounced execution was carried out June 20, 1947, at the Beverly Hills home of Siegel's girlfriend, Virginia Hill.

If the very same characters operated today's casinos, Don Trump and Bob Stupak would have turned up missing years ago.

In death, Siegel became a legend.

Time and Hollywood have colored the image. In the big-budget movie, Warren Beatty played the part of Siegel.

The fact is, the genuine article, who wore tailored suits and loved to surround himself with Hollywood stars, confessed to taking part in a dozen homicides. That qualifies him as a mass murderer in some dictionaries. He was a killer with class, perhaps, but a hit man just the same.

The same truth test applies to the original Flamingo. It's historical, but homely.

In a better Las Vegas, a spot would exist to preserve pieces of Southern Nevada's tawdry history. Other than in Lonnie Hammargren's backyard, I mean.

The city's forefathers spent so much time covering their tracks and spraying cologne on their pasts that little of the syndicate's city exists in 1993. It's far too late for sentiment now.

"This is not the Lincoln Memorial," Flamingo Hilton publicity director Terry Lindberg says. "It's a completely different thing. It's not the sort of thing where anybody should be losing sleep over not maintaining a memorial to a mobster."

Instead, the area will become a memorial to the strength of the corporate casino bosses: a 600-room tower, 15 acres of tropical pools, islands and gardens, a ballroom, and a new sports book and buffet.

There will be no plaques, no rose gardens, no busts of the old boss. No tributes, no traces. Some things never change.

On the way out, a sports book pony catches my fancy. I drop a fin to win on Fortune's Gone in the first at Calder, expecting the burro to go lame between post time and the back stretch. Instead, the three-year-old takes the stakes race by a half-dozen lengths, and I pocket enough for bus fare around the new Las Vegas.

On the street, I decide against taking just one more look at the house Bugsy built. Forget about it: Siegel has been dead almost as long as the Flamingo has been a hotel.

In this town, sentiment is for suckers.

See you in the movies, Benny boy. ◆

Update: Flamingo management later changed its mind and erected a small brick shrine to Siegel in the pool area near where the Oregon Building stood.

To those who bet on a neon mirage, Las Vegas matters

December 17, 1993

It's just a sand-swept oasis on a sun-blinded desert, but Las Vegas matters.

Sometimes I catch myself mumbling the refrain while walking through this glorious, Godless, atomic boomtown. (I have to be careful about talking to myself in public. People tend to stare.)

Even as the bulldozer groaned and strained Tuesday morning to knock down the original fabulous Flamingo, I reminded myself Las Vegas matters to the people who have wagered their futures on this neon mirage. Thousands continue to migrate from everywhere for a chance to carve out a life here.

I suspect it is one reason locals so often feel compelled to ferociously defend this town's hopelessly tawdry reputation.

Hoping to hold a few memories before the old city returns to the sand from where it came, I stood and watched the final hours of Ben Siegel's Flamingo and thought of what the other

Las Vegas offered those who sojourned here.

In 1946, the Garvin family came to the desert.

Don Garvin took a job as a key maker and locksmith at the new Flamingo, and quickly moved into the top engineering job. He remained there nearly three decades.

He met Siegel and Gus Greenbaum, both of whom would be murdered. Although he had brushes with the notorious, Garvin spent most of his time in the boiler room keeping the Flamingo running. He raised his family and watched the town fill the valley.

He is 89 now and has his family and his memories. On Tuesday, he sat in a wheelchair amid the racket and reminisced.

"It was a loser to start with, but it turned out to be quite a hotel," Garvin said. "Siegel didn't hurt anybody around here. He helped build the town, no doubt about that. He never caused any trouble at all."

When Garvin was a younger man, the 77-room Flamingo was a palace in the desert. On Saturday, the MGM Grand Hotel & Theme Park opens. It has 5,005 rooms.

"If I'd realized the town would be like this," Garvin said, smiling, "I'd have made some money out of it."

Instead, he settled for making a living for himself, his wife Laura, and their four children.

On Tuesday, Laura wore a red coat and mostly remained apart from the gathering. Her children learned to swim in the Flamingo pool. Some of the fanciest times of her life took place in the restaurant and showroom.

Las Vegas mattered.

"We used to see a lot of the shows," Laura said. "The service was wonderful. The meals were good."

In Las Vegas, only memories remain.

They are postcards, really, mental snapshots of an era that existed not so long ago.

Old-timers I know who had the pleasure of growing up in the Los Angeles of a half-century ago love to tell stories of sneaking rides on the downtown trolleys. Otherwise upstanding fellows from New York, Chicago, or a dozen other big cities grin wickedly when recalling their stolen-apple youths.

Although he is far from an elderly man, I saw that grin on Neil Garvin's face Tuesday. Having a dad who was the godfather of the Flamingo's true inner sanctum opened the way for a few Huck Finn-in-Vegas adventures.

"We used to come out here every weekend. Dad would keep an eye on us, or try to," Neil Garvin said as a bulldozer gnawed on the building.

Neil and his twin brother, Noel, would sneak up into the showroom's light booth to catch a glimpse of Sheila MacRae and Bobby Darin. The Flamingo's catacombs provided countless adventures.

When they tired of playing inside, they took to the nearby desert in a borrowed electric maintenance cart with security guards in hot pursuit.

"You can't have much more fun than that," Neil said through the crush of the past giving way to the future.

Las Vegas matters to the Garvin family and to many families. Now the Flamingo, and the town it symbolized, is a desert memory.

Because history is only sand we take time to give a name, on Tuesday I picked up a chunk of sandstone from the fabulous Flamingo's fallen facade.

A rock to remember a neon mirage. ◆

Las Vegas outgrows the friendly confines of the rotunda

February 14, 1991

As workers peeled off pieces of the Convention Center rotunda like so many garments from a sagging old stripper, I promised myself not to get too sentimental about the demise of the gaudy old gal.

After all, unless you can imitate a dead entertainer, it doesn't pay to feel nostalgic in Las Vegas. Look around. This city has no past, only a big future. Las Vegas perpetually denies its heritage in an endless but futile search for respect from Middle America.

The rotunda is being leveled in favor of a bigger, brighter, and more expensive facility as part of a $50 million renovation of the Convention Center. Oh, boy. Just what we need—more convention space.

Like that squatty old harem girl, the rotunda's years of service have earned it little respect. On Wednesday morning, as workers lifted its skirt and tore at its big top, the rotunda was well on its way to becoming just another funky and wonderful Las Vegas memory.

But, after a little more than three decades, the space ship on Paradise Road could not hold all the memories to which it has played host.

Shaped every bit like a flying saucer, it was constructed in 1959 near the end of what is best described as the George Jetson era of American architecture. The period was defined by the hip heights of Seattle's Space Needle. While not unique, buildings such as the rotunda in Las Vegas was all the rage. When those buildings went the way of the Hula-Hoop a few years later, the rotunda fit nicely into this city's Disney-meets-Dali architecture.

It was not its architecture that made the rotunda special. Its events are what made it an integral and endearing part of the community.

President Kennedy filled the rotunda for a speech in 1963. Civil rights leader Martin Luther King Jr. addressed an audience of 1,200 there a year later.

It also was the site of dozens of circuses, rock concerts, and college basketball games. The community congregated at the rotunda when much of the community could fit inside comfortably.

Siegfried & Roy's act pales in comparison to those first circus experiences at the rotunda, at least in my memory. The clowns and trapeze artists, conjured from the dark by a spotlight and the ringmaster's voice, still retain their color and excitement years later.

Before Jerry Tarkanian put the Runnin' in Rebels, UNLV's basketball team dribbled there. Tarkanian's early Rebel teams, including the nationally prominent Hardway Eight club, packed the rotunda game after game. It was there I fell in love with high-speed basketball.

It was there I became a sucker for Muhammad Ali. He had just finished dancing and slapping his way to a 12-round victory over British boxer Joe Bugner on February 14, 1973. Standing near the ring on a chair I had no business claiming, I called to Ali as he strolled by with his entourage. He paused and smiled at me before continuing on his way. That moment of acknowledgment, when he had thousands of more important fans, sold me for good on The Greatest.

It was at the rotunda I attended an Eagles concert with my first girlfriend. The concert was not particularly memorable, just smoky and loud and very grownup. In other words, a perfect rock concert. As a teen-ager, it is imperative to be very grownup. Years later that relationship went the way of the Eagles, but fortunately I am no longer so mature.

I could wax nostalgic about my high school graduation or any of a dozen other memories that include the Convention Center as a setting, but I promised to refrain from sentimentality.

Fair enough. I'll say it: Las Vegas has outgrown the rotunda. It has outgrown its roads, water, and air. Why not the big, friendly space ship?

As the city continues to expand at its logarithmic pace, the remnants of that small comfortable Las Vegas are trampled. But as outdated as it was, the rotunda was a part of the community of Las Vegas. Not the neon, but the place people live and work and raise their children.

Suffice it to say the rotunda is going the way of progress, which knows nothing of heavyweight champs, circus clowns, first girlfriends, or sentimentality generally.

Did I ever tell you about the time Ali smiled at me? ◆

Old-timer thinks Nevada is losing a remarkable lifestyle

July 19, 1991

You expect unassuming Jerry Cahill to be one of those growth-is-good preachers who throughout the 1980s shouted from the rooftops about booming Las Vegas' unlimited growth potential.

After all, he was the man in charge of registering the hundreds of new businesses that have opened in the city in the past decade. Until retiring last week, Cahill was the city's director of business licensing.

But Cahill is not just another cookie-cutter bureaucrat. He is a proud native Nevadan, and that may be what the city will miss most now that he is gone.

A country boy by birth and politics, Cahill was born in the mining town of Ely and has spent his life in Nevada. He has watched the state, and especially Las Vegas, undergo a rapid and troubling transformation.

"I think any time you grow like we've grown in an almost uncontrolled fashion there's going to be a lot of mistakes made, and I think we're experiencing that now," said Cahill, a Southern Nevadan since 1966. "The air was nice and clean years ago in the valley. There was always a little breeze. Now you see the haze hanging up here like it does on the eastern side of the valley. Frankly, as a longtime resident, our quality of life has been challenged. I don't think it's what it used to be."

What it used to be, he said, was a smaller community whose residents were not forced to breathe down each other's necks and drive in bumper-to-bumper traffic. Now the 10-minute commute from his home to City Hall takes half an hour. Now, the once abundant water is in short supply.

With all this progress throughout the state, Cahill fears Nevada, the wild wide-open place that exists as much in the psyche as on any map, will be gone forever.

It may sound quaint by Los Angeles and New York standards, but that lifestyle existed locally only less than a generation ago. Las Vegas was hardly a desert paradise; it has long possessed a hard edge thanks to the casino industry, but only a few years back the community existing away from downtown and the Strip was not troubled by traffic tie-ups, water shortages, and street crime.

Cahill also noticed changes in the types of businesses migrating to Southern Nevada, namely the raunchy bars and telemarketing outfits that attempted to proliferate locally. Again, it wasn't that the Las Vegas of a decade ago even vaguely resembled Salt Lake City, but it also was not the country's center for sex-tease nightclubs and fast-talking phone sales.

Although the telemarketing industry has undergone a gradual evolution, Cahill said without supervision the local sex trade is bound to get worse.

"In the past five years I've seen a dramatic increase in the types of questionable businesses that we get inquiries on," he said. "It seems like we used to be confronted with some of these things on occasion. When I left, it was almost a daily occurrence."

From topless doughnut shops to a proposed sexual encounter therapy center, attempts to license sexually oriented businesses in Las Vegas have become increasingly creative. They may be lucrative businesses, he said, but they are notorious fronts for prostitution. He also questioned the impact such rackets have on the community.

Maybe Las Vegas has passed Cahill by. If it has, you must ask whether it has passed him going the wrong direction.

A lot has changed since Cahill was a kid in Ely. He knows he can't go home again. While the south has been overrun by development, the north has been raped by corporate mining.

"The miners are literally packing the northern part of the state off," he said. "I have to wonder what's left of Nevada."

As for the near future, Cahill said he plans to travel with his wife Ronda, another native Nevadan, and hasn't ruled out a possible move from the valley he has watched change so drastically in 25 years.

"Who knows, maybe we'll take a trip and go some place else that's maybe a little more conducive to my lifestyle," he said. "Less traffic, less pollution and people. I wouldn't close the door on that."

You know, some place like the Nevada he remembers. ◆

Cowboy and wife to leave valley as Las Vegas crowds in

December 12, 1993

When the road turns from asphalt to gravel, you're almost to Pete Crump's place.

His slice of Southern Nevada spans 3 $1/2$ acres out in what not long ago was called the rural northwest end of the valley. Dedicated mostly to his horses, in spirit his land is a world away from the new Las Vegas.

Back when the valley had room for cowboys and the Western lifestyle, Crump moved his family out past the lights of Las Vegas. His only neighbors were a few grinning coyotes and a covey of quail.

His job as a dealer and floor supervisor at the International (now the Las Vegas Hilton) kept him busy in town, but his heart was on his place with his wife, Lucille, and his kids and horses.

You see, Pete Crump is a cowboy.

Not the two-bit drug-store variety, but the genuine article. Being a cowboy is not about hats and boots. It's a country philosophy, a way of life.

Crump is barrel-chested with a broad neck and shoulders. His mitts are thick, his handshake firm. He welcomes you to his home with a hot cup of coffee and unpretentious conversation.

Raised on a ranch outside Augusta, Montana, Crump rode horseback to enter his first rodeo at age 11; he won a month's pay that day and narrowed his career goals to one precarious profession.

He went on to become a championship bronc and bull rider and qualified for the first five National Finals Rodeos. Over 24 years, Crump was written up in many national newspapers, and the great sports scribe Red Smith penned three columns about him.

"It was a great life," he says, acknowledging that it cost him 10 leg breaks. "I loved every minute of it."

With the NFR in Las Vegas this past week, the city took on a distinctly Western style. Blackjack dealers and store clerks donned Wranglers and pointed-toed boots in a playful tribute to the rodeo crowd. Almost half a century ago, before Ben Siegel opened the Flamingo, the Western theme defined Las Vegas.

It's part of what attracted Crump to the area, part of what he misses as he contemplates leaving after 25 years. There isn't much space left for the Pete Crumps of the valley.

He has fought constantly with county bureaucrats, who have been all too eager to claim a piece of his land for road easements and charge him for their sewer lines and asphalt paving. He has won a few battles, lost a few more.

He never figured he'd have to hire an attorney to protect his right to live in the country, but that's about the size of it. No matter what he does, the city keeps coming. Out his back door, where once only Sunrise Mountain obstructed his view to the east, housing developments now are 40 acres away.

To people raised in the city, that may seem like a great expanse.

But not to a cowboy.

Crump is not unique. Hundreds of longtime Las Vegans know his plight. Approaching age 65, he figures he is just young enough to do something about it.

"I think the traffic and the influx of people, the congestion, is the thing that gets to you after a while," he says, careful not to criticize the town that enabled him to earn a good living. "It's just getting a little too close for me. I've been out in the country all my life, and I want to live there."

Lucille says, "It's only a matter of time before they won't let you have horses here. We didn't think we'd ever be close to town."

They're not alone in that feeling. When they weren't looking, the town went and became a big city on them.

So, Pete and Lucille Crump are selling out, moving north to Cody, Wyoming, where their daughter and son-in-law own the Proud Cut bar and restaurant. Crump has his sights set on an eight-acre parcel with a view halfway to heaven and no one to crowd his Western soul.

"I'll be able to look out my front door to hundreds of acres of open space," Pete Crump says, smiling.

He'll go grudgingly, but he'll remember when the desert coyotes called near his back door.

Las Vegas has changed forever, and a cowboy needs room to roam. ◆

Busybodies' bull run: bovines in booties bypass blockheads

June 6, 1998

I was a cowboy once.

Actually, more than once. A few times is more like it.

Like almost all kids, there was a time I was fascinated with riding and roping and romanticized the lifestyle.

From an early age I wanted to be a cowboy. Not forever, mind you, but just long enough to try my hand and be reminded that some activities are best left to the experts.

Whenever the opportunity presented itself, I grabbed a rope and tested my luck. Turns out my luck was all bad.

I roped a range cow and hung on as it yanked me out of the saddle and dragged me through the brush.

I rode a steer once. Three seconds later, I was picking gravel out of my scalp.

I even tried to wrestle a steer once. Not off horseback, but man to cow.

Getting an arm around one isn't nearly as hard as the takedown. Turns out cows prefer not to wrestle. I encircled the animal's neck like a string of puka shells and finally let go when the steer pressed me against the fence with his 500 or so pounds.

Haven't had a taste for red meat since.

Yeah, it was pretty stupid. But then no one ever accused me of having the sense God gave a cud-chewer.

Besides, the freedom to try something stupid is what made this country great.

As you might be able to guess, I think the running of the bulls July 11 in Mesquite is a great idea. I can't imagine how it became controversial. Other than the day I spent in Pamplona, Spain, many years ago drinking wine and posing in front of the Hemingway monument, playing the role of the occasional cowboy is the only experience I can relate to such a marvelously warped and foolish activity.

Cutting loose a dozen bulls and letting them charge a few hundred half-witted Hemingways is bound to attract a crowd and plenty of media, too. Mesquite's economy will benefit, and a good garden hose with a high-pressure nozzle will clean up the blood stains.

And if someone gets stomped beyond recognition?

Hey, people die on the highway every day—and car accidents aren't nearly as entertaining as watching a 1,200-pound animal have its way with a tourist.

Having watched the political battle of the bull run develop in recent weeks, I have reached the conclusion that the real problem is not with the event, which is being promoted by Phoenix businessman Phil Immordino, but with the folks on the sidelines.

Not the thousands of gawkers who are sure to take in the spectacle, but the whiners and the fretters who care more about little things like lawsuits and animal husbandry than the time-honored art of drawing a crowd and selling T-shirts.

In approving Immordino's knockoff of the annual event that brings a sea of humanity to Pamplona, Mesquite officials made him promise that participants would refrain from imbibing prior to the running of the bulls.

There's one promise the promoter can't keep. Nor should he.

If anyone deserves a few long pulls off the bota bag, it's a bunch of misguided macho men who are inviting full-grown farm animals to chase them down and do the fandango on their foreheads. Anything to kill the pain, I say.

Then there's the issue of the number of animals to allow into the event. The number now is a dozen, but that's nowhere near enough. If you're going to have a running of the bulls, have an all-out stampede.

Turn loose a couple hundred head of seething, snorting, fire-breathing, fighting bulls and let those muddle-headed matadors have at it.

Next. This balderdash about not allowing the promoter to use Mesquite Boulevard because it is a state road must cease. The Nevada Department of Transportation has determined all those hooves are bad for the asphalt, but diverting the event to some side street or back alley would defeat one of the purposes of the event: to showcase Mesquite as a town where people can come, pay their money, and do something really idiotic.

How is Mesquite going to become known as the moron Mecca of North America if the bureaucrats don't stop all this regulation?

What will they want next, foam-rubber horns?

Back-pocket protectors for all participants?

Truly angry bulls replaced by merely perturbed Holsteins?

Two guys in a cow suit?

No, I say this regulation must cease immediately. It's the only way to preserve the true spirit of the event.

At the very least there will be no need for the participants to wear helmets.

I suspect there won't be much in the way of brains to protect. ◆

UPDATE: The Mesquite bull run was a smashing success. There were no reports of fatalities.

Company calls Primm a proper name for State Line

January 19, 1996

All my early memories of State Line begin before dawn on Saturday with my father dragging me from sleep and coaxing me into the pickup.

In minutes we were southbound on Interstate 15 headed for the family mining claims at a high rate of speed. Riches were waiting in the sun-tanned mountains beyond the border.

The claims were staked at the edge of the Ivanpah mining district on Clark Mountain, a dozen jarring miles back into the hills, and my father and grandfather worked them for years without making the millions they felt certain were buried there.

As it turns out, their feeling was right.

Their calculations were just slightly off.

Once inside the pickup, I resumed sleeping for the 40-mile drive to State Line, where my father slowed the truck long enough to get a cup of coffee and top the fuel tank.

Coffee, gasoline, a cold beer. A pause on the bumpy trail to the elusive glory hole.

State Line, which everyone called Whiskey Pete's, was a roadside rest without a single attraction. A few slot machines and some bad food. Not exactly big-time marketing.

Maybe that's why I won't shed a tear when the place officially becomes Primm, Nevada.

My personal choice would have been Desperado, Nevada, but Primadonna Resorts officials forgot to ask my opinion. Primm might not be the flashiest name a Nevada city ever owned. It's a little too staid for folks who take their boomtowns with a double shot of hyperbole, but it's certainly a fitting moniker.

Depending on whose version of history you believe, the spot was known as State Line Station not long after the tracks of Montana Senator William Clark's San Pedro, Los Angeles & Salt Lake Railroad were laid through Ivanpah Valley.

The map speck could have been called Clark, but the senator already had a mountain and county named after him. Besides, State Line Station was little more than a water tank.

And nearby Roach Lake wasn't an inviting name for a town. Or a motel, for that matter.

By the 1920s, "Whiskey Pete" McIntyre is said to have offered bootleg hootch and gasoline to travelers making the journey from Southern California to Las Vegas. McIntyre's nickname became synonymous with the California-Nevada border.

Whiskey Pete's still wasn't much to look at in the early 1950s when Ernie Primm bought 400 acres for $15,000. He received another 400 acres under the Federal Land Grant Act, which compelled him to grow crops on the parched real estate. He actually harvested barley, which would have made McIntyre the bootlegger proud.

Primm built the first casino at State Line in 1977. Although he died before seeing it explode into the neon-lighted boom town featuring three casinos, hundreds of rooms, and a 209-foot-high roller coaster called the Desperado, Ernie Primm changed the border forever.

Initially, Primadonna Resorts' Chairman Gary Primm, Ernie's son, figured he would name the town after the corporation, which happens to be one of the most successful outfits in the casino industry. It not only made for great publicity, but it also would clear up any confusion created by the fact that the state line at Lake Tahoe also is called Stateline.

But it didn't take long before Gary remembered the importance of being Ernest's son. This week, the corporate boss decided that it was more appropriate to honor his father by making the name change official.

So, it's Primm, Nevada.

Ernest would have sounded too sincere, and Ernie probably seemed too much like a bar.

Until Ernest Primm and his son began building, it wasn't much more than an exit.

Not that it lacked for history.

The Old Spanish Trail crosses there. Of course, it has been

obliterated by off-road vehicles.

Once-prosperous mining camps, such as the one at Old Ivanpah, dot the landscape. But there isn't much left, other than broken bottles and played-out glory holes.

One of the area's most cantankerous residents was a character named Pop Shire. He owned a gypsum mine and ranked as one of the desert's severely troubled souls. He once gut shot an interloper, roped his feet together, and dragged him off what he considered his territory.

Customer relations have improved measurably since then.

Although nothing in this state ought to be too prim, it's all Primm out where Nevada kisses California at Interstate 15.

As for my family, we never got rich digging in the ground.

But it's heartening to know my father and grandfather weren't too far from the pay dirt, after all. ◆

Taking time for tortoises

October 4, 1991

Late as usual, coffee splashing my pants and the seat of the pickup, I barrelled up U.S. 95 toward the city.

Ahead, a familiar lump in the asphalt.

Gopherus agassizi.

Uh, I mean, a desert tortoise.

It was no road kill, not yet anyway, and I still had a few seconds to decide whether to save it from certain death or squash that sucker flat. It was a tougher call than you might imagine.

After all, mashing it is not a crime. Picking up a Mojave desert tortoise in the wild is a violation of federal law. Although it is sometimes difficult to tell where the so-called wild ends and civilization begins, the plight of the threatened species in 1991 begs a philosophical question:

To swerve or not to swerve?

As Southern Nevada rattles and races toward the 21st century, it is answering that question in a peculiar and uniquely American way.

Only in America could the quiet, weed-eating, desert tortoise cause so much controversy. Only in America could the spotted owl command so much respect while so many citizens go homeless. Only in America could an ice-bound whale be coddled and fed while children go abused and hungry.

Then again, it's not the birds' and the beasts' fault our nation's sense of ethics is so screwed up.

So there I sat behind the wheel with time running out on Tortoise X. Either I meet the tortoise, or the tortoise meets his Maker.

Saving the desert tortoise has become a multimillion-dollar shell corporation, of sorts. Between local attempts to create a habitat and federal intervention, it is estimated developers will pay $12.3 million in tortoise taxes and protection money. Naturally, the tortoises do not get to split up all that dough among themselves.

A recent *Review-Journal* article revealed that researchers and consultants are getting far fatter than the threatened beasts. From the Nevada Department of Wildlife to high-priced private firms, millions will be spent to remove and relocate the desert tortoise.

The County Commission recently set aside thousands of acres to create a desert tortoise sanctuary near Searchlight, where rumor has it citizens are thrilled at the prospect of all that commotion.

All this in the name of the desert tortoise, and a reasonable profit, mind you. Well, that's America.

We may not be doing everything possible to save it from extinction, but at least we're keeping tortoise consultants and myriad experts employed. That's reassuring.

Of course, seeking logic in an absurd society is asking too much. It's all we can do to keep from crushing ourselves into extinction.

In case you were wondering, I swerved.

I pulled over, dodged an 18-wheeler, and scooped up the grumpy-faced little jerk. By touching him, I put him at risk of catching a fatal respiratory infection. I probably made the little ingrate constipated for a month.

But I made sure Tortoise X would live another day. You know, with those sad eyes he looked just like Jerry Tarkanian.

Disregarding the official federal advice, I did not cross four lanes of maniacal traffic and risk being puréed by a two-ton piece of hurtling metal in order to deliver the tortoise to the other side.

Why did the tortoise try to cross the road?

To tick me off and make me late for work, that's why.

Surmising that he was lost and did not actually intend to take U.S. 95 to Tonopah, I hauled him about 50 yards into the desert and set him down next to a nice juicy cactus.

"Read 'em and weep, you little malcontent," I told him. "I saved your reptilian life. Now shut up and sit still."

What do I know, he probably hates cactus. He probably hates being hauled by humans. He probably wanted to commit suicide.

Meanwhile, I've been feeling guilty for violating federal law and upsetting man's delicate Marlon Parkins-meets-Salvador-Dali other Nature balancing act.

Why, I can almost hear the sirens now. The tortoise police surely are on their way. For all I know, Greenpeace will probably send one of those rubber dinghys after me.

If I concentrate, I can see the headline: "Columnist Molests Hitchhiking Desert Tortoise, Pays Fine, Does Hard Time."

What can I say?

Underneath this gruff exterior beats the heart of a sappy, tree-hugging, tortoise-toucher.

So sue me. ◆

Tortoise treatise ought to help police sort out shell game

October 25, 1991

It's long overdue, but Metro finally is receiving desert tortoise sensitivity training.

The change soon will be heralded wherever the tortoise is held in highest esteem. It warms the heart to know cynical local cops soon will share a deep and abiding respect for those ancient little army helmets with legs.

Thanks to a letter from a Clark County management analyst, the officers are now being informed of the latest techniques in surveilling, approaching and, only when absolutely necessary, apprehending the creatures.

The four-page treatise was addressed to noted amateur tortologist and sheriff John Moran and recently circulated through Metro's City Hall complex. In the interest of science, I have received a copy of the document.

"This letter is to inform you of new regulations and procedures concerning the handling and treatment of both wild and pet desert tortoises," the letter begins.

It goes on to explain the difficulty amateurs have distinguishing docile pet tortoises from their wild ill-mannered cousins. It's a mistake any cop could make; they sometimes have difficulty separating the good guys from the bad guys.

Millions are being spent to dig up the threatened critters and ship them to friendlier climes. The county recently announced its plan to spend $432,000 in tortoise defense funds to acquire the rights to a dandy habitat near Searchlight. The fact the federally owned land was inhabited by a relatively small number of range cows is beside the point.

Given recent events, police protection is a logical step in preserving the desert dweller. Nothing is too good for the tortoise.

The letter makes it clear they are to be handled only by trained experts, as improper treatment can harm the tortoises and result in nasty bites. It does not explain why hundreds have been adopted as pets by families with children, who treat them like battery-operated Tonka trucks. Surely an oversight.

If an officer encounters a wild tortoise, or a tame one on a drunken binge, he is instructed to approach with caution and call the proper authorities.

"The Mojave Desert population of the desert tortoise (the wild, free-living tortoise) is now federally listed as a threatened species not to be touched, harmed, harassed, moved, or collected from the desert," the letter instructs.

On the volatile subject of tortoises found wandering in developed areas, the letter settles all speculation: "You may have been directly and/or indirectly involved with these tortoises in the past. These tortoises and others will now be handled differently depending on where they are found. A special hotline has been established to direct individuals with inquiries about these tortoises to the Dewey Animal Care Center."

Remember: "The pet tortoise may have the owner's phone number on the shell and these owners should be called to pick up their tortoises. In developed areas the fate of a wandering tortoise without a phone number will depend upon where it was found."

Fortunately, police have plenty of spare time to address this issue.

In recent interviews, the cops made it clear unruly wandering tortoises will be prosecuted to the full extent of the law. Metro takes no guff from street gangs, public drunks, or *Gopherus agassizi*.

Early reports indicate the wild tortoise, although feisty, is relatively easy to subdue and take into custody. Just spook him into his shell, pick him up like a fumbled pigskin, and lateral him into the trunk.

Bingo, bango, bongo.

No handcuffs required.

Then it's downtown with Mr. Smart Guy, where he is toe-printed and receives a room for the night at taxpayer expense. It's Bermuda grass and water until he makes bail.

That'll teach the little hellion to roam free in developed areas.

Fortunately, costly scientific studies prove the vast majority of desert tortoises are sober peace-loving individuals who want nothing more than to meet a nice female *Gopherus* with a shiny shell and settle in a burrow out in the suburbs. Call them simple dreamers, but most enjoy the quiet life.

The troubling reality is, the suburbs are taken. So, it's off to the Searchlight Tort Ranch, where scientists have begun to study whether wild tortoises and pet tortoises will be able to harmoniously coexist.

It is a wonder how the creature survived all these centuries without our expert assistance, police protection, and government housing. ◆

Test site signs may be watershed in tortoise absurdity
February 2, 1992

It being winter and all, I hadn't heard much from the endangered desert tortoise and his thousands of dedicated human protectors.

The silence seemed logical enough. Tortoises hibernate this time of year, and their advocates tend to give the reptile rhetoric a rest until spring. Then, they renew their fight to save the little hard-shelled weasels from extinction and lesser man-made discomforts.

In recent years the tortoise helpers have been largely responsible for raising the public's environmental consciousness, slowing Southern Nevada's reckless growth, and separating government agencies from a fair piece of change. For that they deserve praise. Frankly, I wish I had thought of it first.

Beyond angering some and profiting others, the plight of the lovable desert tortoise also has helped reveal a few of the absurd ironies at work in our society.

Without so much as a single peaceful protest, the tortoise has made residents think about the delicate nature of the desert.

Moreover, the tortoise has managed to control area growth without making one campaign promise, consulting one political image-maker, or collecting one dime in special-interest contributions.

For that, if no other reason, the tortoise deserves to live long and prosper.

Given the recent record of the diminutive beast, perhaps I should have taken the winter's eerie quiet as an omen.

This week, the Department of Energy made a singularly splendid announcement. In the name of all that is sacred where the crawling critter is concerned, the DOE is placing "Caution Tortoise" signs in choice locations on the Nevada Test Site, as well as the acreage set aside for the proposed high-level nuclear waste repository at Yucca Mountain.

According to a press release, the signs will vary, but will have one common purpose: to warn truck-driving workers to be careful when steering in tortoise territory. Pickups tend to treat tortoises like mobile speed bumps, and tortoises hate it when that happens.

You see, the test site "has a long history of supporting research and work with endangered species." Thus, the recent announcement and the informative brochure distributed to the 10,000 test site workers. You can't be too safe where endangered tortoises are concerned.

Uh, wait a minute.

The test site is concerned about desert tortoises?

This may be a watershed in tortoise absurdity.

Unless I missed something, the test site also has a long history of exploding atomic bombs and conducting research that would curl a tortoise's hair, if he had any.

Since it began lighting nuclear fuses in 1951, more than 700 atomic bombs have been detonated at the test site. About 200 blew up above ground. With the enactment of the 1963 Limited Test Ban Treaty, the explosions were moved below the surface.

For the purposes of discussion, let us presume desert tortoises existed above and below ground during those years.

Although contamination levels vary, it is known that excessive amounts of uranium, plutonium, tritium, krypton, and other radioactive materials are present in test site topsoil. A farmer probably could grow cabbage there, but only the bravest soul would dare eat the cole slaw.

The half-life of uranium-235 is 700 million years; even the hardiest durable desert tortoise would have trouble lasting that long.

As for the Yucca Mountain repository, propaganda aside, its supporters promise to carve deep caverns in the earth and drop tons of harmful-if-swallowed high-level nuclear waste down the holes.

It's hard to imagine even the most politically correct nuclear dump site being good for desert tortoises. Then again, I haven't heard what Ron Vitto has to say on the matter.

Given the nuclear-heated history of the test site, it seems a little late to go around hammering tortoise crossing signs into the desert.

If the lowly test site desert tortoise can survive four decades of atomic bomb blasts, sporadic radiation leaks, and countless government bureaucrats, chances are good it can endure a Ford pickup.

Somewhere under the parched forbidding desert, thousands of endangered tortoises are laughing their shriveled little heads off. ◆

Tough shell no protection from changing tortoise rules

July 12, 1995

Despite the wet spring and abundance of grass in the Mojave, these are not the best of times for the humble desert tortoise.

Its habitat is crisscrossed with asphalt and is fast being replaced by mauve houses and strip malls. In recent years, the tortoise has padded through the bureaucratic wasteland that exists between endangered species status and a threatened classification.

Nature has outfitted it with a tough shell, but not a lobbyist.

East of extinction, west of Summerlin, the tortoise plods along with more enemies than allies. For environmentalists, it is a symbol of the vanishing desert. For developers, the sorry squatter represents a mountainous nuisance.

Before breaking ground, land owners pay the county $550 for every acre of raw real estate in the name of tortoise preservation. This tortoise tax has generated millions toward saving the critters from earth movers and securing their habitat for years to come. No doubt, some developers have acquired an enlightened soft spot for the hard-shelled creatures. Other builders probably would like to use their lumpy carcasses for a landfill.

If the desert tortoise has seen better decades, wait until it feels the steam-roller impact of the pending change in its status on land slated for development. The U.S. Fish and Wildlife Service is scheduled to announce this week its decision on the county's application to exempt the desert tortoise from Section 10A of the Endangered Species Act, which details the rules regarding taking the creatures in question from areas under development. The current system makes it mandatory for developers to seek out and remove tortoises from harm's way. The county's Desert Conservation Plan, which offers tortoise strategy for the next 30 years, argues for an exemption to the act's "incidental take" permit process.

In other words, it seeks to make removing desert tortoises from harm's way voluntary instead of mandatory.

The county's short-term plan is scheduled to expire at the end of the month. By presenting a detailed strategy, the way will be cleared to develop other desert real estate in Southern Nevada, while ensuring the preservation of tortoise-friendly areas.

Short of suddenly sprouting the legs of a greyhound, it appears lowly tortoises residing in developing areas are about to assume the stature of corn tortillas.

Since the tortoise was listed as an endangered species in August 1989, then reclassified as a threatened species the following April, more than 900 hours of public meetings have been held to discuss its health, habitat, and future. In the past five years, approximately 1,700 of the little knuckleheads have been plucked from the desert by well-meaning environmentalists. Of those, about 375 have been gathered from the path of development.

"It is very much our hope that the developers do survey and removal on a voluntary basis," desert conservation plan administrator Christine Robinson says.

If not, then it's tortoise tostada time. Unfortunate members of the species not only will be threatened, but flattened as well.

Robinson says developers who wish to comply will be assisted in the pick up and relocation of the tortoises. But they will not be monitored or commanded to clear an area of those toothless reptiles.

There's the irony. In the odd war to save the desert tortoise, the waifs residing in the path of development have become expendable. They are no less wild than the rest, merely less lucky.

The limited conservation dollars will be used to help preserve the species in the wild. Besides, advocates of the plan say, tortoises often perish after being removed from their own neighborhoods. They also tend to develop a deadly upper respiratory disease. Of course, they also often die if they remain behind.

In the interim, the little round refugees will continue to reside in a compound at the end of Rainbow Boulevard near State Route 160.

The others will be voluntarily removed by guys who drive heavy equipment for a living.

No, this definitely is not the best of times for the desert tortoise.◆

Hope for the wild horse of Red Rock

December 8, 1991

We picked through the rocks on strong horses in the hills a half-mile north of State Route 160. The autumn sun softened the afternoon chill, and the pillowy clouds that had dumped an inch of rain a day earlier were no longer threatening.

I rode with Bureau of Land Management cowboy Bob Stager and horse enthusiasts Randi Robertson, Karen Lewallen, and Eddie Longhurst. Most of my horse experience is limited to falling off and picking prickly pear out of my back pocket.

Assured by the wild-eyed Stager that my massive mustang, Big Boy, was completely schooled in the art of balancing Rexall rangers on its broad back, I attempted to keep up without losing my hat, notebook, or hide. I dropped the first two but kept the third.

It was a delicious day in the desert at the Red Rock National Conservation Area, and our animals stepped easily over the loose shale and pressed the damp red clay. It would be a worthwhile ride whether or not we spotted wild horses.

We were still close enough to the road leading from Las Vegas to Pahrump to hear the traffic drone when the Old West apparitions appeared. One sorrel and two pale palominos grazed on bush muhly, big galletta, and Indian rice grasses on the hill ahead. Wild horses are glorious sights.

They didn't spook, but stayed 100 yards beyond our reach.

"A bachelor band," said Stager, whose official title is Wild Horse and Burro Specialist. He explained the three horses had not yet started collecting mates.

Then he reminded me they easily were within shooting range.

Since 1988, 45 of Red Rock's wild horses have died: one from natural causes, 10 by drought, 16 by automobile, and 18 by gunshot.

"That's a lot of horses in three years," he said, maneuvering through the Joshua.

The kind of cruel mind that could shoot an animal just to

watch it fall is hard to imagine. The horses do not run at the sight of humans. They are easy targets.

At last count, the Red Rock palominos number fewer than four dozen. Although more than 5,000 wild horses still roam the range of mountains outside Nellis Air Force Base, the Red Rock area is the only place where a casual traveler is likely to see one in Clark County.

They stir thoughts of what the region was like a century ago when it was inhabited by Indians, hard-rock miners, and ranchers.

The land has its share of litter and motorcycle tracks. Despite recent conservation efforts, urban expansion threatens to carve up the area and ruin its beauty.

The small herd of horses and 55 burros, who mooch snacks from passing motorists, run in an increasingly cramped world.

What will be their fate?

Management is a partial answer. Relocation helps. Animal adoption, like the one taking place through Wednesday on the Strip near the Excalibur, saves some of the animals. Cooperation between ranchers and miners and governmental officials in managing natural water sources is essential.

A little respect wouldn't hurt, either.

As the palominos moved west, we rode toward the foothills. We crossed what was once part of the Wilson Ranch, high desert that had cattle from the 1850s through 1968. I tagged along feeling very much like a fat friar on a $2 donkey, and the real riders tried their best not to laugh.

In time we bombed through rolling clay banks all the way to Mud Springs, where a cooperative effort between the Silver State Pleasure Riders, the Friends of Wild Horses, and the BLM has resulted in an overflowing trough of spring water. The water benefits all the area's wildlife and would not flow without help. The springs have enabled mule deer and desert bighorn sheep, depleted by hunters generations ago, to return to the area.

Near sunset, with the smoky pink and yellow pastel of dusk filling the air, the horses slowed and the riders relaxed.

Off in the distance, with the brush in silhouette and the red sand turned crimson, Longhurst spotted a single wild horse. A sorrel with a white patch on its forehead. Old West history, real and romantic, flashed before my eyes.

The horse stood a mile off the highway, 20 minutes from Las Vegas, and a century out of time.

Our actions will decide whether it will be there for others in an increasingly uncertain future. ◆

Wings but no prayer for Nevada's newly condemned crows

April 2, 1998

Black slashes in a Van Gogh blue sky, common crows call to lonesome souls on solitary roads.

Like old love's memories, they exist in the distance. Out of reach, but close enough to catch the eye and fill the mind.

They mate for life, these birds, and decorate their nests with shiny objects like bottle caps and tin foil. They walk when it's windy, pick roadkill and seeds for meals. They are honored in Indian lore for their wisdom and their magic, and soon they will need every ounce of their spiritual charm.

These black birds, a nearly identical cousin of the larger and internationally protected raven, are not made for eating. I suppose they are edible, the way an old shoe is, but only an idiot would look forward to a steaming brace of crow.

Alas, it appears Nevada has almost as many idiots as crows.

On Saturday, the state Board of Wildlife Commission narrowly voted to create a crow hunting season: 10 birds per day, spring and fall seasons. Lock and load, fellas.

Of all the boneheaded moves pulled by state government in recent months, this has to be the dumbest. The wildlife commission members who voted for the regulation ought to be ashamed. Nevada's hunting community ought to be embarrassed into demanding the regulation be cleaned and plucked.

After all, does any self-respecting hunter really want to be known as the person who shoots crows just because there is a season?

Forget the fact only a starving coyote would eat one.

That's not hunting. That's simple cruelty.

What next, house sparrow season? Forty per day? (They're small, you know. Barely a bite apiece.)

Bluejays make a lot of racket. Better give them a little double-barrel therapy, too.

Any hunter who would shoot a crow ought to have his head examined by an experienced geologist. Imagine the mortification a real sportsman would experience if he stuffed the bird and displayed it next to his bull elk antlers and bighorn sheep. Now there's a conversation piece:

Hunter Bob: "Where'd you bag that black beauty? Looks like a real mean one."

Hunter Ray: "Why, right off the backyard power line. Knocked out the lights for two days, but I got him."

Hunter Bob: "Tough shot, eh?"

Hunter Ray: "Nailed him with the twelve gauge. Took hours piecing him back together."

Fact is, no good argument exists to start shooting crows. Not even Nevada's farmers and ranchers can say with straight faces that they needed a hunting season to eliminate these affable black birds. If crows are ruining the alfalfa in Yerington, no Nevada farmer ever got arrested for protecting his land from a predator or pest.

But the crows aren't devastating crops, slaughtering sheep, or carrying off toddlers.

Well, what's done is done. A call to Governor Bob Miller's office would be useless. He's a lame duck.

Wildlife Commission Chairman Don Cavin had the good sense to vote against the regulation. Cavin, 73, has been hunting and fishing in Nevada since shortly after arriving here in 1933.

"I've eaten a lot of crow on the commission, but not of the meat kind," Cavin says from his Hawthorne home. "I know there are some recipes for crow, but I've never tried one and I don't expect I ever will. I don't believe in shooting for the sake of shooting."

Federal regulations allow farmers who somehow feel threatened by crows to get rid of them, he says.

The real danger is not only to the crows, but to the protected ravens. Although generally larger than crows, from a distance ravens look like their common cousins.

"Crows and ravens are so much alike it's even difficult for an experienced bird-watcher to tell the difference," Cavin says. "When they start arresting people for shooting ravens, people will be up in arms when they're hauled into court. Adult crows and young ravens are basically the same size."

In Southern Nevada, Cavin says, there are relatively few crows, "but there are hundreds and even thousands of ravens."

And that means potentially thousands of violations. Assuming, of course, the offending hunters are caught by a game warden or are willing to turn themselves in.

As you can tell, I like crows.

Listen closely, and you'll hear them have the audacity to say no, no, no to man.

Unfortunately, some men take a sinister pleasure in destroying animals that dare to disagree with them.

May these common crows' dying calls haunt their killers' dreams. ◆

UPDATE: Attempts to halt the crow hunt were unsuccessful.

Phone sex workers put themselves on the line every day

August 5, 1998

A hot tip recently led the state attorney general's Workers' Compensation Fraud Unit to investigate the Shining Star company of Las Vegas.

Perhaps it was a Deep Throat source, or maybe someone sent a letter, but the result was that investigators opened a case against a company they first believed was a telephone sales outfit suspected of not paying workers' compensation premiums on its 27 employees.

After making a few calls, however, the investigators very nearly blushed when they found out the product Shining Star's dedicated crew was selling was sex.

Not the actual act itself, but the fantasy. To be more explicit, phone sex.

Now, I'm not sure how a phone-sex-company employee might injure him or herself on the job, but out of a sense of journalistic devotion I endeavored to find out.

The short answer is, you don't want to know.

The long answer my boss won't let me print.

Suffice it to say the potential for phone ear is great. And word is workers occasionally suffer from fantasy block, a debilitating malady in which a phone sex vixen just can't think of one more dirty thing to say to a stranger.

Undaunted, I called Kevin Higgins, chief deputy attorney general and director of the workers' compensation fraud unit.

In a perfectly polite baritone, without one ounce of irony or inflection, Higgins said, "We certainly don't go out looking for phone-sex companies to investigate."

Shining Star officials assert their workers are independent contractors.

The Shining Star case serves to illustrate a point: not about Southern Nevada's broadly diverse business community, but about the nature of workers' compensation insurance. With some exceptions, employers must carry workers' compensation insurance for their employees, either through a private company or the Employers Insurance Company of Nevada.

But what constitutes an employee?

The Nevada Revised Statutes has plenty to say on the subject, and it is riddled with exceptions.

For instance: All construction workers must be covered, but farm laborers are excluded. (Phone call for Mr. Chavez, Mr.

Cesar Chavez.)

Musicians are covered, except if their performances are "merely casual in nature and not lasting more than two consecutive days." Or unless they're really awful, in which case they are heavy metal rockers and are so wealthy they need no insurance.

Rabbis and other members of the clergy are excluded from the law. Apparently, doing God's work has a built-in insurance policy.

Part-time state legislators are covered, but part-time prostitutes are not. Go figure.

There is a special provision for members of county advisory boards to manage wildlife, but the state's description of wildlife is inconsistent with Shining Star's definition.

Household domestics, chicken pluckers, real estate brokers, and telemarketers are exempted.

So are entertainers.

This includes topless dancers and "any person engaged as a theatrical or stage performer or in an exhibition." And Steve and Eydie, no matter how they're dressed.

Even though they work harder than most casino executives, chorus line dancers by law can be excluded from coverage.

But nowhere in the state statutes does it say that professional heavy breathers are exceptions to the rule. Telephone sales persons, yes. Exotic tassel-twirlers, yes. But not the telephone tarts.

Seems as if the Shining Star folks fall somewhere between categories. Perhaps if they danced while they talked, then the phone-sex company would be off the hook.

Alas, it appears Shining Star's owner might face a misdemeanor charge and a fine.

In recent years, the AG's office has investigated approximately 5,000 complaints of workers' compensation fraud. About half of those are focused on workers, the rest on companies that have neglected to insure their employees.

"People should care because it's a hidden fraud that raises the prices of everything," Higgins says. "We all pay for it. It's really not the insurance company that's paying for it. We're all paying for it in the form of higher prices."

Threatened with the potential of being forced to pay a few thousand dollars in tardy insurance premiums, the phone-sex company has cut back its workers to a dozen.

For the record, I attempted to talk to the owner of Shining Star. She declined a request for a telephone interview.

Which, I suspect, is a first for her. ◆

Founding Fathers blush as First Amendment hits gutter

March 6, 1992

The First Amendment received a resounding Las Vegas-style endorsement Thursday in District Court.

Bill of Rights, you're beautiful, babe. Basic freedoms, you're numero uno, and I mean it.

More flexible than an exotic dancer, the First Amendment received a considerable workout in District Judge Donald Mosley's courtroom as owners of opposing publications advertising outcall entertainment services squared off in the name of freedom.

Freedom of the press.

Freedom of speech.

Freedom to get lucky.

Namely, freedom for eerie-looking characters on Strip sidewalks to pass out handbills advertising dance and entertainment businesses that promise "adult satisfaction," "red hot and lively," and "totally nude" babes direct to your room. At reasonable rates, of course.

Lest the naive Las Vegas newcomer be misled into thinking the town is brimming with Isadora Duncan types, outcall dance services are notorious fronts for prostitution, which is illegal in

Clark County unless you win elected office.

On one side of the constitutional concern, tawdry street tabloid publisher and outcall service operator Eddie Munoz. On the other side, publishers of the aforementioned handbills and related rags.

Munoz has strategically positioned news boxes on the Strip jammed with his *Adult Informer*. The others, six in all, have strategically positioned guys distributing handbills on the street corners.

But Munoz's attorney James "Bucky" Buchanan argued the shoe-leather ad men were nothing but sidewalk solicitors in disguise. It takes a privileged license to operate an outcall service. Why, those guys probably don't even have a license to drive.

Buchanan wanted the judge to force the Clark County Business License office to get the hustlers off the sidewalk and away from Munoz's *Informers*.

"They're promoting a business for which they have no license," Buchanan said. (As fate would have it, his client has a license.)

"You mean you need a license to send a nude person to a room?" Mosley asked amid titters.

Affirmative, your honor.

But once the dancer gets to the room, disrobes, works up a sweat, and mars the coffee table with her high heels, the customer is not allowed to pay her for sex.

The naked dancing is moral, the sex stuff is immoral.

Go figure.

"I don't want to pronounce a moral judgment on what we're talking about here," Buchanan said.

Which is good, because watching a judge die laughing would be a terrible thing.

Las Vegas' gutter-level sex racket aside, something much greater was in question. (Drum roll, please. Cue the unfurling of the Stars and Stripes.)

It's the First Amendment thing, babe.

Although embarrassing to county commissioners, Strip casino operators, and locals not employed in the trade, the news racks and bothersome bill-passers have a right to exist. More specifically, as long as the hawkers aren't harassing tourists or advertising prostitution, they can hand out harlot hype until Elvis phones home.

Deputy District Attorney Chuck Paine, charged with representing the business license office in the matter against Munoz, said the argument is simple and as old as America.

"We cannot restrict the use of a public forum in any way," Paine said. The sidewalk constitutes the forum, the bill-passers constitute the public. County ordinances ban selling goods and services on the street without a license.

But advertising is different.

"You cannot tread on the people's right to voice their opinion," Paine said. "The sidewalk is literally totally painted with the First Amendment."

By neon light, the First Amendment looks a lot like cigarette butts and discarded handbills advertising hoochie-coochie girls.

Fortunately, Mosley agreed with Paine and the Constitution and tossed the case back into the street.

It appears Munoz will have to concoct another way to put his competition out of business. His boulevard rivals can thank their sleazy stars the First Amendment extends from the penthouse to the outhouse.

Meanwhile, the Founding Fathers are blushing, babe. ◆

Drug addict hopes Southern exposure will change his life

September 23, 1990

He sat back with a Corona in the permanent shade of Frankie's bar and said he wants out. Out of the street life, out of the endless cycle of drug abuse, out of this seductively dangerous city.

He said he has dealt drugs for more than a decade and has an extensive arrest record. A phone call confirmed his criminal history, but left little indication of his street status. Assault with a deadly weapon registered on his record was enough to make the meeting less than comfortable.

I could not think of a reason why a tattooed hustler would want to exaggerate his role in the local methamphetamine racket. Although his credibility and sincerity were suspect, I decided to listen. Besides, he said he was an avid reader and I need all the fans I can get.

Over two hours he told stories of trips to jail, threats of prison, and a stint in a mental ward. He has lost wives, children, friends, jobs, and money, yet he still spoke with a strange reverence for drugs and the street lifestyle.

But now he wants out. This time, he means it. At 37, he senses his days on the street are numbered, and the number is low.

"You wind up either being dead or being in the joint. And being in the joint and being dead is the same thing," he said. "My intentions are I'm going to escape this. I'd just like to see something happen for the brothers who can't go with me. I'd like to see if there's a way to change the program."

His escape route includes drug rehabilitation treatment and putting Las Vegas in his rear-view mirror, never to return to the speed or the city.

The treatment will have to come from elsewhere. Nevada's system of drug and alcohol rehabilitation is almost nonexistent. If you are nearly penniless, it is all but invisible. Someone who makes a living selling drugs, for instance, would feel compelled to sell dope in order to be able to afford a program.

"I've left numerous times," he said. "I always wind up back here."

Las Vegas is seductive that way. For humans with cravings, it is the most seductive city since Sodom. But every town has drugs, and in most places the street life is just outside the front door.

As he prepares to leave Las Vegas—this time, for the last time—he will not be traveling the road without his ghosts. There are ex-wives and eight children, including two young ones.

In particular, there is one teenage son already caught up in the drug trade. He has been arrested on charges of selling speed.

The ironic adage floats like cigarette smoke: like father, like son.

It was the last thing he wanted. Even speed freaks and drug dealers love their children.

"He is the product of a lifestyle that I led. Now I'm sorry I did," he said. "I don't want to be a junkie. I've got two new babies. I've done my best to detour. I don't want these two children to grow up in that environment."

In 1976, when he began experimenting with drugs, the environment was enticing. It soon led to street sales of speed and marijuana as well as a circle of dangerous acquaintances.

"When I started getting high, it was really a rush," he said. "There's more money in selling the stuff than there is in a paycheck working eight hours a day."

There is also the downside, of course. Thanks to drugs he has carved out a thoroughly wasted life that now, despite a kilo of excuses and good intentions, isn't worth much on the street or anywhere else.

But he is still alive.

"I've been a speed junkie more than anything else, and I don't want to fall back on that lifestyle," he said. "When I get down South, I want to go back to what I was prior to seventy-six. I was a fairly straight citizen then. The rule's been in the Bible for a hundred-million years. When you live by the sword, you die by the sword."

Drugs have taken everything else.

He does not want to die.

In that desperate bad light, it was better to believe in a Southern recovery than to keep considering the alternate reality. ◆

Thanks to owner, bar no longer haven for drug dealers

November 21, 1993

The Long Branch Saloon features a horse on the roof and a free taco for every Bucket o' Bud you buy.

It will never be confused with Cafe Michelle or TGI Friday's. With its pool tables, ponderous moose head, and cowboy memorabilia, the unpretentious neighborhood joint sits on the island between Fremont Street and East Charleston Boulevard.

The rooftop surveillance camera is less visible, but the bar's marquee gives away the little secret:

"The Long Branch Saloon Says No to Drugs."

The message appears trite and insignificant. Unless you know the area.

Then you can begin to appreciate what Jerry White has accomplished with the notorious bar once known as the Vegas Lounge. When he bought the bar 2 1/2 years ago, it was a magnet for crack dealers, dope addicts, street whores, and even the occasional transvestite prostitute.

White accomplished the feat with long hours, angry confrontations, and not a dime of city redevelopment funds. His kind rarely qualifies for such largess.

When White bought the filthy dive next to his motel, he received little help from the cops, either. They were suspicious of his motives: Unless your business is drugs, purchasing a crack bar doesn't make much sense.

In a way, White had no choice. Those bar patrons were ruining his struggling motel trade. Something had to give.

After hosing out the debris, he changed the name, repainted the exterior, and redecorated the interior. He hung signs and installed surveillance cameras.

Then he served notice on the dealers, crack whores, and booze-addled barflies: He didn't want their money or their static. He started sweeping the dregs from his place with all the genteelness of a railyard bull tossing hobos from a freight.

"Hit the door, whore," he'd call to a street chippy looking

for a place to roost. The pushers and addicts received similarly warm welcomes.

Within a few weeks, White lost 30 percent of his customers. Within a year, most of the rest disappeared into the night.

In the interim, a change took place.

His old regulars gradually were replaced by new ones, mostly blue-collar workers and a better class of migrant job-seekers. The police took notice and assisted in the transition.

"I used to get more stretch limos out here the first six months of operation than Caesars Palace," White, 53, says. "When I took the place over, it was an absolute haven for drug dealers. They dealt freely in the restroom. They had spotters sitting at the door. Drugs were killing my business. It was so dirty you wouldn't want to sit in here, anyway. The bar was beyond human comprehension."

After White confronted the dope-seeking cab and limo drivers in the parking lot, they quickly got the message that now is bannered on his marquee:

"The Long Branch Saloon Says No to Drugs."

But Jerry White has no illusions; his fight isn't finished. He sees some of his former customers on the street every day and occasionally confronts them for standing too close to his establishment.

"All I can do is work on the properties, but the street is their domain," he says. "Understand something: I don't hate these people. I feel sorry for them. They've destroyed their lives."

He just refused to let them destroy his business.

"I by no means feel that I cleaned up the area. Some of those drug dealers have been on the same corner for nine years," he says. "I did it mainly from a business standpoint. It's a squeeze play. Everyone in business has to do the same thing. You have to make them unwelcome."

But he's right. White swept out his bar, not the street. Today, those same crackheads and hookers hustle a few blocks away and are someone else's problem.

Our system caters to the powerful, pays lip service to the pitiful. Street fighters like White are left to fend for themselves.

Fortunately, a few fighters remain.

Consider Jerry White the champ of East Charleston. ◆

UPDATE: White lost his "championship" a year later to the decaying neighborhood.

'Date' upends woman suspected of being trick-roll artist

April 26, 1992

The night Jim Moses fell for the big blonde, the lights went out and he felt funny in the head.

Chance meetings by neon light will do that to a person, and some enchanted evenings are full of dark magic.

Although they had never met, and he would not call it kismet, Moses knew the big blonde at the bar looked familiar.

A squat 5-foot-3, with a wide gap between her front teeth, she did not exactly constitute the girl of his dreams. But when she immediately warmed up to him after he struck up a conversation, he figured he was onto something.

Moses and men like him had waited four years to meet the woman, and he wasn't going to blow his chance. He was a big player from Australia and had the money, jewelry, and accent to prove it.

He was about to get lucky.

The big girl said she was a tourist who loved to gamble. Her girlfriend was away with another man, and, as luck would have it, she had a few hours to kill.

Late night became early morning, and over drinks he suggested they move from the bar at the Barbary Coast to his room at Caesars Palace. She gladly accepted.

Some guys have all the luck, and Moses' fortune was too good to be true.

After a short conversation upstairs, they had breakfast and

coffee in a Caesars cafe and returned to the room. The big blonde continued the friendly banter in the hotel room, and offered a back rub.

By then, Moses was a poor conversationalist.

His coffee had been laced with Lorazepam, a powerful tranquilizer. He was in a drug-induced stupor.

The big blonde was the woman known as the "Fat Girl Robber," and she figured she had successfully completed another in an incredible series of trick rolls authorities allege had netted nearly $2 million in cash and jewelry from unsuspecting gamblers.

Fortunately for Moses, a sergeant working undercover with Metro vice, his friends maintained consciousness and picked up Pamela Davis soon after she left his hotel room with $548 in cash. According to police reports, Davis is one of the most notorious trick-roll artists working Las Vegas.

A three-time felon for fraud and grand larceny, Davis is scheduled to go on trial on robbery, burglary, and trick-rolling charges in District Court.

"We've been trying to catch her for four years," Metro Lt. Bill Young said. Young spotted the suspect first and organized the sting. "She had a really unique description."

To say the least. Unlike traditional trick-rollers, who often are young prostitutes, she was older, less attractive, and did not display a hooker's aggressiveness.

Moses watched her hands closely, but he said she still managed to slip him a Mickey. He later suspected she had drugged his coffee.

The formula, police insist, was successful from Florida, through Texas, to Los Angeles.

"She's known by a million names. She's worked this stuff all over the country," Young said. "She's spent a lot of time here in Vegas the last four years. She hits on a guy who has been gambling quite heavily. This is the perfect place for her pickings."

Young estimates Davis was involved in 100 trick rolls and spent much of the money feeding a voracious gambling habit.

Prostitution-related trick rolls are on the rise, Young said. The night life and river of cash flowing through the casinos make Las Vegas ideal. Because of the nature of the crime and expertise of the criminal, some victims are reluctant to cooperate with police.

A search of Davis' apartment revealed pawn slips for men's jewelry and a bottle of Lorazepam. Young said she had enough tranquilizers to continue her late-night business indefinitely.

"This girl was really slick at it," Young said. "She was good."

On some enchanted evenings, the strangers you see are very strange indeed.

Fortunately, some chance meetings aren't meant to be. ◆

It would be truly insane if experts fail the Haven of Hope

September 26, 1990

The ragged fellow babbled loudly, but no one seemed to mind. He righteously scolded himself, then went silent and sipped his cold drink.

Other clients at the Haven of Hope relaxed quietly in the cool air and listened to oldies rock music. As staffers prepared a simple lunch for their mentally ill acquaintances, I wondered about the minds at work in Washington who had seen fit to slash the tiny center's funding.

Obviously, some forms of insanity are more acceptable than others.

The Haven of Hope is a nonprofit operation affiliated with Catholic Community Services and located in the catacombs of the St. Vincent Plaza on Las Vegas Boulevard. Its goal is simple: to identify and assist mentally ill street people. Accomplishing that goal is an arduous and largely thankless task.

Mere mention of mental illness makes people uncomfortable. Most upstanding citizens would prefer those kinds of people just disappeared. Thanks to our nation's revolving-door policy toward the mentally ill, the streets have become riddled with indigent schizophrenics. That's where the Haven of Hope comes in.

One recent client insisted he was from another planet. He suffered from delusions, but was helped with kind words and medication. The more stable his life became, the more stable his universe became.

Another young Las Vegan heard voices so loud he tried to drown them with a Walkman turned up to full volume. When that didn't work, he banged his head into walls until he bled. With medication, the voices were reduced to murmurs. It was a small victory, but a sweet one.

With medication, many mentally ill people can become stable. While most never will return to the mainstream, they at least can remain safe, clean, away from downtown casinos, and out of local jails.

On the street, they forget to take their medication. When they forget to take their medication, they exhibit the unacceptable—but absolutely predictable—behavior that gets them in trouble.

The nine-person Haven staff has cared for 750 clients in 2 1/2 years and has an active file of 120.

But that does not begin to describe the work involved. Because the mentally ill often do not congregate near the so-called normal street people, they often must be searched out. Because most have ceased taking their medicine, they are likely to exhibit schizophrenic characteristics. It sometimes takes weeks to persuade a person to seek help.

The wonder is that nine people could be found to attempt such a difficult job. While most of the center's social workers have advanced college degrees, their average yearly salary is about $15,000. Obviously, they're not in it for the money.

"If it wasn't for their commitment to the work, there's no way they would work here. They'd be crazy to work here," center director Howie Bieber said. "Everyone is involved and [taxpayers] are getting quality at Kmart prices."

Now cutbacks threaten to snuff all hope. In 1989, the center received $249,000 in federal funds and was awarded another $249,000 in services from the state. Their 1990 request of $289,000 seemed reasonable enough, but they instead received $190,300. The state will match only what the federal government allocates.

Beginning October 1, the staff will be reduced to as few as five. That means five people will be charged with helping the hundreds of Southern Nevada's mentally ill street people.

Now comes the most absurd aspect of this tale: The cutback won't save money and will only make the problem more convoluted. With fewer social workers on the street, more schizophrenics will be unsupervised. They will walk the streets downtown and disturb tourists. Police will be called, jails will be affected. More trips to the county hospital will be made when they are victimized.

"I'm sure the police will tell you the bizarre actions on the street have diminished tenfold," the center's clinical psychologist Ken Hehr said.

That will change. It is logical that the mentally ill street people will become more visible. They will be seen somewhere. If not at the center, then in a downtown casino or on a street corner near you.

The center is not the answer to mental illness. Answers do not exist. It merely offers a little hope. If the quality of a society is measured by its compassion for its helpless citizens, then this cutback represents a sociopathic mind at work.

What is truly insane is the thought that experts would fail to value the Haven of Hope.

But some forms of insanity are more acceptable than others. ◆

UPDATE: The Haven of Hope eventually closed.

Local angels offer compassion and caring to those in trouble

May 24, 1998

The nine-year-old thought she had a problem, so she came to Ruth McGroarty's place.

The kid, accompanied by a relative, didn't get a lecture. Instead, she got a hug and help from an energetic angel nearly 80 years old.

Fortunately, the kid's test proved negative. The child was relieved to find that she was not pregnant. Where she would have gone without McGroarty's Life Line pregnancy assistance center is anyone's guess.

Tens of thousands of other girls and women can say the same thing. Without their angel, they would have been lost.

Las Vegas is a nightmare for pregnant teens, but in various locations McGroarty has managed to keep the doors of Life Line open for 23 years. Today, Life Line is housed in a handsome spacious building at 1330 East Karen Avenue.

Inside the door, McGroarty's place buzzes with activity. The air is full of English and Spanish and the sound of children's voices. There is laughter and some crying, but no one waits long for help. There is little time to waste.

Last year in a cramped office, McGroarty, Executive Director Lynn Richmond-Scales, and their small staff handled 11,474 cases. Most were teen-agers, but a few were much older.

"Easily that number will double just by this location," Richmond-Scales, 44, says.

Life Line provides pregnancy counseling, day care, and educational training ranging from English as a second language to high school math. Beyond the parenting seminars and diaper distribution, McGroarty and her troops relocate abused young mothers, issue adoption information, pay power bills, find and furnish apartments, and provide employment services. Now Life Line features a first-time fathers group, in which young dads receive instruction on how to treat their roles as parents responsibly.

Many of the clients are poor. Many more need their children to be cared for while they attend classes or work toward a General Equivalency Diploma. There is a crisis every hour.

Because abortion consultation is not part of Life Line's program, at times the center has received knee-jerk criticism from those who are perhaps unaware that McGroarty has been lauded by Planned Parenthood and the Nevada Women's Caucus.

In a city filled with false hope, she really cares.

McGroarty started Life Line in the mid-1970s after reading a newspaper article about pregnant teen-agers who were being thrown out of their homes. It was that simple. A need was identified, and she set out to see it met.

She doesn't draw a salary. Never has.

"I didn't know what to do, but I wanted to help," she says. "It just grew and grew from there. When Lynn came in, it just mushroomed. She can put any idea to work. She's proven that with all the things she's done. We try to figure out what every girl needs."

Those needs have grown complex with the passing years. When children have children, the needs transcend providing food and clothing. The counseling never ends.

For Richmond-Scales, 16-hour workdays are common. Her beeper rarely stops buzzing. She also handles most of the fundraising and worked closely with Senator Joe Neal during the '97 Legislature to secure Life Line's first state grant.

Get to know her, and it becomes clear that her articulate assertiveness provides inspiration to the center's many clients.

Her candor on the subject of teen pregnancy doesn't stop at Life Line's door. With the exception of the Boyd Group, which has embraced the program, she says the nonprofit center has received no help from the community's cash-rich casino industry.

"I understand that the state makes money off gambling, but this lifestyle has its costs," she says. "This is not an easy place to raise children. I don't know if I could have raised my daughter here. You would think I was asking for money for something that didn't exist, that it was a figment of my imagination."

But it's not, of course, and every year the statistics grow more alarming. At a time of unprecedented growth and economic prosperity, Nevada ranks third in the country in the rate of teen pregnancy.

It is a national embarrassment. It is our shame.

The numbers are daunting, the reality sobering. And complex.

"There's a real misconception that only the young single moms, the teen moms, come here," Richmond-Scales says. "I have 40-year-old moms who come in with the same problem. And they're just as frightened."

Thanks to a couple of angels in this tough city, they have some place to go. ◆

Society pays for abuse epidemic despite its indifference

February 16, 1996

You think your week's going bad, and then you glance at Sue Battaglia's appointment book and cringe.

A toddler with a fractured skull, an octogenarian with a broken arm, an infant autopsy. Spouses with black eyes, busted ribs and, sometimes, knives protruding from their chests.

There are corpses and court appearances, and the cases just keep on coming.

Battaglia is a civilian abuse and neglect specialist at Metro. Her job gives hardened homicide detectives the willies.

Death is easy. Interviewing human beings who brutalize children and exploit old people is hard. Encountering the victims of unthinkable cruelty on a daily basis is enough to generate infinite cynicism in the department's laughably small seven-person abuse staff. But, somehow, they're not so cynical.

Oh, they would like to strangle the creep who shakes his baby into a coma or breaks a toddler's ribs and blames it on the dog. There's no question they're angry.

They just haven't lost hope.

Considering the 7,000 battery and domestic violence cases that cross their desk each year, and the 1,400 criminal cases involving children and seniors, and the hundreds of calls each month that fall somewhere short of criminal abuse, that's saying quite a lot.

It's something to think about the next time you consider paying for more cops.

What flabbergasts Battaglia is not the meanness and the mayhem, but the relative indifference of society when it comes to appreciating the broad scope of the problem.

In this era of stone-cold conservatism, where the very notion of asking the public to fund increased police protection is the subject of talk-radio laughter and tax-paranoid invective, it's not as if society can escape footing this bill.

It comes due every day.

It's more than the stress on places like Child Haven and juvenile hall. One shaken baby can suffer from mental, emotional, and physical problems the rest of his life.

"These are crimes," Battaglia, 35, says. "There's this notion that a lot of people still have that children are property...Most of our serious abuse cases, where death or serious disability occurs, are in infants. These people can't protect themselves."

Beyond the hundreds of obvious cases of abuse, there is the stack of incidences of neglect. The infant pool drowning is one example.

"I think people still see it as a terrible accident, and of course it is, but someone is also responsible for that child," Battaglia says. "Accidents do happen, but when a child drowns in a swimming pool I think it's obvious that parents are not providing a safe environment."

Until last August, the abuse and neglect detail would have fit comfortably in a Yugo. It included only supervisor Sandie Durgin, a 23-year veteran, Frank Casey, and Battaglia.

Not exactly an army.

Even with seven persons, including one detective, they're not keeping up with the caseload.

Battaglia and her cohorts build cases, make court appearances, attend autopsies, conduct polygraphs, remove children and seniors from abusive environments, interview physicians about everything from shattered ribs to cranial bleeding. And they deal with legions of parents.

"A lot of parents are ignorant about how to care for a child, but a lot of them are horribly vicious," she says. "I think Las Vegas has a lot of stress factors."

From gambling and substance abuse to late-shift work and the lack of an extended support system, surviving in the boomtown never was easy. It plays hell with families.

But Battaglia is not a social worker. She's an investigator and a witness to immense cruelty.

When political experts talk about bond issues, they invariably concentrate on increasing the number of cops on the beat. But there's more to it than badges, bullets, and black-and-whites.

"Babies' ribs don't break easily," she says. "Babies' skulls don't crack easily."

No matter how ignored or underfunded, the problem isn't going away. The principal is due, and the interest is compounding.

"It's ugly," Battaglia says. "We don't want to talk about it, but if we don't address it we're doing a terrible disservice to our children. They are our future."

Preserving a small portion of that future is part of what the abuse and neglect detail is all about.

Instead of whining about crime and taxes, maybe we should be grateful that anyone is willing to do the job. ◆

Exploited workers build everyone else's hopes, dreams

January 18, 1996

Outside the Lamb Boulevard union hall, the hand-painted sign read, "Junta De Asociacion."

A meeting of the association.

Inside, trade union representatives from across the valley assembled to listen to the concerns of a few representatives of a large but little-recognized group of Southern Nevada residents: Latino construction workers.

Many spoke only Spanish, and undoubtedly some were undocumented aliens.

They are descendants of the Chinese, Irish, Italian, and countless other ethnic groups who helped build America, then had to fight like hell to be able to enjoy the dream.

All those present Tuesday shared a common interest in improving their working conditions at area housing tracts. Depending on who is counting, there are up to 15,000 Hispanic construction workers in Southern Nevada.

Their presence on job sites is one of the worst kept secrets in the construction trade, and it is a sore point with the trade unions. Organized labor lost this lucrative turf years ago.

Developers commonly argue that the presence of a cheap labor force is one reason Southern Nevada home prices, despite increases in the price of land and materials, remain within reach of so many residents.

Not for the Hispanic construction workers, mind you, but then they don't appear to count.

And they are the last ones to generate sympathy from the tax-paying citizenry. If they don't like the working conditions, then they can go back where they came from.

The Chinese, Irish, Italians, and others heard the same thing a century or more ago.

The fact is, few consumers lose sleep after purchasing clothes manufactured in Asian sweatshops. Not many homebuyers care whether the people who built their dream home had medical insurance or enjoyed a 40-hour work week.

The Latino carpenters, drywall hangers, cement finishers, painters, and tapers are helping to build a Las Vegas not many of them can afford. They are ripe for organization.

The new construction workers are a boomtown contractor's dream: They often work long hours, are paid in tax-free cash, can't complain about job safety and conditions because of their illegal status, are kept quiet by labor brokers, and rarely receive the medical benefits that have become standard in other trades.

Not that they fail to receive medical coverage; they usually wind up seeking treatment at the county hospital. Which costs taxpayers plenty.

At the meeting, the workers complained of being cheated by their bosses and expressed the fear of being fired or, worse, being apprehended by the immigration service.

Although their predicament would appear to provide an ideal opportunity for organized labor, it is anything but that. The language barrier is a problem, but the number of bilingual organizers is increasing.

The real problem is the workers' illegal status. Although many qualify for green cards and legitimate citizenship, few trust the system enough to go through the process. They not only risk deportation, but also are gambling on losing what in Mexico would be considered high-wage jobs.

But, then again, they're not in Mexico.

"These guys come to work when the sun comes up and go home when the sun goes down," Carpenters Union Executive Secretary Dana Wiggins said. "They've frozen wages, and they're taking advantage of the people. They fear immigration. It's our intention to improve the industry for everybody."

Painters union Business Representative and Financial Secretary Jerry Kmetz added, "They're never paid overtime. They have no medical benefits for their families and they're in fear of their jobs all the time because they're told there's always someone who will take their place. They're intimidated. Fear is their biggest enemy."

Getting workers to attend meetings isn't easy. The unions have begun advertising with Spanish-language radio stations and newspapers.

Still, it's hard to consider the association much more than a fledgling movement, though the numbers have tripled in each of three meetings.

The meeting of the association is sure to be criticized as a thinly veiled attempt to organize a potentially potent workforce.

But that criticism doesn't change the fact that increasing numbers of these low-wage craftsmen have begun searching for a place to voice their grievances.

The faces have changed, but everyone still wants a piece of the dream. ◆

Widow finds her nest egg cracked by investment company

January 25, 1998

Marge Lorenzo isn't an accountant, but then it doesn't take a financial expert to appreciate her predicament.

She receives $481 each month in Social Security benefits and pays $300 per month to lease a space for her double-wide trailer at the Sand Creek mobile home park on Lamb Boulevard.

Add utilities and expenses for such extravagances as food, and Lorenzo exists below the poverty line. In truth, she is nearly destitute. There's something else.

Marge Lorenzo is 88 years old.

Born in Dexter, Missouri, in 1909, she moved to Las Vegas in 1937. Long before Southern Nevada had supermarkets, Marge's husband, Dick Lorenzo, once owned the Fifth Street, Hyde Park, and L Bar L grocery stores.

Her late husband left her $40,000, which she invested with Harley L. Harmon Mortgage in a first-trust deed for a construction loan. She was promised a 15 percent interest return.

Beginning in 1995, she began receiving monthly $500 checks from her friend, Harley Harmon, whose family she had known for more than 40 years. That four-decade relationship was a primary reason she trusted Harmon with all her money.

Late last year, those checks stopped coming.

In December, Harmon's license was suspended by the state Financial Institutions Division in the wake of what threatens to become one of the biggest mortgage scandals in Nevada history. Harmon is alleged to have allowed millions in investments to be "dissipated" from the company without authorization. As of November 1996, $22 million in Harmon Mortgage loans were outstanding.

Today, a court-appointed receiver is working in what investors fear is a vain attempt to recover their millions. Investor complaints also have led to a Securities and Exchange Commission investigation into the business practices at Harmon Mortgage.

In a recent interview, Harmon was confident the vast majority of the company's 350 investors eventually would recover their money. He also said he has experienced some bad luck, but has done nothing criminal. Time will reveal his role in protecting the assets of the company's many investors.

Such promises instill little confidence in Marge Lorenzo, who has neither time nor money to waste.

"I've been sick since this happened," she says, sitting in her mobile home surrounded by knickknacks. "It's like I can't move anymore. I can't sleep. And when I do, it's the first thing I think about when I wake up in the morning. I need my money. It's not for special things. It's a matter of survival."

Although the effects of a recent heart attack prevent her from working, Lorenzo is unaccustomed to sitting idle. She held a job as a store clerk until she was 82.

"But I'm too old now," she says. "I hurt my right hand a few years ago. I can't go back to work. It's sad what he's done, and it has taken a lot out of me."

Lorenzo's $40,000 was invested in the ill-fated Greenpoint mobile home park, which brochures touted as a luxury community for active seniors. In all, "250 extra-wide lots," as well as a pool and spa, were to be created on land at 5252 N. Fifth St. not far from Craig Road.

Today, Greenpoint is silent. And Lorenzo is near poverty.

She recently received a form letter from state-appointed receiver Bernie Chippoletti of Terra West Realty/Development Corporation, in essence stating that "sufficient time" will be required before any action can be taken. The extent of the liabilities of Harmon Mortgage are not yet fully known. Meanwhile, she has been advised to consult an attorney.

Not that she has been entirely out of contact with Harmon, whose family has been a part of the Las Vegas valley since 1907. She drove to his office each day for a week in an attempt to discuss her investment with him. She has been told repeatedly that her check is in the mail and her investment is secure.

"He looked me right in the face and told me, 'Don't worry, you're taken care of,'" Lorenzo recalls. "I'm taken care of, all right. Thank God I have my trailer paid for. I may have to sell it. You don't know how this has affected me. When I think about it I can feel my heart beat faster."

Harmon has blamed disgruntled investors for his troubles, arguing that, given sufficient time, he would have stabilized his company and made good on the investments.

Time is something Marge Lorenzo has precious little of. ◆

Pity the poor huddled masses without pals who are county pols

June 30, 1998

Maybe it was the heat. Blame it on El Niño, a stroke, or too many late nights.

For the life of me, when I awoke Monday morning I could not remember the definition of the word "disadvantaged."

Frankly, I was alarmed. Here I am a newspaper writer, a person who supposedly has at least a few dozen words in his vocabulary, and I couldn't even remember the meaning of such a simple word.

Suddenly sweating, I thumbed through the dictionary and found the word just down from "dirty tricks" and only a stone's throw from "disgrace" and "dishonesty."

There it was: "Disadvantaged, adj., deprived of a decent standard of living, education, etc. by poverty or a lack of opportunity; underprivileged."

Sounded vaguely familiar, but it had a hollow ring to it. As if something was missing.

In the wake of Saturday's ruling by the Nevada Ethics Commission that County Commissioners Yvonne Atkinson Gates and Lance Malone committed ethical violations by using their influence to help friends land lucrative concessions contracts at McCarran International Airport, concessions reserved for "disadvantaged" persons, such as women and minorities, I have lost all sense of the definition of the word.

So I went for a drive to clear my head. (I know what you're thinking: Clearing a head so close to empty shouldn't take long.)

Driving north on Martin Luther King Jr. Boulevard, I entered a predominantly black neighborhood and noticed a few businesses open. Then I went east on Owens Avenue and passed other stores and shops that struggle year after year to remain solvent.

It isn't the richest neighborhood in Las Vegas. Entrepreneurs aren't exactly flocking to Owens Avenue to open a business. So you might think these hard-working people doing business in a depressed section of Southern Nevada would be the first to grab one of those lucrative airport concessions reserved for disadvantaged persons.

But you'd be wrong.

The next time you visit the airport, you'll notice that it takes a bank loan to buy a beer and only close friends of the Sultan of Brunei can afford dinner.

What you will not notice is an abundance of shops and markets owned by business operators from Owens Avenue. Look all day if you want, and can afford the parking. You won't find them.

From Owens I made my way over to Bonanza Road and slipped all the way down to Eastern Avenue, where Southern Nevada has a burgeoning Hispanic population. Spanish is spoken in many of the stores there, and the neighborhood possesses some excellent hole-in-the-wall cafes.

But, let's be frank, no one is making a killing in business

down in that neighborhood. The families are poor, working class, and middle class.

The people down on Bonanza and Eastern, like their counterparts on Owens, should get medals for bravery for even attempting to carve out a living there. As locations go, there are many better than these.

But these people won't get medals.

They won't get one of those juicy airport concessions, either.

And so I drove back to the office, crisscrossing through business districts that have seen better decades, up Fremont Street and over to Charleston Boulevard. In less than one hour, I drove by dozens of businesses whose owners could use the kind of once-in-a-lifetime break an airport concession might provide.

Then I thought of some of the people who had received those concessions. There was Mike Chambliss, commissioner Gates' political crony. And there was Democratic National Committeewoman Judy Klein. There were the friends of the wife of Commissioner Lance Malone. Political spinmeister Sig Rogich received one, too.

Although Commissioners Myrna Williams and Bruce Woodbury were not found to have violated state ethics laws, their friends somehow managed to receive lucrative concessions, too.

Most of those people, it should be noted, had not previously eked out a living in some rundown neighborhood. They might have lacked monetary wealth, but they possessed a wealth of political contacts. As anyone who has lived in Las Vegas long enough to unpack his duffel surely knows, political connections are like money in the bank.

Or, in this case, a concession at the airport.

It has taken months, but thanks to the Ethics Commission I now remember the true definition of the word disadvantaged.

It means, "Any poor sucker who isn't tight with a county commissioner." ◆

Kidney caper: the making of a myth nobody can miss

March 30, 1997

It's the ultimate Las Vegas vacation offer:

Three days, two nights, one kidney removal.

Why, not even Bob Stupak in his heyday could have offered such a deal.

The city is known for its off-the-wall marketing concepts, but something tells me the Discount Kidney Junket is destined not to catch on. It turns out that when people take vacations, they don't mind dropping their money, but they hate to leave behind internal organs.

Cash, yes.

Kidneys, no, sir.

Surely by now you have heard the one about the Las Vegas tourist who meets the willing woman and escorts her to his hotel room, only to be drugged, knocked out, and become yet another Man Without a Kidney.

Hey, why doesn't this ever happen in Reno?

Anyway, after his kidney is plucked out, the dupe is stitched up, bandaged, and set in a bathtub of ice. You know, to prevent the pain and discomfort that often accompany such surgical procedures.

By the time he wakes up, his kidney is being brokered hundreds of miles away on the human-organ black market, where this week there's a two-for-one special on hearts and livers. Personally, I don't shop there because they don't take coupons and their produce is weird, but that's another subject.

As it turns out, the kidney incident always happens to a friend of a friend.

Ah, urban legends. You gotta love 'em.

As fast as you can put a puppy in a microwave and sing "Pop goes the weasel," the Las Vegas kidney-kidnapping story has circulated the planet.

Las Vegas Convention and Visitors Authority spokesman Rob Powers continues to field inquiries from curious travelers and travel agents regarding the secret kidney-snatching story. So far, his bosses aren't considering changing the convention authority's current slogan, "Las Vegas: Open 24 Hours," to "Las Vegas: You've got to be Kidney," "Las Vegas: Urine the Money," or even "Las Vegas: Bladder Ask Your Travel Agent."

As an aside, the "I Lost My Kidney in Las Vegas" T-shirt is an anemic seller at downtown gift shops.

But I digress.

"The vast majority of people with common sense would realize that it's a silly story that has no basis in fact," Powers says. "We see it as one of those urban folklore things that the vast majority of people with common sense will see for what it is—a silly story."

But then it figures he'd say something like that. The guy works for the convention bureau.

The fact is, this silly story has gone off dialysis and taken on a life of its own. Powers says virtually every call his office has received has come after the caller has encountered the tale floating on the Internet. At least some of the Internet stories have appeared under the heading "Traveler's Warning." Apparently that attracts more attention from browsers than "Suckers, Read This."

The Las Vegas police homicide section is aware of the kidney story, too. Its detectives have heard breathless tourists and head-scratching cops from out of state report the tale of the hooker who knocks out her customer and swipes his kidney but, apparently, leaves his wallet and watch. (A fact which surely proves the story is not based in reality.)

After many years investigating real stories of mayhem, mutilation, and murder, Sergeant Bill Keeton shrugs at the urban legends that buzz like gnats around the city. The frequency of the kidney story did, however, lead him to place a call to the convention authority to inform its officials of the bad news.

Keeton, the homicide section's unofficial urban myths curator, likens the kidney caper to the smelly old story of the dead prostitute stuffed under the bed at the Strip resort and discovered after she began to get gamy. The story was false—do you really believe union housekeepers never vacuum under the bed?—but it has persisted in various versions for a decade.

For my part, I have been contacted on the subject by journalists from out of state, at least one of whom figured she had entered Pulitzer territory with the kidney story. She was pretty disappointed when I told her there was no truth to it. I imagine the British author who recently wrote to the newspaper for assistance in researching the American kidney-theft phenomenon will be downright depressed when he finds out there is no big story.

Meanwhile, the calls keep coming.

"It's absolutely ridiculous," Keeton says.

Easy for him to say. He didn't have a friend of a friend lose a kidney in Vegas. ◆

Cocktail waiter doesn't give a hoot about stereotypes

November 17, 1995

The photograph of the burly Hooters guy in the blond wig, Dolly Parton falsies, and cute orange shorts surely brought laughter when it hit newspapers across the country.

A man with breasts makes for a pretty cheap chuckle.

Hooters, the restaurant operation whose waitresses are known for their figures and friendliness, is locked in a losing battle with the Equal Employment Opportunity Commission to prevent—dare it be uttered—men from serving beer and chicken fingers to customers who prefer to watch the babes fetch the Budweiser.

In response to the menacing government intrusion, the company has produced an advertising campaign featuring a bruising boy toy with a mustache, a day's growth of beard, and a message for federal bureaucrats: "Washington, Get a Grip!"

The restaurant chain's officials argue that Hooters has built its reputation on the frame of its lithe hired help, and that reputation will be irreparably damaged if a bunch of hairy-legged men don the uniform.

After all, they snicker, what sort of man wants to be a cocktail waitress, anyway?

Meet Mark Dreitzler.

Occupation: Cocktail waiter.

The handsome 34-year-old Las Vegan has worked more than a year running cocktails to casino customers at the MGM Grand.

And you can bag the stereotypes, buster.

He's a straight guy who does not wear skirts and three-inch heels to work. He doesn't shake his tail feathers or wear a push-up anything. In his black slacks, tux shirt, and vest, he looks more like a blackjack dealer than a geek with a strap-on bosom.

Like his female counterparts, his feet hurt at the end of the day. And he occasionally experiences every cocktail server's occupational hazard; the smart remarks, fanny pats, lurid stares, and outright come-ons go with the territory.

Although Dreitzler realizes he is breaking fresh ground in chauvinistic Las Vegas, he does his job for a more basic reason.

It's the money, honey.

It's easy work that pays the bills with dough to spare. At the MGM, home to some of gaming's highest high rollers, he has received individual tips that look like two weeks' pay for a heavy-equipment operator. And Dreitzler doesn't have to lift anything heavier than a double martini with extra large olives.

A guy could do worse.

He has held good tip jobs at the MGM's Charlie Trotter's, as well as at the Excalibur and Mirage. It was at the Riverside that he first worked as a cocktail waiter. Beyond the occasional funny look, he did all right for himself.

"In this town, the money is made in the cocktail department," Dreitzler says. "It's probably one of the best jobs in town, and one of the easiest, too."

He has experienced almost no opposition from his co-workers, whose only real complaint is the fact that he gets to wear pants and their uniforms are designed for maximum leg exposure.

"Most of the girls like it," he says. "They say that it's about time. Some of them say, 'You shouldn't be wearing a shirt. You should be wearing nothing but that vest.'"

What do they think he is, a piece of meat?

And, in case you're wondering, he has no intention of adjusting his footwear to fit the latest fashion.

"My feet hurt wearing flats," he says. "I can't imagine what it's like to work in heels."

Nor does he have any intention of finding out. A few customers have thought him odd, but far more are supportive. He has received hugs from female gamblers who are pleased to see time change on the Strip.

Who knows, it might take a guy like Dreitzler to open doors for other men. It also might lead to changes for cocktail waitresses, too.

With the job market in constant flux, Dreitzler would like to think that he could apply for a cocktail waiter's job anywhere in the city. But he knows that's not the case. Some resorts, he says, have shown no interest in changing a Las Vegas tradition.

"I have one of the best jobs in the casinos," he says. "It's fun to me. I like working with customers, and they seem to like it, too."

As for Hooters, Dreitzler figures the restaurant chain is taking its babes-only image a little too seriously.

"I think that they really don't have a leg to stand on," he says. "Times have changed."

Hey, man, it's only cocktails. ◆

The Huntridge: from heroic Heston to the Skankin' Pickle

August 3, 1995

There's this great scene at the end of *Planet of the Apes* where Charlton Heston and his cave babe ride bareback on the beach. They have escaped the angry gun-toting apes—the worst kind of simians—and have emerged as a sort of post-apocalyptic

Adam and Eve.

Then Heston sees the big picture and collapses in a fist-pounding lament. He knows the world has changed forever and that all his memories are lost after seeing a big chunk of the Statue of Liberty perched in the surf.

For your basic end-of-the-world ape movie, it's pretty dramatic stuff.

Standing in the parking lot of the Huntridge Performing Arts Theater, gazing up at the big familiar sign, and then at the oddly worded marquee, I avoided pounding my fist on the skillet-hot asphalt. Instead, I settled for my usual bewildered shoulder shrug.

In part, the marquee read: July 28 Circle Jerks July 30 Skankin' Pickle

There also was the news that the Hip Hop Comedy Jam and Kiss band bad boys Peter Criss and Ace Frehley were coming to the Huntridge.

Suddenly, I felt like Chuck Heston on the beach at the end of the world.

Where had I been all these years?

Where was I when the world went ape?

The Huntridge is one of the theaters of my youth. It's the place I saw *Mary Poppins* and *The Sound of Music* and fell in love with Julie Andrews, who, come to think of it, would have made a fine cave babe.

But times have changed and Julie Andrews has given way to the Circle Jerks, which is in no way related to the Von Trapp family.

The Circle Jerks?

It's a rock band, not a Senate subcommittee.

The Skankin' Pickle?

Sounds less than kosher, but it's another music group.

Me, I'm on the beach pounding the sands of time.

I am Mr. Out of It.

I am Mr. Nowhere Man Sitting in his Nowhere Land.

I don't wear an earring, not even a clip-on. If my hair is spiky, it's because my wife cut it crooked. If you see me wearing pump-up shoes, it's because my feet are flat.

I've seen better days, so I know how the Huntridge feels as it blisters and peels in the summer sun. Last Friday, its half-century-old roof collapsed. No one was injured, but the Circle Jerks and Skankin' Pickle concerts had to be postponed. The heavy metal has-beens will have to find another place to bang their heads, too.

So, it looks like you can cancel that devil-babysitter and return your tickets for a full refund. While such news is likely darkening musical moods all over the valley, I had to remind myself that every generation has its own memories.

For me, the Huntridge was a great place to escape reality and the heat for a Sunday matinee and maybe a Coke across the street at the Huntridge Drugs lunch counter. But that was years ago.

Not long after Charlton Heston stopped doing ape movies and started taking an active role in Republican Party politics— at times, distinguishing between the two can test even the sharpest political minds—the Huntridge began to change. Moviegoers were avoiding downtown in favor of the megaplexes that were springing up in other neighborhoods. The Huntridge's parking lot was used as a swap meet, its theater divided into an all-Spanish movie house.

Eventually, someone came up with the bright idea that it would make a funky venue for small-time concerts and Saturday night screenings of *The Rocky Horror Picture Show*. It struggled for a few years, then began to catch on again with young people interested in live music from bands too hip for Strip showrooms and too obscure to pack the Thomas & Mack Center.

With a little promotion and the Friends of the Huntridge Theater, the old movie house had found a usefulness again. This time, for a whole new generation.

Then the roof caved in.

Now the finger-pointing has begun.

The building's structural integrity hadn't been inspected since FDR was in office, and that news has set local political leaders chattering about safety and stucco strength.

Friends of the Huntridge Chairman Richard Lenz, who grew up two blocks from the theater, helped save the building from destruction in 1991. He vows to reroof the Huntridge, which is insured.

But if the fates and fractures are unkind, don't blame the Skankin' Pickle. Don't blame Julie Andrews, either. They're only memories on the beach, and the Huntridge has been home to a million of them.

If you must pound your fist, blame those damn dirty apes of time and neglect. ◆

News Bureau photographers a part of Las Vegas history

June 14, 1992

Arms reaching skyward, legs stretching a mile to Earth, a mushroom cloud cutout concealing the radioactive zones in between, the big blonde is captured forever as Miss Atomic Bomb.

The year was 1957. The nuclear arms at the Nevada Test Site were good for America, and Las Vegas was in its cheesecake heyday.

For the happy hucksters who pitched the town to a world still leery of Sin City, the combination was irresistible.

The fallout of the big blonde's picture, taken for the Sands Hotel by a Las Vegas News Bureau photographer, was felt around the world. Like thousands of other photographs on file at the agency, it is a piece of Las Vegas history.

Fans of Vegas nostalgia will remember other shots in the News Bureau's million-photograph morgue:

• Liberace strums a guitar as Elvis plays a piano. The photo of the baby-faced pop stars has been published in dozens of newspapers and magazines.

• Gamblers in swimsuits test out the "floating crap game" adrift in the Sands' pool. Again, another world traveler.

• President Truman and Jimmy Durante ham it up around a piano. Bill Clinton, eat your heart out.

Then there's the cheesecake. Thanks to the bikini-on-the-brain brilliance of PR man Al Freeman, Las Vegas became known as much for its beauties as its blackjack.

News Bureau photographers, whose job it was to keep pictures of Las Vegas in the nation's press, needed little prompting. Their ingenuity created such deadline delights as Miss Daylight Savings Time, Miss Pickle Week, and Miss Sandwich Week.

The recent decision by the Las Vegas Chamber of Commerce to stop funding the agency's $650,000 annual budget raises the question of preserving Miss Atomic Bomb for all time.

Since 1949, the News Bureau has chronicled the strange but endlessly entertaining maturing of Las Vegas. The city's founding fathers prospered by denying their heritage; they preferred we forgot our marvelously surreal history.

That is what has made the News Bureau boys so important. They have acted as the city's living historians.

That changes on June 28, when the agency itself becomes history. The Las Vegas Convention and Visitors Authority is expected to absorb it, but most of the photographers will lose their jobs.

Word of the tiny crew's demise had a fascinating effect on the local resort subculture. The chamber's decision was made so swiftly it set off a panic among many hotel publicists, who have relied on the 24-hour photo service since the Truman era. Several resort executives, whose properties enjoy the millions in free publicity News Bureau cameras provide, also reportedly are upset about the move.

It's understandable. In the first five months of 1992, its seven photographers handled 1,322 assignments for the hotels and printed about 63,000 pictures. That $650,000 budget generates about $7 million in positive press annually.

The agency has done more than take pictures. Its friendly relationship with journalists has helped place an infinite number of spins on the Las Vegas story.

Chamber Chairman Mark Smith said the News Bureau is finally being transferred to the proper agency, namely the Convention Authority. Convention Authority Executive Director Manny Cortez said the agency will survive with a greatly narrowed scope.

Resorts belonging to the chamber are bound to save money on dues without the News Bureau budget, but the city's publicity machine is sure to suffer. Given the nationwide spread of gambling, any savings may be short-lived.

As for the historically significant photographs, Cortez promised they will be protected.

"Those things are sacred parts of the legacy of Las Vegas. They're also irreplaceable," News Bureau chief Don Payne said. At 63, Payne has spent three decades selling the city to the world. "There isn't a day that goes by that we don't get a request for something out of our archives."

Despite all protests, the tiny agency will not survive the end of the month. The photographers will not be replaced.

Too bad.

July is ideal bikini weather.

As long as Miss Atomic Bomb is preserved in all her radioactive glory, the News Bureau's historians will not be forgotten. ◆

Ralph Lamb clipped more than just the wings of Hell's Angels

July 1, 1998

Ralph Lamb had a lot of close shaves in his tenure in Southern Nevada law enforcement. That's bound to happen when you're the last frontier sheriff in the wildest town in the West.

Somehow, he ran the Clark County Sheriff's Office, and later the Metropolitan Police Department, for nearly two decades and managed to survive with only a few nicks. Early Tuesday morning over coffee at Poppa Gar's, Lamb and I laughed about the way policing in Las Vegas was done not so many years ago.

Then he said he had to get a haircut, I presumed in order to look his best for the department's 25th anniversary celebration tonight at the MGM Grand. But I couldn't let him go without reminding him that he was responsible for the most infamous bit of barbering in Southern Nevada history, an event that says more about the changing times as any hairstyle ever could.

More than 30 years ago, the Hell's Angels Motorcycle Club was best known for its ability to intimidate ordinary citizens and understaffed police departments. The Angels had a reputation for destruction that stretched from New York to San Francisco.

"Today, businessmen, lawyers, and everybody rides bikes, but back then these people terrorized whole towns," Lamb recalled. "They scared people to death."

Tipped to the Angels' impending arrival from California, Lamb and his men turned them back at the state line. The bikers used back roads throughout California and Arizona to get to Las Vegas.

When one of Lamb's precious few patrol cars was ruined chasing the scattered bikers around Southern Nevada, the sheriff got angry. The leader of the pack was brought to Lamb, who told him to take his gang up to Mount Charleston, where the cops wouldn't hassle them.

Lamb loaded up two busloads of uniformed officers and paid them a visit at their mountain retreat. With a cop behind every tree, the bikers were surrounded and taken into custody.

Their choppers managed to make the trip to the impound yard, too. Piece by piece.

Once inside the jail, the chains were removed from the bikers' jackets. They were deloused repeatedly, just in case the bugs were stubborn.

Then it was time for a trip to the barber, a place some of them hadn't been in years. By the time they left the police clip joint bound for a holding cell, the Angels were unmatched for tonsorial splendor. They looked more like members of the Four Freshmen than associates of the most formidable bike gang in America.

Soon enough the Angels contacted their lawyer, and he responded with angry threats leveled at the sheriff and his wild bunch. The lawyer demanded to see his clients, and Lamb was only too happy to oblige.

The attorney got to see his clients up close for 24 hours. In the morning, the lawyer was asked whether he'd had enough time with his Angels or needed another day, but the mouthpiece said he was quite through.

Once bail was secured, the Angels were escorted down Interstate 15 to the state line, where Lamb and his men bid them farewell.

"It might not have been too legal, but the people asked me to do a job and didn't tell me how to get it done," Lamb said. "I did it the best way I knew how, and the next time I ran, I ran stronger than I ever ran in any election."

In the days before sophisticated policing programs, instant litigation, and the omnipresence of the American Civil Liberties Union, a response from Lamb usually meant someone was bound to wind up in the dirt.

Holding a broken nose.

Or worse.

In that regard, the Angels got off lucky.

In addition to his 19 years as sheriff, Lamb knew and worked for Howard Hughes, battled and befriended Frank Sinatra. Lamb battled a Who's Who of the underworld and managed to survive everything from stray bullets to the IRS. He is in no small part responsible for creating police substations in Southern Nevada and consolidating the sheriff's office and Las Vegas Police Department.

But he will forever be known as the man who gave the Hell's Angels haircuts.

That raises a question after all these years. In a complaint to the FBI, the bikers swore the cops shot at them as they rode out of sight.

How about it, sheriff?

"They reported that to the FBI, but that is just a fallacy,"

Lamb said, smiling. "We weren't shooting at them."

"If we'd have been shooting at them, they'd have been missing more than their hair." ◆

New trend in hairstyling leaves local barbers laughing

July 25, 1993

The clean-faced fellow from Utah stopped in for a haircut at the three-chair barber shop. He's receiving the Friday matinee of the Phil and Frank Show at no extra charge.

The subject is the proposed A Little Off the Top hair salon, where lingerie-clad babes will trim a guy's hair while he drools on his barber bib.

"We're going to stay competitive, whatever it takes!" Phil Langham says, laughing and waving clippers.

"Phil's going to shave his legs. I'm going to wear those things on my boobs," his partner, Frank Lombardo, adds, cracking up. "They'll pay us extra to keep our clothes on."

The Utah man's eyes get wider.

You don't get this kind of conversation in Salt Lake City.

Welcome to Phil's Barber Shop, a Charleston Boulevard institution for 25 years. It's a real barber shop with copies of outdoor magazines piled up and a Pepsi machine against one wall. Beyond its gregarious operators, the shop's most distinguishing feature is the gargantuan rubber plant that wraps halfway around the room.

It is not a place a fellow is likely to find a woman in her underwear brandishing scissors. Phil and Frank do their shtick for free with each $10 haircut. Phil and Frank are not to be confused with Frank and Ernest.

Thankfully, they keep their shirts on.

The proposed lingerie clip joint, located in Spring Valley, has been the subject of a petition by the area's angry citizens. They don't want that kind of monkey business in their neighborhood.

In a country that constitutionally protects underwear barbering as a form of expression, the neighbors are losing out to progress and the efforts of the shop's owner, David "Davy-O" Thompson. The Las Vegas native says he has cut hair for 17 years, presumably fully clothed.

The lingerie hair salon idea has been profitable in other cities. Although Davy-O might not want to count on his neighbors as customers, the idea appears a natural for sexually surrealistic Las Vegas.

What constitutes appropriate expression in a residential area, anyway?

For some Summerlin senior citizens, a Mexican restaurant with a liquor license is inappropriate. For Spring Valley residents, it's hairstylists in teddies.

In Las Vegas, drawing the line isn't easy.

"They're trying to turn Spring Mountain into Slut Avenue if you ask me," Frank says. "Why don't they just keep it around Las Vegas Boulevard? That's where the clientele is going to come from."

Obviously Frank is a barber, not an entrepreneur.

Davy-O plans to get at least $25 per haircut. He has something else working in his favor: Most of his clients will be men.

No matter what you've been told, men are not the smartest creatures God gave a libido. Wave anything vaguely resembling a female form in front of them, and men will start panting like Rin Tin Tin after a hard day at the office.

Men will spend their paychecks, drink whiskey, hide their wedding rings, suck in their beer guts, and brag about sports cars they don't even own just to impress a woman half their age and weight.

Barber shops are a bastion of maleness, but they are unfashionable in the unisex '90s. Nowadays, men and women use hair mousse with equal abandon; you won't find big hair or stylish slime at Phil's.

You won't find women, either. Salty stories and old *National Geographic* magazines are about as wild as it gets at a real barber shop.

"There's not a decent woman in town who would come in here," Phil says, grinning.

With the competition wearing next to nothing, the traditional barber shop doesn't stand much of a chance.

A conservative haircut is one thing.

The chance to gawk at a woman's boobies is quite another.

Phil and Frank do not intend to follow the latest trend. Fortunately, a haircut and their comedy routine still are enough for some guys.

"When we go topless, you're going to have to pay the price," Phil says, busting up once more.

The man from Utah, his eyes barely in his head, pays his $10 and departs the barber shop.

It is unclear whether he is headed toward Spring Valley, or the state line. ◆

Even the weather is a big production in the city of neon

July 5, 1995

The old man shuffles north on the Strip in a coat too thin for rain.

Unlike the others caught in the cold downpour, he is oddly oblivious to the drops that fall around him like countless fleeting dimes. The tourists study the sidewalk as they hustle for cover, but the old man takes his time and keeps his eyes on the mean gray sky.

Is it dumbfounded disbelief, or a rainy dream remembered?

Las Vegas is crying, but the old man doesn't mind. He removes his hands from his pockets and holds them palms up to catch the torrent. As if he has captured change, or comprehended the mystery of the New Year, he slips his mitts back into his pockets and leans against the storm.

When you think of rain, San Francisco with its slick hilly

streets, its noisy Chinatown sidewalks teeming with huddled shoppers, comes sloshing to mind. Or perhaps it is Seattle near Pike Place Market, where in heavy weather the guitar-picking street musicians crowd under the eaves of the pastry shops and coffee counters, that defines your stormy day.

For me, it is neon in the rain.

No metaphor Raymond Chandler ever wrote can fully describe this town when the water comes down. The dripping neon reflections come closest.

Las Vegas does nothing in a small way. A city built on vice and hyperbole can't afford to play the piccolo in the orchestra. Around here it's trombones and timpani or nothing at all. Understatement is for Utah.

The theme holds true for weather, too.

In the summer, children play under a sun hot enough to melt sneakers. Poolside tourists turn to jerky before your eyes. In July, Dante is a pit boss in this Hell with Megabucks and air conditioning.

In a downpour, it rains megabuckets.

As a kid in Henderson, I waded in storm-fed ponds as impressive as anything at the Lakes. I have grown to love this town in the rain.

In San Francisco, or some place civilized, people open umbrellas when it rains. Around here, they wave goodbye as their Oldsmobiles float down Oakey Boulevard.

Occasionally, some poor soul slips into the flood and drowns in a ditch. Rescue crews slog through the mud and brown water for hours to recover the body.

A single cloudburst brings out pots and pans to catch ceiling drips at hotels and hospitals. A genuine desert downpour can turn whole neighborhoods into a scene from *A River Runs Through It*.

On the Strip, the themes of the day are chaos and clouds. It's one massive, twisted, driver's education lesson. And all the students are failing. Miserably.

Taxis muscle through traffic with the collective patience of a speed freak convention. They honk at befuddled puddle-jumpers whose sin is driving only the speed limit. In the rain, the cabbies earn plenty.

Even the CAT buses are popular. They'd turn a tidy profit if it rained every day.

At Caesars Palace, the statue of Mark Antony looks more bewildered than regal as it ushers visitors toward dry ground. Only Tony Bennett, who is playing in the showroom, would find something suitable to sing about.

The *Mystere* sign and Treasure Island marquee are all the more mysterious in the storm. At the Mirage, it is hard to tell where the rain forest ends and the sidewalk begins.

The crane atop of the Stratosphere Tower disappears in the fog and clouds. On a day such as this, the skin joints on Industrial Road look more tame than tawdry.

When it rains, the complexion of the city changes. The Mojave dust is washed away and Las Vegas is momentarily cleansed. Its edges are smoothed. The air afterward is briefly sweet, and the flooding reminds you that there's something greater at work than the action.

For all its pirates and clowns, it is not such a tough place in the rain. And only a little sad, like a carnival on get-away day. In Las Vegas, the crowd leaves town and the clouds move on and the carnival remains.

Farther down the boulevard, in the nether world of motels and wedding chapels that survive between the Strip and downtown, the old man stoops to retrieve something from the sidewalk. A penny for his travels, a dime among infinite dimes.

He places the coin in his pocket and slumps on through the storm.

Maybe he is pursuing a memory, or just neon in the rain. ◆

Beefs
With
Bureaucrats

Bureaucrats turn deaf ear to woman's complaint of injustice

October 3, 1991

Enid Thompson is the last person a reasonable human being would expect to be in the doghouse with the city's surreal bureaucracy.

After all, Enid Thompson is deaf.

She suffers from 97 percent hearing loss. She uses a special telephone that enables her to communicate. She wears a hearing aid to help capture the remaining three percent of sound.

She also has help from Erin, a four-year-old springer spaniel specially trained to offset the handicap of her owner.

Thompson, 53, received Erin from Oregon's Dogs for the Deaf center in September 1988. With Erin's help, Thompson now is able to respond to the door bell, a fire alarm, a specially designed telephone, and other sounds the hearing take for granted.

The dog offered something more.

"I would like to say Erin is the light of my life," Thompson said. "She has taken the lonely spot away that seems to be there when you cannot hear."

Thompson's problem is simple. After three years of believing her working guide dog was exempt from the licensing rules governing lesser canines, she has been cited by the city Animal Control Unit.

A city ordinance frees owners of seeing-eye dogs from paying licensing fees. Hearing-aid dogs are not yet included in the ordinance.

And you wonder why the city's braintrust has such trouble redeveloping downtown?

Sergeant Charles Berger of the Animal Control Unit said tentative plans have been made to include the hearing-guide-dog provision in the next update of the city's collection of ordinances. Meanwhile, rules are rules and Thompson has failed to renew her $4-a-year license.

"This is all so stupid over a dog tag the city said was free anyway," Thompson said. "I don't mind paying the four dollars a year. That's immaterial. It's the principle."

The principle is scheduled to cost her a second trip to a local courtroom today, all over a discontinued dog tag.

Her argument is simple. She says an animal control officer gave her a license and an exemption. If an error was made, it wasn't Thompson's.

"Why should I pay for her mistake?" she asked, failing to recognize one of the first rules of bureaucracy: The customer is always wrong.

Thompson said she was issued a citation to appear in court for failing to buy the tags she was told were free for her working dog. She faces a small fine, but she is not concerned about the money. It's the city's strange system that has her baffled.

"It has me feeling like a criminal," she said.

On a previous trip to court, the bailiffs refused to allow Erin to accompany Thompson into the municipal menagerie. Thompson pleaded not guilty from the hallway.

Ah, Municipal Court. Almost a bastion of justice, almost a rude little kingdom unto itself. It's probably too much to ask the court to serve the people.

Later, Thompson said, she was assured that upon her return to court Erin would be allowed to sit by her side. Well, that's big of them.

Of course, Thompson's trip to court could have been avoided.

Would it have been so difficult for an animal-control bureaucrat to grant her an exemption?

True enough, the hearing-aid provision has not yet been inserted into the official Las Vegas Animal Control Guide and Coloring Book. But one sober move by the city would have saved her time and trouble. It would have given her comfort, not to mention justice.

Then again, rules are rules, and the strange enforcement of this one is just plain dumb.

To borrow a theme from the late dog-lover Dr. Seuss: Go people, go. See people, see. Think people, think.

Frustrated by her legal odyssey not yet complete, Enid Thompson is worried about her companion, Erin.

"I would just be shattered if anything ever happened to my dog," she said. "I will buy a license every year. I would never want to go through this again. I've never had anything like this before.

"It's confusing to me."

You're not the only one who is confused, Enid. ◆

UPDATE: Enid Thompson got her wish and was allowed to bring her dog to court. She won her case, too.

One man's treasures earn him neighbors' wrath, jail time

March 19, 1995

With its peeled paint, rumor of a lawn, and missing boards like spaces in a beggar's smile, the house at 702 Upland Blvd. has seen better decades.

The elm is dead. The drapes are drawn, but the house is neither haunted nor deserted. In fact, it has been inhabited by the same occupants, Vitold and Helen Kaseta, since 1954.

Recently, it was the site of a large-scale excavation of the things Mr. Kaseta had collected over 40 years. He was not present to watch his mountain of bargains hauled away; he had been jailed by Municipal Judge Gregory Barlow for failing to clean up his yard. Neighbors had complained for years; the judge finally made good on his threat. Kaseta was released last week after spending three weeks in jail for first-degree clutter.

More than four decades ago, when Vic Kaseta first went to work for AT&T, he knew and liked his neighbors on the east side of Upland.

There were no neighbors on the west side of Upland in those

days. There was mostly sagebrush and sand. Over the years, that changed. New neighbors with different standards moved in.

Kaseta did not change.

The 76-year-old was the same son of Lithuanian shoemakers who had worked 12-hour days for a few dollars a week. Although Kaseta retired from AT&T in 1986, inside he was still the same boy who had picked lumps of coal from along the railroad track to help heat his family's home in Brockton, Massachusetts.

Because he remembered those hard days, it made it easy to stockpile things he might need. Like wood to burn in the fireplace during winter. Like tools for every occasion. Like fire extinguishers and snowshoes, Kentucky bourbon, and hydraulic jacks.

Most of it is gone now. The eyesores have been removed. The neighbors have gotten their way.

As he stands in a knit hat and plaid sports coat, blue eyes flashing from behind bifocals, Kaseta surveys the void. Epithets pepper his speech as he tries to muster a case against the home invasion, but as he tours his yard the anger is replaced by sentimental anecdotes about the things they carried away and the few things that remain.

Why the snowshoes?

"I paid two or three bucks for them at the swap meet," he says proudly. "I'm not a dummy. I know what to save."

They were a bargain. If three feet of snow ever falls on Upland Boulevard, Kaseta will be well ahead of his neighbors. Until then, they hang on the wall outside his house.

The industrial-size fire extinguishers, all five of them, were another irresistible deal: $5 a piece. The jugs of whiskey went on sale when a Safeway went out of business, and Kaseta bought as much as he could haul. He has genuine Elvis decanters, too.

"I had a million things here," he says, and you don't think he's exaggerating. "I had so much valuable stuff."

Under the carport is a 1959 Triumph TR3 convertible. Out back is another Triumph which, like the house and yard, has seen better days. Neither vehicle runs, but they're collector's items and Kaseta is a collector. Under a canopy in the driveway is a British Rover. Kaseta calls it a poor-man's Rolls Royce.

"They say, 'This is junk. This is not worth one penny. It's loaded with rats, and it stinks like sardines.' Can you smell sardines?" he asks. "That's what these holier-than-thou neighbors said."

But Kaseta acknowledges that, yes, he was warned of the consequences he faced for allowing his yard to become a surplus store. Along the way he also has learned a lesson about the limits of one man's property rights. He always believed that what was in his yard behind a fence was no one's business. He was wrong.

"How in the hell can they fine anybody without being a peeping Tom, which is illegal?" he asks, staring into the empty yard. "Why the hell did they move up here in the first place if they want to live at Sun City? They're holier-than-thou people."

In the end, he stands out against the dilapidated backdrop of 702 Upland and shrugs at the scene.

"I painted it once. It was in the back of my mind to paint it again," the old man says unsteadily. The March sun is shining and the spring sparrows are chirping. He pauses before returning to the shadows of his house.

"I've never been a dummy in my life. Maybe I didn't paint my house like I should have.

"They didn't have to put me in jail." ◆

UPDATE: Kaseta died in 1997.

Retiree wants stream restored to his bit of consciousness

September 13, 1992

The stream that ran through Robert Rusch's Cold Creek mountain property probably wouldn't have inspired a trout-fishing Hemingway.

For one thing, it lacked trout. As a finger of tiny Cold Creek, it didn't exactly roar through the Spring Mountains.

It sort of trickled in a soothing stream, and that suited Rusch fine. Combined with the area's mule deer and wild horses, and the elk herd that roams the hills, it provided a peaceful environment. His handicapped friends liked it, too, when they picnicked on his 3/4-acre piece of heaven set about 50 miles from Las Vegas.

That is, until the day in late August a forest ranger ordered a backhoe operator to block the creek.

Now a dam of dirt, boulders, and brush have turned the stream into a dry wash. It's also turned Rusch, a 39-year-old union cement finisher, into an angry man.

He blames a forest service official for damming the stream for no reason. Rusch built a small deck over the creek on his own property, which may have led to the problem.

From the Owens Valley to the Colorado River, the history of the West is filled with chapters of battles over water. Rusch's skirmish may qualify as the smallest water war on record.

File it under stream of unconsciousness, for that is what appears at the heart of the issue.

Although his story isn't filled with tales of gun battles and courtroom struggles, the issue is no less important to Rusch. He cashed out his union pension three years ago to invest in land he believes possesses the rarest of Southern Nevada features—a natural water source.

"The land is sort of like my retirement fund. Without water it's not going to be worth anything like it was with water on it," Rusch said. He has built a two-story shed and planted a garden on his land. "I've enjoyed it. It's sure a lot cooler than town."

But one man's soothing stream is another man's expendable ephemeral channel. George Perkins, district resource officer with the U.S. Forest Service, said the trickling offshoot of Cold Creek is merely a ditch that runs sporadically when the main creek overflows. Called an ephemeral channel, it lacks the vegetation common to a year-round stream, he said. It also shows signs of human attempts to keep it dug out and flowing.

Nearby landowners disagree. They recall the stream running year-round for more than 15 years and have heard stories of its vitality dating decades earlier. Rusch said documentation exists showing the stream running as early as 1907, when the area was a ranch.

The Forest Service owns the water rights to Cold Creek, Perkins said, and apparently that includes the channel/stream that crosses Rusch's private property. It also includes easement rights on either side of Cold Creek. Perkins did not say the stream closure was an authorized act.

There is no government project in the works. No one was stealing the water. No pupfish were in danger.

Perkins gave no reason why a government employee hired to watch for forest fires feels compelled to stop up the little stream, ephemeral or perennial.

"There is some question as to whether that channel is a natural channel or an artificial channel," Perkins said. "We have been looking at how we're going to handle this whole thing."

That's dandy.

Just for the sake of argument, what would happen if a common taxpayer tried the same stunt?

If you were caught damming a babbling brook or felling a Douglas fir, you would face heavy fines and possible felony prosecution. That includes potential prison time.

When the government does it, well, that's another story.

Rusch isn't looking for trouble. He just wants his creek back.

"This happening has given me an ulcer. My stomach's just been churning, and I've had a hard time sleeping. It's got me quite upset," Rusch said. "Mainly we want the creek opened up how it was before he did it. That's the most important thing."

Given the stream of unconsciousness at work, he obviously is asking a great deal. ◆

A tow truck and trooper crash the calm of mountain

January 15, 1993

I appreciate a creative con as much as the next sucker, but what the Nevada Highway Patrol has going with Indian Springs Towing on Mount Charleston is one for the books.

Or, in this case, the column.

To begin, I have lived the past 18 months in a little place at Mount Charleston. I heat with wood and spend hours each winter week shoveling snow and chipping ice. It's not exactly a "Lifestyles of the Rich & Famous" episode, but it's about the best world possible on reporter's pay.

There's nothing like spotting a mule deer browsing on a mahogany trimmed hillside to re-energize my too-cynical spirit. The 40-minute commute and occasional Donner party-like snow experiences are an accepted part of living on the mountain.

The eerie arrangement between a wrecker and trooper is not.

On the mountain, the snow and ice can be treacherous. The snow-removal-equipment operators have a difficult job. That's why I moved the four-wheel-drive pickup on loan from my father to a spot just off the state highway that runs behind my house. The truck was in line with two other vehicles and allowed plenty of room for the plow to maneuver. It was practically in my backyard.

I use the four-wheel drive only in emergencies and hadn't moved it in a week. That's where it was Saturday when trooper Mike Wiltse decided to let his friend from the towing company hook it up as an abandoned vehicle.

It was neither abandoned nor blocking the highway, but here's where the story turns.

Although the wrecker hadn't finished his paperwork when I frantically inquired about the pickup, Wiltse said I would have to pay the $49 towing fee to have the vehicle unhooked. It's the law, he said.

The law?

Because I don't carry a set of the Nevada Revised Statutes

with me, I was forced to accept the trooper's word for it. But I planned to find out whether he was telling the truth, and took down his name.

It was then he asked me how long I had lived on the mountain and where I worked. It was none of his business, but I told him.

Then he said, "Well, since you're going to put my name in the newspaper, I guess I'm going to have to cite you."

The words nearly made me fall in the snow. What did this person expect me to do, wilt under the pressure of possibly receiving a lousy ticket for an abandoned truck that wasn't even abandoned?

To put it politely, I don't take threats very well.

Especially not from glorified meter mollies.

When I repeatedly told him to write me the ticket, his disposition changed. He returned my driver's license and forgot about the citation. I still wonder what his reaction would have been had I sold shoes for a living instead of newspaper stories.

How many people get clipped $49 over someone else's mistake?

It doesn't take a CPA to figure the result would be lucrative for a wrecker based in a town 45 miles from Las Vegas.

Then I called the officer's boss, Sargeant James Dennis, who was the picture of professionalism as he explained Highway Patrol policy on roadside vehicles and towing. He said troopers have the authority to have towed any vehicle left on the roadside more than 72 hours.

When I asked whether the towing procedure was, in fact, the law, the sergeant said no. It was policy, not statute.

Well, now, that's something.

NHP troopers legally can shill for towing companies.

Anyone see a potential conflict?

I don't expect troopers to be the brightest people to whom the good Lord loaned a badge, but I'll be damned if I expect them to mislead the people who pay their salaries.

I also hate to write about petty personal squabbles in this column. Readers are too busy with their own important problems to care about mine.

But if this happened to me, it probably has happened to

dozens of people who never will get the chance to respond in print to one little tyranny.

The lesson cost me $49. Maybe writing about it will save other potential suckers a little tuition in the future. ◆

Mount Charleston hermit faces eviction by Big Brother

October 28, 1990

Near the gravel road to Harris Springs, seven dogs greeted me with varying degrees of mock malevolence.

The animals probably violated a federal statute, but they seemed harmless enough. Like all dogs, they were a reflection of their master: In this case, a little gruff, but harmless and sweet once you get to know them.

Moments later, their master, Kelly McKinney, welcomed me to the camp in the Spring Mountains she has called home for the past 13 years. Barring a late change, it is a camp she will have to break at the end of the month after losing a court battle with the U.S. Forest Service.

While her camp was under the jurisdiction of the Bureau of Land Management, McKinney lived peacefully. When the Forest Service took control of the area in 1989, her status changed from harmless hermit to law-breaking squatter.

For more than a year, Forest Service officials did their legal best to attempt to relocate McKinney. They contacted social workers to analyze her, animal activists to employ her, and reporters to illustrate the dilemma. She refused to budge.

McKinney likes her camp. It has been her home for more than a decade. She takes her drinking water from a nearby stream, walks four miles to the main road when she needs a lift into the city, survives on the few dollars she makes knitting quilts and selling her blood. It is not a life many would want to emulate, but it is her life.

"I consider it a pretty wonderful lifestyle," she said.

Government officials, however, consider it a nuisance. They have the law and federal might on their side. Soon enough, they will win.

Perhaps they believe that if McKinney is allowed to maintain her camp, then they will be inundated with unauthorized homesteaders.

Such logic fails. Were it so, the hillside already would be dotted with campers. Few people possess the toughness essential to live in a broken-down Volkswagen van for 13 years. Winter around Harris Springs is freezing and snow-filled.

She poses no threat to national security or the delicate desert tortoise. Off-road enthusiasts and pistol-packing pot-shot artists are a far greater threat to the environment.

In many ways, McKinney has been a guardian of the land and its critters since arriving at Harris Springs in 1988. Back then, she was awed by the area's wildlife and was especially taken by a burro herd. With a battered van and a few necessities, she made it her home. She has been watching and naming the animals ever since.

"One of my little witticisms at the time is that welfare would have been a step up," she said of the leanest years.

Since then, she has acquired a few more possessions, including a radio to hear baseball games in summer and some camping equipment to make life a little easier.

It is a life that does not include welfare.

"I won't take it. I haven't cost the taxpayers one dime," she said. "I'd like to know when it became a crime not to leech off the taxpayers."

Occasionally, she receives unsolicited packages from her neighbors in Kyle Canyon. She also enjoys the spoils of the Harris Springs dump, and her dogs eat well thanks to kind cooks at the Mount Charleston Hotel who save them table scraps.

"Sometimes they eat better than I do," she said, without malice.

McKinney is not merely a rural bag lady. She is articulate, opinionated, and keeps a clean camp. If her soul and mind are terribly touched, then many of us are in trouble.

"Basically, I'm not a nine-to-five person," she said. "If I wanted to be a bookkeeper, I could be a bookkeeper. I have nothing against bookkeepers, but I don't want to be one."

All she wants is to be left alone.

Historically, independence has been tolerated in America. Why, we even named a day after it. As our population has increased, the country has shrunk. Laws multiply like blowflies, sending independence the way of the nuclear family: Everyone remembers it, but few can find one when they need it.

McKinney is not so strange. She just doesn't fit our national neurosis.

She does, however, admit being cantankerous: "You can't hang somebody for a lousy disposition, or three-fourths of the world would be hanging from some tree branch."

But the government can force her to move.

While it lasts, her simple lifestyle can teach us about the fleeting nature of independence and the relativity of our material world.

Kelly McKinney, the harmless hermit, deserves to be left in peace. ◆

UPDATE: McKinney continues to live with her dogs in the hills outside Las Vegas.

Not everything is well for water users getting the shaft

November 23, 1997

The history of water wars in the West is as long and turbulent as the Colorado River, but Ellen and Leland Hinricksen are most concerned with the battle in their own backyard.

It's a mismatch, really.

It's Ellen and Leland vs. the state Division of Water Resources and the Las Vegas Valley Water District. No bookie in town would set a price on the Hinricksens prevailing against the Great Nevada Waterworks. The real question is whether the water system will work for them or bury them in debt.

For 21 years the Hinricksens have drawn water from the 250-foot-deep well on their two-acre property on West Fisher Avenue. When they first moved there, no street ran in front of their place, and the lights of the city were miles away.

The ensuing years have brought the city, and the water system, to them. City water is a few hundred feet from their door, but several thousand dollars out of their price range.

These days, their well is acting up and needs to be recased. At $6,334, the price isn't cheap.

But it's downright affordable compared to the $13,500 estimate they have received from the water district to connect them to the main line. Add the price of capping their well as required by state law, and it could cost $18,000 to join the city program. In theory, some of the outlay could be recovered after others hook up to their line.

That excludes a monthly water bill that, for a mature two-acre residence, is bound to parch their throats.

"I was prepared to hook up to city water if it was a fair price," Ellen says. "I don't think it's a fair price. So I'll probably just fix my well."

The Hinricksens are one of a growing number of well-dependent Southern Nevadans stuck in the past. Although some cling to their wells, others would happily give them up if the costs weren't prohibitive.

Why not just sink the well a little deeper and continue pumping?

Nevada law, as interpreted by the state engineer's office, prohibits drilling a well where district water is available.

In some ways the Hinricksens are fortunate. One of their neighbors, Dinora Sharpe, has received a $35,494 estimate to hook up to "available" water. Another neighbor, M. Elaine Cole, hauls water in 55-gallon drums and is dependent on neighbors for showers because she can neither deepen her well nor afford the estimated $13,557 the district is asking to hook up. While her fruit trees are dying, the connection costs keep on rising.

And the fees must be paid up front. No installments, no amortization, no breaks.

Those well owners had better time their transfer carefully. The estimated wait for service through the district is six months to one year.

The state, meanwhile, does nothing.

"The State Engineer is aware of your situation and of others like yours and he is sympathetic to your problem," Deputy State Engineer Hugh Ricci wrote the Hinricksens. "However, his decision must be made with the health of the entire ground water basin and the future of that basin in mind."

It's easy to be sympathetic when you shower at home.

But this is what happens when a developer lays a water line through a once-rural area. That pipe, in effect, forces some well owners to spend thousands to comply with the law and subsidize development.

Developers pass along their costs to home buyers, who pay the price a few dollars a month over a 30-year mortgage. The developer has his money, the home buyer his payment plan.

The private well owner has the shaft and a war he cannot win.

It's something to remember in light of the Clark County Commission's recent rejection of a quarter-cent sales-tax increase to pay for $3 billion in water and sewer infrastructure improvements. The tax increase would have given home developers and homeowners a break on water rates, but it wouldn't have rescued the Hinricksens and others like them.

A groundwater advisory committee meets Tuesday to discuss Southern Nevada's changing water philosophy. Months from now, their discussions might become policy that, years from now, might help the Hinricksens, who need assistance now.

"The developer did not put the water down my street to improve my life," Ellen Hinricksen says. "He put the water down the street to sell his damn houses. The cost is outrageous. Are people supposed to get a second mortgage on their house for water?"

In the backyard water war, these people are about to become refugees. ◆

Senior bird-feeder runs afoul of North Las Vegas' trivial pursuit

May 31, 1998

Marion Goodwin is not your average jailbird.

First, there's his nickname. Forget Lefty Two Guns, Mumbles, or the Slasher. Friends call him "Goody," which has to rank as the worst handle for an unrepentant repeat offender in the history of jailhouse monikers.

At 77 years old, he is a retired member of the armed services who worked many years for the *Los Angeles Times*. For 21 years he has lived quietly in North Las Vegas. He pitches for and manages a senior softball team.

But, make no mistake, Goody Goodwin is a repeat offender who early Monday morning was cited, arrested, and booked into the North Las Vegas Detention Center.

The charge: littering from an automobile.

As an experienced scofflaw, Goodwin was handcuffed and hauled from near the scene of the crime, a parking lot at 2560 Las Vegas Blvd. North, to the city's lockup. A friend later paid $170 to bail out Goodwin, who spent $102 to retrieve his van from the impound yard.

Given North Las Vegas' pathetic history of enforcement in such areas as the dumping of medical waste, it can be argued that the local police were just trying to take precautionary measures. Considering the fact North Las Vegas has one of the higher violent crime rates in America, one might presume the officers were investigating one of the myriad shootings, stabbings, rapes, and robberies that take place there each year.

Except that, well, Goody Goodwin wasn't dropping medical waste. Nor was he tossing a hot pistol from his getaway car.

He was feeding the birds. The stuff he dumped out of coffee cans from the window of his green Ford van consisted of pieces of bread. Day old, mind you, but edible.

As he does on many mornings near his home, Goodwin was feeding the sparrows and pigeons when he was observed by traffic officer Phil Hicks.

It wasn't the first time Goodwin has run afoul of the law.

Hicks, in fact, last cited Goodwin on April 22, 1996, for littering from a vehicle. The officer went easy on Goodwin that time. He didn't hook him and book him, just handed him a ticket. The case was dismissed by then-Municipal Judge Gary Davis.

This time was different. Goodwin declined to renounce bird-feeding and go straight, and in his van were, to quote the officer, "three plastic containers full of discarded foodstuffs situated in the front passenger seat and floor area of Goodwin's vehicle."

Aha. Busted. Nabbed. Caught with the goods.

Use a crumb, go to jail.

A Polaroid was taken of the offending bread and placed into evidence. Goodwin was taken into custody.

The hassle to make bail and get back his van wasted the entire day and upset Goodwin, who is not interested in becoming known as the Bird Man of Northtown Jail. As an aside, the detention center is riddled with prisoners who pass the time by feeding the yard birds that land inside the walls. Now Goodwin will have to waste even more time on June 25, when he is scheduled to have his day in court.

What does the defendant have to say for himself?

"Where I'm feeding them, there's no houses," Goodwin says. "It's away from buildings and isn't bothering anybody. It's edible, and it's eaten right away.

"I love birds. God created them the same as he created us. As it says in the Bible, he put us here to take care of the animals. I'm taking care of God's creation."

While we're on the subject, what in God's creation are people thinking arresting an elderly man for feeding the birds?

Are there so few criminals running loose in North Las Vegas that bored officers must nail a softball-playing St. Francis?

Let's be frank. Defacing Las Vegas Boulevard North isn't easy. Many have tried. That stretch of thoroughfare near the scene of the crime is lined with more than its share of used-car lots, saloons, and motels. Most self-respecting pigeons won't hang out there.

Goodwin wasn't even contributing to the delinquency of a mynah. Nor was he defacing private property. Pigeons will do that without any help from their self-appointed patron saint.

Forget the ACLU. Somebody call the Audubon Society.

Modern living is full of little tyrannies and injustices small enough to fit in a coffee can. Marion Goodwin is out more than $272 in anguish and irritation alone, but, for the record, he says he will continue to do God's work a crust of bread at a time.

If it's not safe to feed the birds in Northtown, then something is foul, indeed. ◆

UPDATE: Marion Goodwin's case was eventually dismissed.

Police slash prices to liquidate inventory of fine used vehicles

June 17, 1998

If that family four-banger is giving you trouble, you should have been at Manheim's auto auction Tuesday afternoon. You would have had to fight the crowd and pick through a few lemons, but some real bargains were available.

Many of the best vehicles up for bid would have looked familiar. There were 70 automobiles and motorcycles previously operated by the Metropolitan Police Department. Approximately half the cars were 1996 Chevrolet Caprices still under the 75,000-mile factory warranty.

Although one panting patrol car had nearly 140,000 miles on it, many of the odometers hadn't reached 60,000 and some were under 50,000.

The vehicles retail for more than $20,000. The wholesale blue book averaged $11,000.

Most sold Tuesday afternoon for around $6,500, which is an improvement. Usually, the vehicles go for under $5,000, Deputy Chief Dick McKee says. That does not include the lights, siren, and gun rack—they were removed prior to sale—but it does include the transferable warranty.

Lest you worry that officers will have to take to the street on foot, the police have a new fleet of vehicles due to go into service next month at the beginning of fiscal year 1998-99. Many of those cars are year-old Fords with low miles. As working stiffs know, previously owned cars are less expensive than the kind that come fresh from the factory. The latest fleet of vehicles, for instance, will cost only $19,000 each.

If the math doesn't add up, and you're having difficulty finding the logic in selling two-year-old vehicles at a fraction of their blue-book price, then you can appreciate my bewilderment. Of course, it is possible I am bitter. My pickup has 115,000 miles on it.

But only a few years ago, the police pleaded with the public for a new fleet of automobiles in the name of public safety and reliable transportation. Sheriff Jerry Keller and his cops got their wish, but now it appears they have more cars than they know what to do with.

At the auction, Captain Ron Niemann of the department's General Services Bureau kept his comments brief.

"I've been directed to sell them," Niemann said.

McKee, Niemann's supervisor, assured skeptics that appearances are deceiving. Auction is the only way to relieve the department of its vehicles, he said, and letting these cars go is the only way to ensure the department's fleet remains reliable.

On average, a patrol car puts on 25,000 miles every 12 months and lasts three years, McKee said.

The fact you probably put more miles on your finicky family car, and keep it far longer, is not part of the department's fiscal strategy.

"It just so happens seventy-five thousand is a good life cycle on a car," McKee said, uttering words sure to make the folks at Ford and Chevrolet cringe. "How comfortable would you be in taking a car with fifty-thousand to sixty-thousand miles on it and driving it twenty-four hours a day in traffic conditions?"

Frankly, chief, a lot more comfortable than I am now. But, as I say, I'm probably bitter.

Is the department coming up short of ready cash as its fiscal year ends?

Sources within the department said they were directed to cut back on spending until July, when the new budget begins to flow.

McKee countered that the fiscal-year-end auction is an annual event and is not meant merely to replenish the till. The money generated at auction does, however, go directly into the general revenue stream.

McKee added that nearly nine of 10 department vehicles are in service. Cops are not in danger of wearing out shoe leather or waiting long periods of time for patrol vehicles. McKee's assurance runs contrary to department sources, who claim that late-shift officers have waited up to two hours for an available black-and-white.

In an election season, the department's budget is sure to be attacked. Incumbent Keller, who likes to say his officers do more with less each year, is a fierce defender of the department's $211.7 million budget. He also enjoys a staggering popularity, according to the latest *Review-Journal* and KTNV-TV Channel 13 poll conducted by Mason-Dixon Political/Media Research.

Why should you care?

Replacing the automobiles sold at auction will cost more than $1.2 million. You're footing the bill.

There were some real bargains available on Tuesday, and you could have made a killing on those cars.

That's only proper.

You've already paid for them once. ◆

Hot firefighters overheating on ban of steamy television

August 2, 1990

Thanks to a few vigilant city officials, we can rest a little easier now that local firefighters no longer are corrupting themselves by watching the heathen Playboy Channel or steamy videotapes featuring naked humans in various stages of repose.

Perhaps fearing dozens of firefighters would go blind from eye strain—or, maybe out of concern for potential harassment suits—the city has decided to outlaw the viewing of the sexually oriented television programs down at the station.

The change has caused a grumble among some city firefighters. It is unclear whether the disgruntled are upset at being treated like overheated adolescents or are mad about missing a little T&A TV.

No matter. The city has stamped out those erotic fires for the good of all concerned. What a relief.

While some people would argue the films are no more distracting than a football game or a Bogart classic, others believe it's inappropriate for city workers to view movies with titles like *Frisky Fillies, Lusty Leprechauns,* and *So Many Women, So Little Pennzoil.*

"They are city employees on city time and we expect them to act accordingly," city affirmative action officer Diane Santiago Cornier said. "Our position has been that we will take proactive steps to ensure that the city is in compliance with civil rights legislation and, secondly, that our employees are working in an atmosphere that allows them to perform their work."

That makes sense, but what about the firefighters' point of view?

• The change smacks of Big Brother creeping through the bedroom window of privacy and rifling through the underwear drawer. Firefighters spend about one third of their lives at the station; doesn't that give them some privileges?

• While the stations are co-ed, no complaints have been filed.

• The movies don't dominate the TV and the public is unlikely to see them. The station is closed to civilians at night, which limits an outsider's viewing to matinees only.

• The firefighters pay for all optional cable service, including other more acceptable networks that also show R-rated movies. Station houses have more than one TV, making skinflick viewing optional.

Still, such programs make some people uncomfortable—especially city officials. City Fire Chief Clell West said the change is in everybody's best interest and that the Playboy Channel isn't actually banned.

"I have no idea what Playboy shows," West said. (Sure, chief, we believe you.) "I understand that they will be able to subscribe to the channel as long as they don't watch sexually explicit programs."

But, chief, Playboy isn't known for showing a lot of "Mannix" reruns.

"I understand they show documentaries and some things that people might want to subscribe to," he said, revealing his sincere ignorance of Playboy's format.

Documentaries?

Perhaps those *National Geographic* programs with the dancing tribal maidens and their rhythmic bongos get big air time on Playboy. Maybe a one-hour special on the prolific pollinating skills of Mr. Honey Bee and his friends the Daffodil Sisters finds it way to the screen.

Documentaries? Why, of course. Just listen to the bookish conversation down at the station:

Firefighter A: "A documentary's starting on the Playboy Channel."

Firefighter B: "*Debbie Does Dallas* is a documentary?"

Firefighter A: "Well, uh, maybe it's a tour of the Lone Star State."

Firefighter B: "Yeah, that's it."

Firefighter A: "See what I mean? Get a look at that hill country."

Whatever the firefighters are doing, it must be working.

Despite their off-hour interest in human anatomy, they have a prized Class 1 national rating. Extracurricular activities aside, they are ranked among the top fire extinguishers in America.

West said he is proud of the Class 1 rating, not the X-rating. But don't misunderstand. He's no prude.

"I wouldn't even attempt to mandate morals," West said, realizing the department appears to be doing just that, "but I do think we have to control the work environment."

That means no blue movies and, in theory, no dirty magazines or nude pinups. If the stuff is deemed offensive, then it could be removed from the workplace. So, it appears those firefighters will just have to spend a little more time winding their hoses and mopping the station.

But what if—heaven forbid—they run roughshod over department policy, watch one of those girly movies, and get all overheated?

Well, at least they'll know who to call if a fire breaks out. ◆

Death and taxes

August 25, 1991

The accountant thought it strange when a letter from the Internal Revenue Service arrived at his office regarding the delinquent taxes owed by two elderly clients.

After all, the clients in question had been deceased for months.

The husband had died of natural causes the previous August. The next February, the wife followed her husband into the great tax shelter in the sky.

Three months later, the IRS letter arrived.

Well, the accountant thought, these things happen. He penned a letter explaining the circumstances and made it clear the surviving family would make good on any tax debts. The figure in question was about $500, which apparently was owed from two years earlier.

Five weeks passed.

A letter arrived from IRS regional headquarters.

"The letter thanked me for the inquiry," said the longtime Las Vegas accountant, who has a healthy mistrust of the government and requested anonymity. "Then it talked about the clients' right to privacy and that the IRS can't discuss the case without first establishing a power of attorney."

The dead have been known to vote in Chicago, but they do not pay taxes in Las Vegas. With that in mind, the accountant wrote back and explained that obtaining the power of attorney would be difficult, considering the elderly couple enjoyed a lawyer-free eternity.

Five weeks passed.

The IRS sent another bill, this time adding penalties and interest. The accountant again explained that his clients, although loyal taxpayers in life, were somewhat less beholden to Uncle Sam in death.

Five weeks passed.

The accountant received a threatening letter demanding his clients remit or face the federal consequences.

Again, the accountant outlined the truth. This time, though, he explained the elderly couple had changed addresses and gave the IRS the couple's new digs, including the plot numbers.

"I assume they took it to be a trailer park," the accountant said. "I don't know what they could do to dead people. They were going to do it to them, whatever it was."

Five weeks passed.

The accountant received a thank you letter. The IRS was investigating the matter.

Four months later, the head of collections from the Reno IRS office called the accountant.

"She said, 'When are your clients going to pay this tax bill?' I said, 'When are you going to answer my letter?' She said, 'What letter?'"

Until then, the accountant had been corresponding with a

computer.

"After she got done laughing, she said, 'I don't believe you.' Eventually, she wrote the whole thing off, and we never did find out what the bill was for.

"That's your IRS at work."

Obviously, most of the time the tax process works without incident. The tax man's job, ever the butt of cynical jokes, is performed with quiet—if sometimes ruthless—efficiency.

One problem is the lack of warmth inherent in separating citizens from their earnings. Another shortfall is the staggering size of the system.

"The IRS is so big now, it's not that the left hand doesn't know what the right hand is doing, it's that the left hand doesn't know there's a right hand," the accountant said.

Recently, I read that Governor Miller has instructed his battalion of state bureaucrats to not share tax information with the IRS. Although Miller's decision may win him a few friends in Nevada, I have to wonder whether he anticipates an audit.

Around these parts, there are plenty of auditors to go around. According to a national tax watchdog group, the IRS is far more likely to scrutinize Nevadans than residents of other states. Although that is logical given Nevada's cash-oriented economy and long history of resistance to federal pickpockets, it only adds to the image that the big impersonal government is out to get us.

"They are people not to be trusted, believe me," the accountant said. "They are weird people."

Although a few ounces of paranoia flow through his veins, his attitude embodies the views many Nevadans have about the IRS. It also serves to illustrate that widely quoted adage regarding the internal revenue.

The next time someone says the only two certainties in American life are death and taxes, believe them. ◆

Government efficiency rolls along in humble travel trailer

April 5, 1998

By most standards, the 38-year-old Champion mobile home is a humble abode.

A salesman would call it a manufactured home, but it's really just a travel trailer with a thyroid condition. It is 12 feet wide, 60 feet long.

And, according to the Clark County assessor's office, $11.24 in debt.

Until recently, the single-wide sat on a two-acre piece of desert real estate owned by Kenneth and Carnelle Greene. Until last week, the Greenes also owned the mobile home.

Now that the Champion has been auctioned for back taxes, all $11.24 of them, it also is the subject of litigation.

As lawsuits go, the Greenes vs. the Clark County assessor's office is not a sexy one. While multimillion-dollar filings are common in our court system, this action hinges on that $11.24 debt.

It's not a clerical error. You probably have more money than that stuck behind the couch cushions.

While society is riddled with far more costly concerns, this $11.24 gives insight into what some people find so damn bewildering about the machinery of county government. In that regard, this slender litigation may be priceless.

The Greenes owned two mobile homes on their Sandy Valley property. One they rented out. They lived part-time in the Champion.

Beginning in July, the trailer's tax bill went unpaid. Joe Ullom, the county's chief delinquent tax collector, began the process of attempting to locate the Greenes. By any standard, Ullom did his job and then some. For the next six months, he posted a seizure notice, mailed certified letters, and advertised the trailer's impending seizure in the *Nevada Legal News*.

He called several phone numbers, contacted the local justice of the peace and, finally, held an auction Wednesday. The Champion sold to the only bidder, Newman Vann, for $125, the approximate amount owed the county for the taxes ($11.24), penalty ($25.12), travel expense ($41.95), advertising ($45), and sale fee ($3).

Immediately following the auction, the Greenes discovered the problem and offered to pay the taxes and delinquencies. It was too late.

The assessor's office appears to have more than satisfied the letter of the law, which demands that all tax debts of $5 or more be pursued with no exceptions. But, then, the law is precisely not the issue.

This is, after all, the same county government whose treasurer, Mark Aston, in 1997 was reprimanded for dismissing nearly $2 million in penalties against people who failed to pay their property taxes in a timely manner. Be assured few of those tardy taxpayers owed as little as $11.24 for a single-wide in Sandy Valley.

Aston, who served 11 years in office, now serves probation and house arrest for thievery after he solicited thousands of dollars from private donors for a State Fiscal Officers Association conference and pocketed thousands in proceeds.

Assessor Mark Schofield cringes at the comparison.

"The law requires us to collect it," Schofield says. "The last thing we want to do is sell a manufactured home."

Ullom adds that few of the approximately 35,000 mobile homes in Clark County are seized and auctioned. The taxman tries to be reasonable.

"When a guy next door has paid his taxes, he gets a little mad when the guy next door hasn't paid his," Ullom says. "We do follow the letter of the law."

The county can't just return the trailer. Then it would face litigation from Vann, who was named in the Greenes' lawsuit filed by attorney Robert Knott Jr.

Knott argues that not only did his clients offer to compensate the county, but also that the paltry sum could have been generated by selling other items on the property. It was, he charges, unnecessary to sell a mobile home for a chump-change tax debt.

Schofield counters, "We have to treat all taxpayers equally whether it's $10 or $10,000."

That's a pretty thought, but it's painfully naive to believe that government fails to favor the wealthy. I recall a tax break for wealthy art owners, but when was the last time a lobbyist argued at the Legislature for relief for mobile-home owners?

That's what angers some people about their government. At the bottom end, government works with jack-booted efficiency. Rules are rules and, as a taxpayer, you're expected to follow all of them to precise specification. Or else.

Or else your Sandy Valley single-wide is snapped up in the name of the statute.

For $11.24? ◆

Tax season brings not-so-happy returns for Redd Foxx

April 6, 1990

When I arrived at the sprawling ranch-style home just off Eastern Avenue, a fellow who looked like Fred G. Sanford was busy unpacking his junk.

Not just any junk, but good junk. Personal junk. Boxes and boxes of it.

But Mr. Sanford, also known as comedian Redd Foxx, was not a happy man. In fact, he was surly and snide. The Internal Revenue Service had seen fit to release a few crates of the material goods its agents had confiscated from Foxx, but he did not appear overly grateful.

As the 67-year-old Foxx unwrapped his possessions, which appeared to hold as much sentimental as monetary value, he seemed anything but a comedic character. He looked like a sad, bitter, old man.

Friends and helpers scurried around, and he verbally abused them. A couple of reporters asked easy questions and a photographer fired off a few shots. He was curt to the reporters, belligerent to the photographer, and even accused his photo choice of somehow being prejudiced.

Whatever.

According to IRS figures, Foxx owes the government $2.9 million in taxes, a figure large enough to make most people bitter. Much of his more expensive belongings, automobiles and jewelry, have gone toward paying the debt. The rest of his stuff confiscated in November was returned to his home Wednesday.

Marc Risman, Foxx's attorney, said a payment schedule has been negotiated with the IRS. Because Foxx owes more than he is worth, the government can redefine the amount of his indebtedness.

During the course of the brief interview, Foxx was asked how he planned to repay a debt most people would consider staggering.

"What am I going to do about the two and a half million?" Foxx asked, figurines in hand. "Go back to armed robbery."

A good line. One worthy of a comedian who has enjoyed the rewards of success and celebrity.

Then he returned to the sour dour whining.

"If I had any friends, they [IRS] wouldn't have taken my stuff," Foxx said. "The people I thought were my friends got their own problems."

Millionaires, even bankrupt ones, should never whine. It doesn't look good on them. But Foxx is right on one account: Everyone has problems.

It is likely more than one Las Vegan would like to have the opportunity to have Foxx's money problems. To get that far behind financially, one would have had to start out much further ahead.

Foxx no doubt has had his share of life's sorrows and now

must be going through tribulations. But he also has had plenty of success as a stage comedian, on television in "Sanford and Sons," and in the movies, of late *Harlem Nights*. He has been admired and even adored by the public for his blunt wit.

Foxx still lives in a nice house, has plenty of people buzzing around him, and made at least enough money to get behind a couple of million bucks in taxes, according to government figures.

Perhaps unintentionally, the release of Foxx's boxes came in the waning days of the income tax season. The government's message is clear: If a rich man gets in trouble for failing to pay his taxes, then just imagine the kind of hell the rest of us will be forced to endure.

If a wealthy public figure's plight doesn't intimidate the middle class into beating the April 15 deadline, then it is likely nothing will. The IRS was unavailable to confirm my theory.

I thought about asking Foxx about the course his life has taken, but he was too busy berating the photographer.

It was a pathetic scene.

I couldn't wait to leave.

Turning to do just that, I reminded myself to mail that damned tax form as soon as I found it under my own pile of junk.

At the edge of the driveway, a small wooden sign caught my eye.

It read, "Only Little People Pay Taxes!" Signed, "L. Helmsley."

It must have been meant as a joke, but I decided not to ask Redd Foxx if he had found the ironic humor in it. ◆

Leaders give new meaning to term 'Deadhead'

June 4, 1992

Deadheads, meet the Blockheads.

They don't like your music, manners, or morals. They don't like your grooming or your grooving.

They want you to take the next VW bus headed for Haight-Ashbury and never return to our little silicone-enhanced Mayberry.

After all, Dead Elvis is good for our image. Deadheads are not.

Figure that one out, and I'll buy the drugs.

If it weren't such a broken record, the barrage of hypocritical ranting over the recent visit to Las Vegas by thousands of Grateful Dead fans would be amusing. Instead, it's like being forced to watch old lounge comics: It's not funny, just pathetic.

Thousands of members of the tie-dye fraternity made the long strange trip to Las Vegas last week for three Grateful Dead concerts and set an attendance record at the Sam Boyd Silver Bowl. The fans generated $2.7 million in ticket sales, $910,000 in state sales taxes, and $26 million in countywide revenue.

They also incurred the wrath of Circus Circus President Mike Sloan and Clark County Commissioner Paul Christensen for failing to display the respect due Las Vegas. Sources insist these fellows are not tripping on bad acid; they've merely overdosed on Vegas rhetoric.

It seems those shaggy rock fans didn't gamble enough. They also dressed funny. The former is a mortal sin. The latter is no mean feat here in leisure-suit land.

But a casino executive has spoken: It's better dead than Deadhead.

Sloan called the fans, known for their open drug use and scandalous free-form dancing, a slovenly horde. He also questioned the Deadheads' morals.

Sloan is a casino boss, political mechanic, and corporate attorney.

Clearly, morality is his strong suit.

His sorry lament echoes his annual whine over the frugality of the 100,000 computer heads who gather for the Comdex convention. Perhaps hotel operators down on Deadheads should treat them like the Comdexicans—gouge the wanna-be hippies on room prices to offset the lost casino revenue.

You see, jacking up room rates isn't bad for our image.

But the Deadheads are.

Just ask Christensen.

On Tuesday, he blamed the Deadheads for crowding the jails, flooding the hospitals, and overwhelming the police. Hell, they're probably behind this global warming thing, too.

Christensen's assertions are false. The concert promoter paid the security and ambulance costs.

But Christensen did personally experience one Deadhead's violent tendency. A wayward fan, possibly on drugs, used his body to dent the hood of the commissioner's classic 1967 Porsche coupe.

No wonder he's so mad.

I hate it when the hood of my Porsche gets bent.

Police made only a few arrests in three days. Laughing-gas sales ranked high among the transgressions. Another big violation was misdemeanor ticket scalping, which is offered as a minor at UNLV.

Presumably, more egregious sins were committed; other than malicious Porsche pouncing, I mean.

The Deadheads are bad for business and murder on resale values.

"The people I've talked to say they sleep ten to a room," Christensen said. "They don't appear to be the type to be employed. I wouldn't hire any of them."

Undaunted if not undented, such comments are common from Christensen. He often shoots from the lip using zip-gun logic.

"There was no way to control the drug use," he said. "They bring a group in here to promote the illegal use of illicit drugs and just wink at it."

Carl Sagan couldn't explain what goes on in the space between Christensen's ears on some days.

True, the cops could have made 50,000 two-bit pot arrests and turned the Silver Bowl into a county jail annex. That would have cost taxpayers plenty, but at least the Deadheads would have been reminded to Just Say No.

Surely one day soon someone will inform Sloan and Christensen the Grateful Dead scene is largely an affectation. Yes, Deadheads crave their three basic food groups: sex, drugs, and rock 'n' roll. Indeed, the band has thousands of diehards who follow it cross-country.

But for every penniless vagabond in the mellow crowd there was a gainfully employed American Express card-carrying yuppie pining for a little nostalgia.

Unlike Blockheads, Deadheads don't discriminate. ◆

Zero tolerance makes zero sense to grounded local pilot

October 10, 1991

Skyway Jet Charter wasn't the biggest airline flying, but it suited Las Vegan Billy Munnerlyn.

Munnerlyn was the pilot, co-pilot, and chief executive officer. He was a regular one-man flying circus and proud of his little operation's record. He piled up more than 9,000 flights and hauled everything from businessmen to disaster victims in his Lear Jet.

Today, the jet is gone. Skyway Charter is ruined. Munnerlyn's life is in a suicide stall as he tries to make sense of what he has experienced in the past three years.

On October 2, 1989, Munnerlyn picked up a passenger in Arkansas at Little Rock Airport, flew him to California, and deposited him at Ontario International Airport. Munnerlyn said he believed his passenger was Randy Sullivan, a banker who carried with him four boxes of documents.

Upon arrival, Munnerlyn's jet was met by Drug Enforcement Administration agents. Sullivan's real name was Albert Wright, a 74-year-old convicted cocaine trafficker. In reality, the document boxes were filled with $2.8 million in cash. Wright, agents believed, was on his way to launder the money with the full knowledge of his pilot.

Munnerlyn, experienced pilot and one-man company, was charged with drug trafficking and slapped with $1 million bail.

Nearly three days later, the charges were pulled and he was released.

Although he went free, his jet was seized by the government in its war on drugs. The seizure is one of dozens made each year in an attempt to separate drug traffickers from their ill-gotten gains.

The problem is, the only thing the government has been able to establish is Munnerlyn's solid record as a pilot. He never has been shown to be a criminal, much less a dope peddler. In this case, the government's theme of zero tolerance makes zero sense.

"I've done nothing," he said. "They can dig up all they want and go to anywhere they want and they're not going to find nothing on me. I haven't even had a speeding ticket in twenty years."

He has lived in Las Vegas 22 years. A pilot since 1966, the Arkansas native had flown commercially for a dozen years. He has been grounded since the seizure.

So sure they had captured a drug trafficker, agents subpoenaed his bank records, pulled his flight logs, and tore up his house looking for evidence. Somehow, this high-flying cocaine mule did a great job of disguising himself as a legitimate charter pilot.

In a three-day trial held a year ago in Los Angeles, a six-member jury ruled the seizure was inappropriate. The jet was to be returned to its rightful owner.

The U.S. Attorney's office had other plans. It quickly refiled its case, and kept the jet.

Over the next few months, Munnerlyn said he received several offers to settle. For $66,000, the jet would be released. Munnerlyn refused. First, the jury didn't say anything about owing any money. Second, pigs would fly before he would have $66,000 again.

In time, a second offer was made: The jet for $33,000. Later, the figure was reduced to $15,000.

In June, the figure was slashed to $6,500 for the privilege of having returned to Munnerlyn a jet a jury ruled was improperly seized in the first place.

Whether you choose to believe Munnerlyn was oblivious to his passenger's actual identity or was less naive is not the point: The fact remains a jury ruled in his favor.

So much for justice.

"If I had been a person who's been an underworld figure or that junk, then fine," Munnerlyn said. "We've been a local family. For this to happen, it's just bizarre. It should never happen."

Perverted justice aside, the jet sits collecting dust and cobwebs at a Midland, Texas, airfield. After more than two years, Munnerlyn estimated it will take $50,000 to return it to FAA standards.

$50,000?

Munnerlyn said he would be hard pressed to put together $500.

These days, the government's big-time drug trafficker rolls up and down the interstate hauling produce in an 18-wheeler. Instead of flying the friendly skies, he motors the menacing highways. The job gives him a lot of time to think about his jet and Skyway Charters. Maybe too much time.

"It just shouldn't happen to anybody," Munnerlyn said. ◆

Sporting
Life

Betting a lifelong game for Las Vegas Club's Mel Exber

February 27, 1994

Brooklyn, 1937.

Darkness rolls in like a blue fog on the asphalt ball yard, and the players are anxious to finish while the late light lasts.

The game is stickball, the bet is a nickel a man, and the contest is close.

A mother appears at a second-floor window of a nearby apartment.

"Melvin, your father's home!" she calls. "It's time for dinner!"

It's not her fault. Adults rarely understand the importance of the game. This could be the Dodgers vs. the Yankees, a genuine Subway Series, and an adult wouldn't see it.

Time and light are short.

"Throw me down a sandwich, Ma," the boy responds. "The game's not over yet."

Six decades and 3,000 miles from that Brooklyn street, Mel Exber sits back in his office at the Las Vegas Club and contemplates the game of his youth and his life.

"When I was a kid, the game was more important than anything. We never played a game, I don't care whether it was basketball, softball, punchball, stickball, without making a bet," he says. "We bet on everything. This was dog-eat-dog. We pitched pennies, matched coins. Whatever we did, we bet. It's the way it was."

The stakes have risen considerably, but for Exber the game hasn't changed. When historians ponder the evolution of Las Vegas, they will heap credit for the city's growth on the casino operators. But if the card-and-dice men are responsible for developing Las Vegas, the bookmakers should get credit for blazing the trail that leads to the Strip. The founding fathers not only knew the score, but they could give you the odds as well.

Exber, the son of a Brooklyn tailor, is one of those. The 70-year-old is a piece of living history, which makes him sound like a fossil. He's far from it. The guy looks 50, and only a fool would bet against him on the golf course.

When he rolled into Las Vegas with his brother on the Fourth of July in 1947, Ben Siegel had been dead less than a month. The Strip featured three casinos, but most of the action was downtown at the El Cortez, El Dorado, Pioneer Club, Golden Nugget, and the Las Vegas Club.

The action ate him alive. His Army Air Corps mustering-out pay vanished before his eyes, and he took a job as a ticket writer at the Las Vegas Club for $15 a week.

"We were broke within a week," he says. "I stayed."

In those days, most of the action was bet on thoroughbreds.

He gradually learned the lay of Fremont Street and the casino racket. He booked and bet and bided his time, joining partners in the Saratoga and Derby betting parlors with an Omaha sportsman named Jackie Gaughan. In 1961, with the help of downtown legend Kell Houssels Sr., they picked up the rickety old Las Vegas Club.

His business interests have expanded over the decades, and Exber is comfortable by anyone's standards.

No matter what the mirror says, Mel Exber is 70. He stopped making $15 a day a long time ago. He could retire and play golf more than once a day. He could travel full-time in an endless summer with his longtime pal, former Dodger Maury Wills.

Why doesn't he?

To ask such a question is to miss his reason for being.

Think about Brooklyn all those years ago. It's the game. He's never stopped playing it, or loving it.

That's one reason the walls of the Las Vegas Club are lined with autographed sports memorabilia. It's a dream for a fan of baseball, football, basketball, or hockey. The walls reflect his personality.

"I'd go nuts if I didn't have this place to come to," Exber says. "It's the game. It's a helluva game, and that's why I do it. I don't ever want to grow up as far as sports is concerned."

That's why you'll find him almost every day behind the counter of his unpretentious sports book, gnawing on a cigar, and pushing the numbers back and forth.

At the end of the day, he sleeps like a kid. Sometimes he wakes in the middle of the night, flips on the computer that links him to his sports operation, and studies the betting lines.

Win or lose a contest, he knows he's a lucky man.

After all these years, Mel Exber is still playing the game of his youth and his life. ◆

Si Redd a vision of Vegas as he keeps building business

May 2, 1993

The place is the Las Vegas Country Club, but at this moment it resembles nothing more than Si Redd's personal showroom and stage.

Wrapped in an intriguing black and gold sports coat, a big gold bolo tie hanging from his neck, Redd is dressed for a spot on "The Tonight Show." He waves to members of the lunchtime crowd, pauses to embrace two executive types, flirts with a waitress, and finally lands at the table dealing one-liners and country yarns like aces from a sweetly stacked deck.

At an age when most folks are satisfied just waking up in the morning, the founder of International Game Technology is ready to embark on a multimillion-dollar business venture. At 81, the rail-slim former farm boy from Philadelphia, Mississippi, is in a rush to make a little money and have a little fun before the day is through.

Redd personifies the entrepreneurial spirit of Las Vegas. He is one part huckster, one part savvy businessman. One moment he is the grinning son of an itinerant Southern preacher, the next minute he is the hustler who survived doing business with some of the world's toughest customers.

Men like Redd have enabled gambling to evolve from back-alley racket to billion-dollar industry.

His business education started with 21-mile barefoot sales

trips around the greater Philadelphia area, which is to say through cotton fields and across clay flats. World War I was ending, and Si was seven years old. He sold *Grit* magazines to the share-croppers who could read, Cloverine salve to the rest.

"There's no question I was an entrepreneur," he says, attacking a Caesar salad with a poor boy's zeal.

He had the sore feet to prove it.

"My father was a jack-leg preacher, a holy-roller with the Church of Christ. I was embarrassed by him at the time, but I have come to respect him. He had the courage to stand up for his beliefs. But he didn't have the slightest idea that you were supposed to have money."

Family finance became Si's job. He turned nickels into dimes and earned up to $9.75 a week pressing clothes and shining shoes. He saved up enough cash to buy a penny-a-play pinball machine.

Placing it carefully on the dirt floor of a Decatur, Mississippi, greasy spoon, Redd returned days later to find the cash box bursting with cents, $32 in all.

His days of walking farm to farm were over.

From Mississippi to Massachusetts, Chicago to Reno, he has run in fast company and managed to keep his head on his shoulders and his wallet in his pocket.

In Philadelphia, he founded Mississippi Vending Company and riddled the countryside with juke boxes and pinball machines.

In Sterling, Illinois, he started Northwestern Music Company with the same product.

In Boston after World War II, Redd Distributing put Wurlitzer juke boxes in cafes and saloons.

As the founder of Reno's Bally Distributing, Redd helped revolutionize the slot machine business. By the time he sold his share of the company in 1978 and created IGT, he had more money than a farm boy would know what to do with.

Today, IGT stock is among the best buys on Wall Street. Redd left the company six years ago, but, give or take a share, he owns about $60 million worth.

The fact is, Redd has had a hand in most of the big ideas to come along in the slot machine business. From the Big Bertha slots to the Video Lottery, he has experimented with one hand and sold machines with the other.

But our man Si isn't waiting around for someone to bronze his likeness and place it in the town square. He is taking over the Peppermill Casino at Mesquite, building bigger and better slots, and selling 26,000 poker machines to 5,000 bars in Massachusetts.

"It's going to make millions for the state, and old Si ain't going to do too bad, either," he says, laughing. Imagine a preacher's son speaking in terms of millions.

"And I ain't stopped yet. It's in my blood. I like people. I like to make people laugh. And I like to make money."

In a couple years, he plans to spend a little of it at his friend George Burns' 100th birthday celebration at the Palladium. Redd will be the kid in the front row.

"I guarantee you I'm going to be at that party."

No one ever got rich betting against this country boy.

At the rate he's going, Si Redd will be the opening act. ◆

UPDATE: Now in his 80s, Si Redd shows little sign of slowing down.

World Series of Poker's excitement truly one big deal

May 17, 1996

With the hype and punditry billowing thicker than the fog from the cheapest cigar, it's easy to forget what gambling is all about.

I thought about that as I stared through the haze Thursday at a fortune in chips moving back and forth across the final table in the 27th Annual World Series of Poker at Binion's Horseshoe.

It may not sell in the Bible Belt, and it might not make for wise political policy in Congress, but this is what it's all about.

Between the national political intrigue and the daily local casino moves, the gaming industry is a constant source of news and entertainment.

To the moral crowd, it's a dark-hearted monolith representing everything that is wrong with America. From teen-age blackjack junkies to check-bouncing grandmothers, there's a soapbox for every critic and a fretful feature for every taste.

To readers of the Business page, there's the industry's jaw-dropping success story. Casino stocks have been the talk of Wall Street for years. What's bad for the nation is good for business.

For people who love Las Vegas and consider it the heart, soul, and center of America's casino subculture, all that other stuff is just a bunch of noise.

The World Series distills this whole surreal phenomenon to its essence: risk and reward. There's a little danger in every deal.

On Thursday, the makeshift grandstands were jammed with pretty good players as they watched this year's masters. Place extra emphasis on this year, for there is nothing as fickle as the flop of the cards.

Surely longtime fans noticed the absence of Johnny Chan and Phil Hellmuth Jr., but they were rewarded with the presence of a new kid in town.

The $10,000 buy-in No-Limit Texas Hold 'em tournament was won by 27-year-old Las Vegan Huck Seed, a most unlikely name for a big-city card player. The name conjures images of a barefoot country boy with hay in his hair, and his casual dress and two-days' growth of beard added to the image.

But Mr. Seed was anything but a simple fellow on Thursday. A veteran of several major tournaments, he bulled his way through hand after hand on the way to defeating a table lined with players twice his age.

Normally, watching other men play cards is about as exciting as watching an accountant fiddle with a tax return. The Friday night nickel-ante game isn't much of a spectator sport, but there's something oddly American about poker. There's skill and there's luck, and we hold both traits almost as dearly as life, liberty, and the pursuit of happiness.

Even with the emcee calling the hands and the TV cameras hovering above every move on the table, the big game illustrated everything that really matters about gambling. Whether you're playing for a fin or a fortune, the real thrill is in the playing.

No kids, no clowns, no executives expounding on the virtues of casino "entertainment." Thankfully, there wasn't much chatter at all.

On Thursday, the players quietly bet the price of a four-bedroom house time after time as they jockeyed for position.

"I have to wait for a guy to win a million bucks so I can go home," one World Series regular said facetiously.

The World Series is that kind of tournament.

At times it appears that the industry possesses a million maladies. Gambling has been criticized in publications ranging from the *Holy Bible* to *The New York Times*. With the crowd murmuring as the chips traded hands, one woman was oblivious to the drama being played out before her. She was mesmerized by a quarter slot machine, and could barely contain herself when it hit a $75 jackpot.

Serious poker enthusiasts, who spoke in hushed tones and treated the action at the final table with the respect most people reserve for religious ceremonies, stared at her as the coins clanked in the bin. She didn't notice at all as a $120,000 bet was placed nearby.

"All right," she cried above the crowd. "Whew. Oh, yeah."

Hey, pal, 75 bucks is 75 bucks.

That's the best part of gambling.

The thrill is in the playing. And the winning, of course, but winning is something the house eventually takes care of for you.

It's the playing that counts. That's what it's all about. ◆

Shed no tears for former jock blowing his latest chance

November 11, 1991

Football jock-turned-compulsive-betting poster-boy Art Schlichter continued his pathetic fall Thursday by miring himself in a $400,000 federal bank-fraud case.

Save your tears, sports fans.

He was an odds-on favorite to be exposed sooner or later. Despite declaring sports book sobriety years ago, he hasn't missed many bets through the seasons.

Art Schlichter's story was a tragedy a decade ago. Today, it's a felony. From the looks of things, several.

Schlichter, who wore No. 10 and starred at Ohio State before later fumbling away a National Football League career in the name of the latest line, worked of late as a local radio sports talk show host. He is accused of stealing thousands from numerous people and writing $175,000 in bad checks over four months.

It's not all that complex. In brief, he is accused of taking advantage of his celebrity, collecting friendships and business contacts, and then exploiting those associations. It's not exactly news for Schlichter, whose once-promising career included being a high first-round draft pick of the Indianapolis Colts. He celebrated by being suspended from the league for a year for gambling.

Two years ago, when he was arrested in Cincinnati on a bad-check charge, Schlichter was said to have suffered a "gambling relapse." Oh, please. He had been handed a quarterback assignment with the Cincinnati Rockers of the Arena Football League and rewarded its owners with the intercepted pass of a $3,000 check.

Over the lost seasons, dozens of sympathetic feature stories have been written about Schlichter and his terrible disease. His career has been used to illustrate the awful effects of compulsive sports betting, and he's taken advantage of that, too.

You see, Schlichter's betting habit was the worst-kept secret in Strip sports books. He even has been suspected of taking and laying off bets.

"I love to gamble. I've always loved to gamble. It's been a problem, but that doesn't mean you can't talk about sports or be around them," Schlichter once told *R-J* writer Stephen Nover. "It's tough anywhere you go trying to make a living and feeding your family."

Oh, yes, feeding the family is a difficult thing. Especially when you're betting the kiddies' inheritance on the Rams-49ers game.

Compulsive gambling is a terrible affliction, but so is throwing away a stadium full of opportunities. Schlichter has done that and more in the decade-plus since he was discovered to have the sucker's disease. He was thousands in debt while still in college and didn't take the hint. He botched his professional football career and didn't understand that the joke was on him. He was given chance after chance to shake himself and get on with his life and just didn't get it.

But wait. Here comes the bad news. Before the ink dries on the federal indictment, Metro intends to file felony fraud charges against the former football hero.

Metro sources disclosed Thursday that Schlichter is suspected of defrauding Southern Nevada residents out of as much as $250,000 through a series of check-switching scams. Schlichter traded personal checks for as much as $6,000 with several locals. Among those victimized are an Air Force colonel and a Las Vegas optometrist. North Las Vegas police also are preparing a case.

Schlichter was bailed out time after time. Not because he was a sweetheart of a guy with innumerable good qualities, but because he was a jock who once upon a time could throw a football better than most.

Don't misunderstand: Compulsive gambling is a nightmare worthy of Dante. It's just that countless other guys with the same problem and inferior arm strength have long since blown their jobs, mortgages, families, and futures by attempting to turn the chaos of the numbers into a quantifiable science. On their way to breaking even, they've broken their lives.

Maybe the cab driver gets two chances to save himself. Maybe he gets 10. But nobody gets as many hand-wringing apologists as successful athletes. They comprise America's celebrity Animal House.

Unlike lesser beings, whose drug addiction is far more likely to land them in the penitentiary than on a weepy Barbara Walters special, celebrities receive sympathy and a trip to the Betty Ford Clinic. Membership has its privileges, but after a while the maudlin morality play gets a little stale.

So save your tears for all the minimum-wage mopes who lost their livelihoods for chump change and lacked a fan club willing to make their bail and swallow their excuses. They're the victims in this sordid story.

Old No. 10 has had his day in the sun. ◆

G.L. Vitto remembered as a true Las Vegas institution

October 30, 1991

Those who consider Howard Cosell the Mouth that Roared never watched the Great G.L. Vitto torture the midnight airwaves in the name of the Castaways casino, surreal sports betting, and good weird fun.

He was Cosell with a funny bone, Leo Durocher with a rubber chicken. He was a wonderfully absurd pitchman, the Las Vegas institution who belonged in one.

Vitto died Monday morning of a heart attack and left behind a wife, five children, and thousands of Las Vegans still scratching their heads at his sincerely insane sense of humor.

His hilariously spastic commercial breaks almost always were better than the movie. But nobody ever received an Emmy for hosting a late-night flick. A rubber chicken, perhaps, but not much more. If they awarded a bronze chicken, G.L. deserved a hundred.

Of course, the one-liner was not his strength. Vitto thrived on stream-of-comatose humor that hounded the viewer into a smile. His schtick was so dumb it hurt, but he could make the Grim Reaper grin.

And man could he sell soap.

As the Great G.L., he expounded on the infinite virtues of parlay cards and $1.99 dinners. All the while he wove some of the strangest scenarios this side of a Ray Bradbury novel.

Maybe it was the late hour. Perhaps it was the mock locker-room backdrop, his zebra- striped jersey, and the relentless deadpan.

Whatever it was, the guy made you laugh. And groan.

When it came to the Great G.L., you either loved him or hated him. Or both.

People laughed in his face and he took it as a compliment.

"Everything was tongue-in-cheek. He'd make these funny remarks with a deadpan expression," former Castaways sports book director Sonny Reizner said. "The L.A. Rams were the L.A. Worms. He didn't like the Stardust, so he used to call it the Starbust."

And then there was Roman Gabriel, of the beleaguered Worms, uh, Rams. In Vitto's vernacular, Gabriel was the worst quarterback to ever fumble a snap from center. In keeping with the relentless schtick, Roman Garbage became the leader of the L.A. Worms.

So it wasn't Groucho Marx.

It kept bleary-eyed insomniacs and swing-shift night owls entertained for years, and it sold plenty of advertising for the Silver Slipper, Castaways, and other hot spots.

With the Great G.L. gone to that late-late show in the sky, local tawdry television will never be the same. Some stiff-collar types will say that's a good thing.

But those critics who allege Vitto was a part of a Las Vegas boob-tube scene that has faded into a Big Chief test pattern obviously don't stay up late. It's getting older, but no better.

These days, the hosts resemble an endless string of absolutely talent-free lounge castoffs lip-syncing "Tie a Yellow Ribbon 'Round the Old Oak Tree" and schmoozing with equally lifeless clowns.

G.L., where are you when we need you?

Of course, there was another side to Vitto's insanity.

"Off-camera, he was one of the most gentle, most considerate human beings I've ever encountered in my life," former Castaways President and General Manager Bill Friedman said.

In the middle of a nameless sports conference several years ago, a slight fellow emerged from the crowd and stood quietly by himself.

It was the Great G.L. Vitto, the human exclamation point.

Expecting cream pies in the face or a joy-buzzer handshake, I contemplated ducking under a table. I waited for a rubber chicken to drop out of the ceiling, but was disappointed.

No pies, no electric shock treatment, no hyperbolic diatribe about the future of the free world riding on the outcome of the next Rams game. He was just a polite little guy with happy eyes and a soft voice.

It was a side television viewers never saw. He made certain of it.

Had they known the Great G.L was a nice, almost normal guy, it would have ruined everything. ◆

Final bell sounds on a life of punches, polkas, and plumbing

October 18, 1995

Eddie Simms stood amid the chaos in Johnny Tocco's downtown gym and breathed in the glorious sweaty scene.

Grinning in his element, alert and bobbing, he wore a sports coat redder than any nosebleed. Eddie was as friendly as a small-town mayor and as talkative as an auctioneer.

He pulled me aside, squeezed my hand, and reminded me of the time he fought the great Joe Louis.

And suddenly we were there.

It was in Cleveland, you know.

In '36.

Eddie went the better part of one round against the Brown Bomber.

Got hit with a lucky shot on the temple, he said. Louis delivered a lot of lucky shots in those days. Went blind for more than one hour, Eddie said. Told the referee he wanted "to go take a walk on the roof."

The fight was stopped, but Eddie recovered.

Tough Eddie Simms always recovered.

Through 205 professional fights, 97 recordings as an impresario of the accordion, bit parts in movies, and long years spent as a union plumber, he was nothing if not resilient.

As many times as I heard the Louis story, and a dozen other chapters in his oral history, I never got over the awe of how this tough old guy loved life.

Some people dine elegantly on experience. Their palate is so refined that they would not deign to eat with their fingers.

Others pick at life's plate. Their tastes are bland and are reflected in a certain pallor of the psyche.

Eddie Simms was a gourmand.

Born in 1908, he lived every minute of 87 years. He died of heart failure a week ago. His family suspected that the true cause of his demise was a broken heart after losing his wife of 42 years. But it will go down as natural causes.

Eddie was born and raised in Cleveland, where he was undoubtedly the best accordion-squeezing boxer of all time. Eddie fought Louis, Max Baer, and scores of lesser men. He was known as a game slugger who could take two, return one, and outlast most opponents. That was in his prime, but every fight fan knows that prime never lasts.

By the time I met him, he wore the history of the fight racket on his face. His visage was a topographical map of every bucket-of-blood saloon and smoky auditorium that became the birthplaces of the best brawlers of boxing's golden era.

Eddie's eyelids were heavy, his eyes fogged with cataracts, his nose almost too flat for glasses. Some of his teeth had been displaced since the FDR administration.

Then there were the hands.

Eddie's mitts were as broad as bricks with knuckles that had dented 200 faces. Those fists remained formidable well into his 80s.

As proof that he wasn't washed up, Eddie put on weekly shows at senior citizen centers.

"I like playing for the old people," Eddie said.

He was past 80 at the time.

"They used to say about me, 'He rocks them to sleep both musically and pugilistically,'" he said.

They used to call Eddie a lot back when he was a quality journeyman heavyweight with a ferocious reputation for toughness. The sports writers loved Eddie with his boxing gloves and jumping accordion.

They called him plenty when he was cutting scads of polka tunes for RCA Victor, Columbia, and Brunswick.

Gifted with a face that launched a thousand hooks, they called him from Hollywood when they needed a guy with a felonious profile.

Eddie liked the movies and the records, but the offers didn't last. He lived quietly in Las Vegas off and on for more than 30 years, only occasionally appearing in newsprint.

When he wasn't playing accordion, he liked to drop in on fight trainer Johnny Tocco and reminisce.

Don't misunderstand. Eddie Simms wasn't punchy. Far from it. His battle-decorated face and husky voice masked a mind capable of instant recall of the slightest details from fights long forgotten.

"In all my fights, I was never knocked down with a punch on the chin," he said with a pride of ownership of one of the toughest jaws on the planet.

No matter how tough life got, he always had a smile, a light step, and a sunny remark for the people in his life.

"It's nice and quiet," Eddie would say. "There's no pain and no strain."

Perhaps because a boxing comeback was improbable at his age, Eddie used his hands to squeeze out jumping tunes from his youth.

"I play a thousand songs, all by ear," Eddie would say, grinning.

And a cauliflower ear at that.

What a wonderful life.

Sweet dreams, Eddie Simms. ◆

Casa Nova loved life

October 2, 1991

The images greeted a visitor just inside the door of Lou Nova's mobile home.

One wall in his small clean place off Valley View Boulevard was dedicated to a boxing Adonis whose press clips had long since yellowed. The image of a classic gladiator with broad shoulders, strong chin, and dark curly hair emerged from two generations past.

The headlines shouted like a street-corner newsy. Nova vs. the great Joe Louis at the Polo Grounds. Nova vs. the brutal Max Baer. Nova the actor on the screen. Nova the comedian on stage.

I glanced at the frail fellow who welcomed me with a bony hand extended and hoped my face didn't tell its shock. The young man and the old one were one in the same.

Then Lou Nova grinned like one of Barnum & Bailey's best buffoons and said, "Like my place? I call it Casa Nova. Casanova, get it?"

He laughed, wheezed a bit, and found a chair, his wife and nurse Teresa standing quietly nearby. That corny line was pure Lou Nova.

Ravaged by cancer, slowed by heart bypass surgery and sour lungs, Nova still managed to laugh at the young warrior on the wall. It did not seem to bother him that the once-powerful athlete who dated Dorothy Lamour and dined at "21" was living out his last days as a sickly ghost in a mobile home. If he hurt, it didn't show.

Don't misunderstand. He hated his shortness of breath, his bum heart, and the cancer that ate away at him daily. It angered him and kept him from working on his ultimate theory about galloping dominoes.

"Sometimes I walk up to the crap table feeling awful," Nova said. "Then, it's unbelievable. There's nothing at all that bothers me when I'm shooting craps. That crap table to me is complete therapy.

"I only wish I could learn to win."

In a world full of arrogant colorless fellows who have let their money define their character, Lou Nova was a rich man.

Easy for me to say. I never made the money he had stolen from him.

To say fortune did not smile upon him would be like saying the Titanic leaked.

Nova fought Louis in 1941 at the Polo Grounds for $125,000, but received only a fraction of the purse. His promoter, manager, trainer, and entourage pocketed most of the dough. Nova won the dubious honor of being knocked out in the sixth round by one of the greatest heavyweights of all time.

He would learn to laugh about it.

He defeated the brawling Baer in two of the dirtiest fights of the modern era and one day would laugh about that, too. Baer nearly killed him before falling, but Nova outlived the brute.

After 87 professional fights, Nova began a career on Broadway, where he starred in "Guys and Dolls" and "The Happiest Millionaire." He went on to appear in dozens of off-Broadway productions and 28 movies. Nova also toured the world as a comedian billed as The Gentleman of Wit. As if that didn't supply enough memories, he once read poetry at Carnegie Hall.

Nova entertained millions, but never became a millionaire. In his fighting prime, he was mobbed on Broadway and harassed in fancy restaurants by hundreds of autograph-seeking fans.

"Back then I used to say to myself, 'One day, just for one day, I'd like to live like an ordinary human being,'" Nova said on a March morning in 1989. "Every day now is like an ordinary human being."

After fighting cancer and lesser maladies for years, Nova died Sunday. He was 78, and died in obscurity like so many who live long enough to hear the deafening roar of silence from the crowd.

But he was different.

Lou Nova was a ring gentleman in an age of cheap cretins, spoiled brats, and glorified thugs.

He was that rarest of fellows, a happy man. Not a millionaire, but one of the happiest guys I have ever met.

That is the image I will remember most: The Gentleman of Wit smiling bravely through his pain.◆

Nevada pugilist entered in bout to save life of one-year-old

August 1, 1993

The Gary Bates story begins with blood, the type spilled in the ring and on the street.

His ability to make others bleed won him a splash of sports-page celebrity, the Nevada state heavyweight title, a few bouts with top contenders, and a certain familiarity with local police.

"Back then, I worked the night shift," the 48-year-old Bates says, smiling about his documented past, which includes a stint in the Marine Corps. He adjusts his glasses, which rest on a nose only a cutman could love. "I had eighty-six fights, in the ring. It's an old joke."

Outside the ropes, differences of opinion usually ended with
someone's nose springing a leak. For a time, he was a magnet
for trouble. In those days, a lot of blood was wasted on ring
mats, sidewalks, and barroom floors.

Why, a few people even mistook Bates for a juice collector
for legendary Las Vegas loan shark Jasper Speciale. Sometimes
people confuse blood with money, but Bates knows the difference.

Blood is life.

The rest is just a waste of energy.

If you can imagine big bad Gary Bates volunteering to spill
his own blood, then you can begin to understand his personal
evolution from knockaround nightfly and Strip Fight of the
Week regular to square citizen and bone-marrow donor.

Bone marrow?

"It was the next level," Bates says. "I'd already given blood
and blood platelets."

In fact, he had given 56 pints (seven gallons) of blood and
another eight pints of platelets through cytapheresis. His wife,
Carmen, has parted with six gallons of blood.

Then Bates asked to do something more. He was marrow
typed and added to that small but important list of nationwide
donors.

Unlike blood typing, marrow matches outside immediate
families are rare. So rare, in fact, that they are referred to as a
Miracle Match. They are improbable, as the bookmakers say,
but not impossible.

The improbable has happened.

A one-year-old is dying of blood cancer in the Midwest. Chemotherapy will scorch the baby's precious marrow. Without
chemotherapy, the child surely will die. Without marrow, the
child will die.

Without Gary Bates, casino floorman and former heavyweight journeyman, the baby has no chance.

About 2,000 miles away, Bates waits. He spends his nights
working as a dice floor supervisor at the Golden Nugget and
his waking hours planning for the August 12 trip to the Research

Medical Center in Kansas City.

Once there, he will undergo a painful transfusion procedure. A needle will be inserted into the top of his hip, and he will become one of approximately 1,700 marrow donors in the history of the process. After about 200 pulls of the syringe, he will be finished.

It will take about two weeks to recover.

It will be painful, but pain is relative. Bates is a fellow who laughs about the time he detached his left biceps in a bout.

Truth is, he can hardly wait to jump into the fight for the infant's life.

"This is an honor," he says. "I think there's an intrinsic strain that runs through me that's a good guy.

"This is like good guy training."

There have been other workouts. There was the time in 1970 he pulled a man from a burning car on Interstate 15. There was the day in 1990 he apprehended a purse-snatcher downtown.

He's not bragging. Just the opposite, in fact. Sometimes he wonders why the fates have chosen him to stand up so many times.

Maybe he's repaying old psychic debts. Possibly his trouble magnet began drawing the right kind of human difficulty.

Or perhaps it has something to do with boxing, with the encouraging words of his old coach, Mike O'Callaghan, and Golden Gloves teammate, Harry Reid. There's nothing like the ring to teach a hard-headed kid to stand and deliver.

"You know how you want the movie to end. You want to be the you that makes you proud in the script...You want to be the hero," Bates says. "I don't want to die and not have had a meaningful life on Earth."

It has something to do with the next level. After all these years, it comes back to blood.

Blood is life, life is good, and Gary Bates is living proof. ◆

Don't confuse things, the public loves the fight game

September 12, 1991

Fearing I had slept for 100 years, I stepped from the back alley into Johnny Tocco's Ringside Gym and was relieved.

The joint looked and smelled the same: heavy bags, speed bags, blood-spattered ring, grumpy old man. Weathered, but with some fight left.

Ghosts of champs and contenders grinned and scowled from the walls. The ring bell tolled steadily, reminding everyone time does not wait. Not for Ali, not for Sugar Ray, not for Mike Tyson.

Boxers raged in the ring to the shouts of mean-faced men. A little blood, a lot of sweat, no tears.

Just business.

The air was warm and stale and free of hypocrisy. I took a few breaths and felt better. With all the whining about Tyson being accused of raping a beauty-pageant contestant, I was worried the nation had grown a conscience and banned boxing in the name of good taste and sensitivity. Obviously, nothing has changed.

Some people are using Tyson's alleged transgression as a good reason to cancel his November 8 fight at Caesars Palace against heavyweight champion Evander Holyfield. After all, rape is an outrageous act of violence. So is boxing. Gee, maybe Phil Donahue will do a show about it.

Others say allowing the fight to go on will give the sport a bad name, which is like saying a tax conviction gave Al Capone a bad name. A quick inventory reveals boxing to be a multimillion-dollar circus filled with violence, sleaze, and a history of mob influence. Those are its good points.

It's also entertaining and feeds the Las Vegas economy. Thus, blood and money win out over the squeamish and the well-mannered every time. That's the reality of Tyson's tribulation.

Granted, Tyson's *National Enquirer* lifestyle is getting embarrassing even for boxing, but let's not get misty-eyed here. The Marquess of Queensberry is dead, pal. A referee deducts a point for a low blow, but usually only after the third one. That's the fight racket.

The truth is, the Tyson-Holyfield fight is a $100 million business venture. Holyfield is promised at least $30 million, Tyson $15 million. Caesars Palace stands to make millions. The tickets are sold, the TV deal is done. The fight is on.

Tyson is hardly the first boxer to run afoul of the law. The great John L. Sullivan beat his women and busted up barrooms. The greater Jack Johnson ran with prostitutes and fought outside the country to evade the authorities.

Not all boxers are animals in the ring. Just the good ones. Although not all are carnivores outside it, we should not be surprised when they brawl, violate women, use drugs, and crash their expensive automobiles. The nation's prisons are full of violent men who would have been fair boxers had they turned professional in the ring and not on the street corner.

Not all boxers use dope, punch out civilians, and rape their dates, but those who do rarely lose sleep. If they are successful, they rarely suffer sanctions, either.

The public prefers it that way.

How else can we explain our behavior at ringside?

When a fellow gets his nose mashed so severely he bleeds a pint down his throat, we call it sport and pay money for a good seat.

When a man grins through the pain of a shattered jaw, we call it courage and applaud his effort.

When a slow-footed journeyman is clubbed so hard by the house fighter he sees his ancestors, we call it a chance for a poor kid to escape the ghetto and find a better life.

Face it, we like to watch.

Boxing hasn't changed, because the spectators haven't changed.

That's why the Caesars show should go on. Not because Tyson is innocent until proven guilty. He is, but we don't really care.

The fight should take place because being offended at such a vile allegation in the world of boxing reeks of hypocrisy.

Fight trainer Johnny Tocco, a survivor of more than 60 years in the racket, said it best: "The public likes that blood. They go to the fight to see somebody get busted up and knocked out."

So let's not confuse the issues.

One is merely the latest chapter in the tragic tale of Mike Tyson's life.

The other is business. ◆

Johnny Tocco trained champions, and Irma trained him

August 15, 1991

It annoyed Johnny Tocco at the time, but it is one of many things he will miss.

Each morning for half a century, Irma Tocco gave her husband a brief quiz.

"I'd get ready for work and she'd say, 'Do you have your keys? Do you have your wallet? Do you have your glasses?' It would bother me. I'd say, 'Why do you always gotta ask me? I'm not a boy, I'm a grown man.'"

He is that. At 81, Tocco still keeps the Ringside Gym open six days a week. He handles a few fighters, works a few corners, stops a few cuts. Once the trainer for Willie Pep, Sonny Liston, and Larry Holmes, most of Tocco's high-paying main-event days are behind him. He works mostly undercard bouts, often with the underdog. Through all the politics and all the disappointment, he keeps working and hopes for one more contender.

Irma comprised the other half of his life. Her love crept inside and softened one of the toughest old fellows you will ever meet. Their relationship is one for the books.

Last year, they were in the hospital together. Her lungs. His heart. Nurses wondered what all the noise was about, and why Larry Holmes was sending all those flowers.

They recovered, but were still fretting over the bills when Irma fell and hurt her hip early this year. She refused to go to the hospital. After spending two weeks in a hospital bed in 1990, she wanted no more of it. Like most old people, she feared checking in would mean never checking out.

Tocco stayed at her side for weeks, running back and forth from the gym to feed her meals and help her to the bathroom. With help from the hands that have patched 10,000 bleeding brows, she gradually recovered enough to move around the house.

He returned to work. Six days a week, nine hours a day, a quiz each morning. Keys, check. Wallet, check. Eyeglasses, check.

Two weeks ago, Irma came down with a flu. On Friday night, she leaned back in her favorite recliner and dozed off. He awoke her shortly before midnight, served her a bowl of soup and Jell-O. She was too tired to eat and returned to dreamland. She did not awaken. She was 84.

Among many loved ones, Irma left behind three fat happy dogs and one tough old man.

She was buried Wednesday, one sweet Catholic lady among the masses. Like most people whose names make the newspaper only when they are born, wed, and die, she was special to someone. In her case, it was a curmudgeon named Tocco.

As a young man, Tocco was more than acquainted with the St. Louis mob. As he grew up around the fight racket, he ran into his share of mob trouble.

He survived all the fights in and out of the ring. He laughs about the time he chased one of Don King's muscle-headed mugs out of his gym with a butcher knife. He shrugs when he relates the story of telling Mike Tyson to hit the highway when he refused to keep his workout appointments. A couple of years ago, he punched out a mouthy construction worker who needed it. You get the idea.

Holmes and lesser champs brought him a modicum of sports-page celebrity and a few good paydays. His gym and his small stable of fighters kept him maddeningly active.

She softened him the way nothing else could.

That is perhaps the least understood but most important effect a good woman has on a man. At her best, she makes him more than what he is. Her kindness and consistency help save him from himself.

During the weekend, a moment of silence was observed in Irma's honor at a local Golden Gloves tournament. Not exactly a fitting tribute, but it's the best boxing can do.

As Tocco went through the family files not long after her death, he came across dozens of notes, letters, and messages she had saved of their life together. As if one woman's memory could not suffice, she kept everything. His eyes brimmed as he reread a simple birthday card.

"I didn't know she admired me so much," he said.

It was something she had been telling him every morning. ◆

New valentine makes heart of boxing trainer Tocco tick

February 14, 1992

Johnny Tocco's heart was a worn-out heavy bag.

The 81-year-old boxing trainer lost his wife of 50 years in August. His two favorite dogs died in the long weeks that followed.

Alone in his house, he wondered how everything had changed so suddenly. The home that once was filled with life and the barking of happy dogs was now a shell.

He still worked six days a week at his gym, still repaired boxers' tattered eyebrows, still argued with everyone who came through the door. He helped train middleweight champ Julian Jackson, former heavyweight champ Michael Dokes, and lightweight prospect Sammy Miller.

But it wasn't the same. He was one of the best cutmen in the business, but not even he could repair his battered spirit.

As he thought about his life, he reminisced about his youth

in St. Louis. He trained fighters, ran a bowling alley, rubbed elbows with everyone from Sugar Ray Robinson and Willie Pep to Johnny Vitale and Blinky Palermo.

There was another girl then, just a kid really. Rosanne Henningsen. A beauty whose relatives were fighters Tocco trained. That was a million years ago.

His life led to Las Vegas; hers remained in St. Louis. He knew she had married, had children. He knew her husband had died many years ago.

Tocco wondered how her life turned out, whether she was still the same gal he once knew.

"I was wondering how long I was going to stay this way. Losing somebody after fifty years, you can't explain it," Tocco said, sipping Italian coffee in his cramped Ringside Gym office. "I took a chance on calling and got a good response."

About 45 years had passed. Almost no time at all, really.

There had been a few changes, of course. Tocco's heart has had more bypasses than the Hollywood Freeway. A pacemaker keeps him ticking.

Rosanne, 65, went him one better. After suffering from cardiomyopathy, four years ago Rosanne received the transplanted heart of a 20-year-old St. Louis woman.

They had just enough heart left for love. After a brief courtship, they were married January 4.

As he sipped his coffee on the eve of Valentine's, photos of Sonny Liston, Mike Tyson, and Evander Holyfield stared down at him from the walls. One photo was entirely incongruous. It was a big color shot of Tocco smiling with his new bride.

Tocco, who has run with the fight racket's toughest customers, still can't believe his luck.

"I think it was the will of God that brought us together," Tocco said. "She's been a big help to me. It's wonderful. She's active, and it's good for me."

Imagine that. An experienced woman with a young heart.

Sounds like every man's dream.

"I guess God didn't want me then," Rosanne said of her past illness. Then she laughed. "There was something I was supposed to do down here, and I hope this is it. It's very comfortable because we've known each other. Things just fell into place."

Time has changed them, but the details don't matter. What they have after nearly half a century is timeless.

"Maybe we were meant for each other," Rosanne said. "We're too old too argue. Everything's great."

To Tocco, Rosanne is still the same vivacious girl he knew so long ago.

"She's always active. She wants to go, go, go," Tocco said, grinning. "I tell her, 'I think it's that twenty-year-old heart you've got.'"

Some will scoff at the very notion of an old man getting married at 81. Others will fret that their hearts are too fragile: that she should have remained in her hometown, that he should have faced the reality of his years.

Lord knows what those people will be doing on Valentine's Day. Sweethearts Johnny and Rosanne have better things to think about.

They have discovered an ageless secret.

In affairs of the heart, time exists only in the present, and love is all that matters.◆

Liston's memory echoes through ancient Las Vegas gym

December 30, 1990

Barely a day goes by that the name doesn't enter conversation down at Johnny Tocco's Ringside Gym.

Today marks the 20th anniversary of the death of Charles "Sonny" Liston, but the mysterious former heavyweight champion remains a constant topic of discussion at Tocco's joint downtown. Liston's memory still echoes through the ancient gym. It is almost as if the big man with the ham-sized hands and the devastating punches will appear in the doorway at any time.

Weathered photos of a grinning Liston hang from walls cov-

ered with posters of champs, contenders, and one-fight wonders. It was at the gym that Liston trained for his final bouts; at
Tocco's Zebra Room Lounge next door he sometimes drank.

Liston was scheduled to make an appearance at the Zebra
Room on New Year's Eve, but he never showed up. Despite
being a loner by nature, Liston's absence caused Tocco concern.
He called Liston's place twice, but received no answer.

A week later, Liston's wife Geraldine discovered the body
of one of the most powerful men ever to lace up gloves lying on
his back with blood covering his face. A small glass of vodka
was on the nightstand with a loaded .38 caliber pistol nearby. A
small amount of marijuana was discovered in Liston's pants
pocket, and one report revealed a minute amount of heroin on
the kitchen counter.

Although Liston's system later revealed traces of heroin, the
amount was nowhere near enough to cause an overdose. There
was a needle mark in his arm, which Tocco insists was caused a
month earlier when Liston was hospitalized after an auto accident, but no needle was found.

Besides, mighty Sonny Liston feared only two things in his
life: airplanes and needles.

Although the Clark County coroner called it a death from
natural causes, a massive seizure perhaps, Liston's demise remains a mystery to boxing fans and Mafia followers.

Liston was the mob's fighter, the 80-year-old Tocco said.
Mobster Johnny Vitale asked Tocco, his acquaintance from the
early days on the streets of the Kerry Patch neighborhood in St.
Louis, to look after the aging but valuable heavyweight.

At 36, Liston was a former heavyweight champion, but also
a fighter haunted by the specter of a taunting Muhammad Ali,
to whom he had twice lost controversial fights. Liston was attempting to make a comeback, and he was looking for a familiar trainer he could trust. He found that person in Tocco.

"I told them, 'Sonny's not going to listen to me,' " he said.
"They said, 'He's asking for you.'"

On June 29, 1970, in Jersey City, New Jersey, Liston battered
white-hope fighter Chuck "The Bayonne Bleeder" Wepner, stop-

ping him in the 10th round and inflicting wounds that would take 54 stitches to close.

When Liston's body was discovered a week into 1971, the speculation started and continues today.

"I get calls from people all the time about Sonny," Tocco said. From *Sports Illustrated* to "Unsolved Mysteries," dozens of publications and programs have interviewed Tocco about his friend.

Tocco has grown tired of the so-called experts who claim to have been good friends with Liston. Two decades after his death, Liston has more friends than he had fights.

Others are sure they know Liston was murdered by the Mafia for not throwing the Wepner fight.

Was Liston killed because he refused to throw the fight?

Was his death linked to the local heroin racket?

Or did he die of natural causes?

"They love to say he died of an overdose or the mob put him away," Tocco said. "The people who say they know he was killed should talk to the police, but they don't. They don't know anything."

But that doesn't keep them from posturing about one of the least understood fighters in the modern era. Sonny Liston, strong-armed ex-con, murderous puncher, brooding loner, was Tocco's good friend. Tocco continues to protect his friend's memory 20 years later.

"Sonny never did call me by my name. He always called me Champ," Tocco said. "Sonny was a person who loved kids. He adopted a white kid and a black kid. He was called the big ugly bear, but that was given to him by Ali, not the press. But it followed him all his days.

"He paid his dues to the public. They should let him rest in peace."

Today, the body of Liston is buried in Row 1 in the Garden of Peace section of the Paradise Gardens Cemetery near McCarran Airport. His marker reads: Charles "Sonny" Liston, "A Man," 1932-1970.

His troubled spirit still resides at Johnny Tocco's Ringside Gym. ◆

Johnny Tocco came out swinging each and every day

August 8, 1997

Johnny Tocco was a good man in a black-hearted blood-soaked racket, an outspoken character in a sport riddled with lackeys.

If boxing had saints, he'd have a halo the size of the St. Louis Arch. He was loyal to a fault and cared so much about the fighters he mentored that he never failed to tell them when to quit.

But there was no quit in Johnny. He was as tough as a heavy bag and ruled his Ringside Gym like a five-star general. Champs or chumps, contenders or pretenders, no man ever forgot who was the boss of the Ringside Gym.

He was a champion at the art of finding out what fighters were made of. He trained them and scolded them, praised them and tested them. And he never forgot that theirs was a deadly serious pursuit.

Although he never boxed professionally, Johnny floored everyone from Tyson and Holmes to no-name undercard pugs with his tenacity and his honesty. Johnny was as honest as Ali's shuffle was quick, as Foreman's right was deadly, as Marciano's record was perfect. He was one for the books, my pal Johnny.

Johnny Tocco fought almost every day of his 87 years. A week ago, he finally got a chance to rest. His funeral is set for 11 a.m. today at Palm Mortuary downtown.

He was my friend.

When I was a sportswriter, Johnny's gym became my second home. It was there, in an office not much larger than a cigar box, that I learned about his life and my own.

I am incapable of recounting all the hours we spent laughing and arguing about the fight game, politics, and personalities. On particularly tough days, I'd run out of work and drop in at his smoggy sanctuary, drink a little cognac, smoke a cigar, and retrieve my sense of humor. In his later years, Johnny smoked more cigars than Castro.

In a world full of phonies and bullies, Johnny was the ultimate B.S. barometer.

For a time I worked out at the gym and sparred, if it can be called that. I worked corners as a spit-bucket second with him and marveled at his ability to stop—in less than a minute—a cut worthy of six stitches. He was one of the greatest cutmen to ever touch a brow.

Johnny was born July 1, 1910, in the Kerry Patch section of St. Louis. As a boy, he sold newspapers on the corner, delivered groceries and bathtub booze, and learned the ways of the street before most kids memorize their multiplication tables.

At eight, he found himself at the gymnasium door watching the pugilists go through their rigorous rituals. And he was hooked.

He hauled water, swept floors, and listened to the voices as they barked out orders. He never lost his love of the gym.

It was in St. Louis that he trained contenders, matched fighters, promoted events. It was there, too, that he befriended the haunted heavyweight Charles "Sonny" Liston.

In 1952, he arrived in Las Vegas for the Nino Valdez-Archie Moore title fight at old Cashman Field and fell in love with the town. He tended bar, ran a keno lounge, bought the Zebra Room, and opened his gym as soon as he scraped together enough greenbacks. It was there he trained Liston for the last time.

Johnny worked closely with champs ranging from Willie Pep to Larry Holmes and played host to countless others. But it's the pugs he let sleep in the back room and the troubled middleweights he got released "on their own reconnaissance" that I'll never forget.

In his life, he argued with everyone: the Nevada Athletic Commission, promoters Don King and Bob Arum. And me.

But we stayed friends. In the last week of his life we spoke on the phone three times. It was small talk mostly. He had a doll for my daughter, a plan to sell his house and move to the hills. He missed his cigars.

And he wanted a new leg.

He lost his left leg to gangrene earlier this year and dispatched me to search for a suitable prosthesis. I started with the

Yellow Pages, determined to find him something that would put him on his feet despite the fact his doctors told him he wasn't strong enough to stand anymore.

By the time I found him a limb, it was too late.

In my life, I have been blessed to know a few wonderful old men who offered genuine friendship for nothing in return. Next to my father, Johnny Tocco was the best of the bunch.

When I close my eyes, I can hear his voice describing the new leg that would get him back in the game he loved so much. Not just boxing, you understand. But life, too.

That's my pal, Johnny.

Fighting to the end. ◆

All the barking about biting rings loud with hypocrisy

July 2 1997

I was going to let it pass, cover my ears, turn the other cheek. But I guess I just snapped.

Like a head butt delivered by a nation of hypocrites, the hand-wringing condemnation of Mike Tyson by the media and public is too much to let slide.

So guard your ears. Here it comes.

Those calling for Tyson's banishment from boxing in the wake of his ear-biting of Evander Holyfield Saturday night at the MGM Grand Garden fail to appreciate a few facts about the sport as it is practiced in Las Vegas.

First, it's not a sport. It's a racket that is heavily influenced by glib gangster Don King. On the way to the top of the heavyweight division, King was a Cleveland street hoodlum who kicked a numbers runner to death, has been accused of extorting millions from legendary heavyweights, and thus far has managed to slip more government investigations than John Gotti.

One other thing. He is a licensed Nevada boxing promoter

with a gargantuan contract with the MGM Grand, a licensed Nevada casino.

And you are fretting over a bite on the ear?

Then there's the devil of the day, Tyson.

His biography reads like a rap sheet. Come to think of it, it is a rap sheet. He was raised by Brownsville wolves. While other kids were learning to ride bicycles without training wheels, he was stealing hubcaps, snatching purses, and pulling armed robberies.

As an adult, he is a convicted rapist who is still on probation in Indiana. Unlike you, at least he's consistent.

And you are fretting over a bite on the ear? Now, to the terrible offense in question.

This just in: One left hook to the temple can cause temporary blindness and permanent brain damage.

Only a rabid animal can kill you with a bite on the ear.

Tyson has had his shots, hasn't he? Boxing is the felonious frolic that refuses to seriously consider the use of any form of headgear to protect participants from possible permanent injury. Although, admittedly, in Tyson's case a muzzle would have been a more appropriate piece of equipment.

Why no headgear?

It's not because they can slip and obscure vision; it's because they would decrease the number of crowd-pleasing knockouts. The fans don't want it.

Then there's the governing body, the Nevada Athletic Commission. The commission is wisely moving swiftly to compel the revocation of Tyson's license and fine him as much as 10 percent of his $29.8 million purse. He is an embarrassment, but he is an earner.

Hate to disappoint the sanctimonious sorority, but Tyson is unlikely to be banished for life. Nor should he be. The commission has repeatedly sanctioned aging George Foreman's fights and has allowed broken-down former champs with ruined retinas to make comebacks in the name of commerce and the peanut-crunching crowd.

If you think Tyson and the heavyweight division somehow

are going to remain persona non grata on the Strip, you need your head examined. With all his baggage and odd dietary practices, Tyson has a history of being good for the casino business. And there's a reason blood and money smell so much alike.

Finally, there are the fans and reporters who have followed Tyson's every move in and out of the ring. Congratulations. You helped make him what he is today. And so did I. We created the animal, then when it bites the hand, or ear, that feeds it we feign outrage. Shame on us.

Now for one last reality check. Boxing exists in all its sleaze and gore because it appeals to our animalistic nature. Mostly, it exists because we like to watch. It is the big-screen bloodbath and Turn 3 at Indy right in your living room. Tyson is a tragically tormented soul who, like his hero Sonny Liston, is well on the way to finding his talent as drained as his fortune. He deserves no sympathy, but neither does he rate a public flogging for playing out his role as the nation's ultimate athletic animal.

So, Mike Tyson bit off a piece of Evander Holyfield's ear.

So what? If you really object to Tyson's behavior, don't buy the next pay-per-view title fight. Pass on purchasing tickets to the next Fight of the Century. Ban the racket entirely, or at least send Don King into retirement. But you won't. After all the whining subsides, the truth is you like to watch. It's in your blood.

So save the outrage for oil spills and crippled kiddies. Besides, the latest juicy rumor has it Tyson-Holyfield III will be a real killer. ◆

A legend of life as well as sports makes a stop in Las Vegas

February 29, 1996

He moved slowly through the buzzing chaos of UNLV's Moyer Student Union like an old man fearful of losing his balance around children.

In the background, a comedian with a routine straight out of the Rush Limbaugh show had a nearby crowd cracking up. He appeared not to notice the crass cackling.

A few people, but not too many, recognized him and smiled. Some sought autographs, one took a photograph.

More than one student mistook a muscular member of his entourage for Mike Tyson. As if Tyson, for all his brawling success and tabloid notoriety, would deserve to be mentioned in the same breath as the old man.

Neatly attired in a black suit, his proud broad shoulders only slightly stooped, Muhammad Ali graced UNLV a week ago as a guest of the Black Student Union Association. His appearance was the highlight of the university's month-long Black History celebration. He was kind enough to make an appearance as a favor to his daughter, Maryum Ali, a UNLV student.

Imagine being able to invite your father to a mature show-and-tell of historical scale. After all, this isn't Sam the Plumber; this is an all-world icon.

As I watched Ali make his way through the student union, with so many people oblivious to his being, I felt like screaming. And crying.

Not just because he has lost the strength that once moved earth and heaven, but because the room did not go silent. Because he was not swarmed by an appreciative throng. Because he was not applauded for taking the time to walk onto the campus and instantly make it a better place.

The world has become an odd neighborhood when people fail to get wide-eyed at the sight of Muhammad Ali.

His presence ought to have been cause for celebration. Not only by black students and boxing fans, but by everyone in the house.

Oh, how I wanted to shout. Put down the Shakespeare and Tennyson—that is, if anyone still reads them—and behold one of America's great poets and political leaders.

Forget that he traveled in disguise as a boxer who won an Olympic gold medal and the world heavyweight title three times. Forget Cassius Clay, the Louisville Lip, the Ali Shuffle, and the rope-a-dope.

In the fight racket, Ali was a prince among pimps. Boxing doesn't deserve him. Never did and never will.

It is only a slight exaggeration to say that Ali was to pugilism what Jesus was to carpenters. Some fellows transcend their trade. Ali did that.

Muhammad Ali was a free black man in a white world, a man capable of outquipping his critics and outboxing his enemies.

He was a giant. He crushed bigots with a grin.

The Reverend Martin Luther King Jr. wrote much of the text for the civil rights movement. Muhammad Ali provided the exclamation points.

While other followers of Islam hurt themselves with hate, Ali never lost sight of the bigger human picture. He loved people and melted hearts even as he infuriated the heartless.

Most champions stay in the game too long, and Ali was no exception. But here's the difference: When Larry Holmes battered an aged Ali in 1980 at Caesars Palace, Holmes pleaded with the referee to stop the fight. Holmes knew his place; he also knew the heavyweight division would have been nothing without the magic of Muhammad Ali.

There was a time not so long ago that Ali's was the most recognized name and face on the planet. More than Elvis. More than Gandhi.

Sports have ambassadors. Nations have ambassadors.

The human race has an ambassador in Muhammad Ali.

He has done more than a dozen telethons to raise awareness of Parkinson's disease simply by contracting it. If he caught the common cold, he might help cure it.

His Parkinson's medication calms his shaking but saps his strength. People mistakenly believe that his mind has gone as soft as his voice. If you listen closely, you will learn from him still.

Even in silence his life story takes on epic proportions.

At 54, he is a giant in mortal trappings. Whether they knew it or not, for a few moments a giant walked among them at UNLV.

If Muhammad Ali is mistaken for an old man in the crowd, then the crowd is infinitely poorer for it. ◆

Little man one of the last big characters from old Las Vegas

May 3, 1998

Bobby Kaye stands in the high-tech horse parlor at Caesars Palace and remembers when he was a big man in Las Vegas.

In Bobby's case, that's saying something. In politically correct parlance, Bobby Kaye is vertically challenged. That is to say, a dwarf. On the street, he is called Bobby the Midget. I call him one of the last great Las Vegas characters.

"I was with Billy Weinberger in this place," he says. "Caesars was the place. I was the best host here, or at least one of the best. I loved to comp players. Billy would say, 'Bobby, Bobby, Bobby, please cut down on the comps, Bobby,' but he let me keep right on signing. Those were good times.

"Today? Today is garbage, you know what I'm saying? It's garbage. The town's too big. Everything's too big. Want to know the two greatest men in this town? The hospice guy, Nate Adelson. And Billy Weinberger. Fine guys, the best."

Bobby was born Robert Krauthamer 70 years ago in Plainfield, New Jersey. He learned about life's long odds at an early age. His father had syphilis of the brain, a condition that led to Bobby's status as a little person. His mother was so impressed with her new son she tried to give him away, but his grandmother intervened.

As a boy, he easily ducked under the turnstile at Yankee Stadium and never missed a ballgame. He can still reel off the lineup of any team in the Joe DiMaggio era as easily as some people recall members of their own family.

At Public School 130 in Flatbush, the teacher marveled at the smallest boy in class, who showed an amazing gift with numbers and troublemaking.

"One teacher said to my mother I'd be a big bookmaker someday," Bobby says. "I was always good with numbers.

"My brothers are six feet tall. I could have been born a dwarf or blind or both. I was only supposed to live until I was thirty-five, but I'm seventy. And handsome, too, don't you think? I'm

Bobby Kaye. Everybody knows me. I'm known from coast to coast like buttered toast."

As a kid on the street in Brooklyn, he worked crap games and booked for the locals, which meant dealing with wild-eyed neighborhood mobsters like Crazy Joe Gallo.

Just when Bobby's front-pocket sports book was thriving, Gallo approached him with an offer: Either they would become partners, or the shorter of the two would get an ice pick in the heart.

"I had eight-hundred in my pocket," Bobby recalls. "Joey said, 'One for you, one for me, one for you, one for me.' Joey says, 'Are we partners?' and I say, 'No, no, no. ' He pulls out that ice pick and says again, 'Are we partners?' and I say, 'Yes, yes, yes.'"

A man must never forget his stature, no matter how great or limited. Bobby Kaye has always known that.

And so he survived his stint at Caesars, which ended about the time mafia bagman Jerry Zarowitz ran afoul of Sheriff Ralph Lamb and the FBI.

He worked for Frank Rosenthal at the Stardust back when the term "The Little Guy" referred to the dangerous Anthony Spilotro and not to Bobby Kaye.

"I like Frank," Bobby says. "He wasn't even in the joint and he hired me."

When called before a grand jury investigating illegal gambling, he was instructed by attorney Oscar Goodman to take the Fifth Amendment. Afterward, he laughed and said, "I took the two-and-a-half."

Bobby the Midget scuffled and hustled and made his way in the world back when Las Vegas was a smaller place, a friendlier place for guys with colorful nicknames and complicated pasts.

At a time when most men his age are retired, he's still hustling the horses, chasing a few bucks, telling stories over coffee. Today, he'll finish up at Caesars and hit two or three other joints. Mostly, he'll remind people of the day the city had time for little men with big hearts.

"Wanna know what one word takes care of everything in life?" he asks. "It's not being a millionaire, either. There are plenty of them who are miserable bastards. But when you got happiness, you got it all. Health goes along with it, but look at me. To be happy, you got to want to be happy.

"You can learn a lot from me, baby. You got to have the right attitude and the whole world will come to you. I'm short, but baby, nobody's got a better personality as a human being."

Personality and attitude know no height requirement, and Bobby Kaye possesses those qualities in Wilt Chamberlain proportions. The town overflows with people these days, but it sure could use more human beings.

In my book, Bobby the Midget will always be a big man in Las Vegas. ◆

Feisty bookmaker talked tough but was no real gangster

February 3, 1994

The word went out from Sunrise Hospital to downtown, up to the Strip, over to Cafe Michelle, and on to Vesuvio.

The Midget knew.

The Lady did, too.

When I heard, I thought about the old Las Vegas and the little dog.

Joey Boston, the feisty Las Vegas nightfly and wise guy, had died of heart troubles and fulfilled Damon Runyon's street-corner philosophy: Life is 6-to-5 against.

Boston, a bettor and bookmaker from the old Las Vegas, knew his numbers well. His number came up Monday. He was 69.

Within minutes, the news circulated through the bars and restaurants Boston patronized to the waitresses and mixologists he sometimes terrorized. His friends knew his heart was weak, but they must have found it hard to imagine anything silencing the cantankerous character with the silver hair and the thick Boston accent.

I think Joey always wanted to be a gangster. Not the genuine article, but the Hollywood kind. As if to celebrate his status, he changed his name to Boston years ago. It had a tougher ring to it than Gurwitz. But he wasn't a tough guy.

He loved the whole idea of being an outlaw. Not for the violence, for he wasn't a violent fellow, but for the romantic image.

And for the chicks.

"You want to meet a gangsta, honey?" I overheard him say one night at Fratelli. "Meet me, my little sweetheart. I'm Joey Boston."

But the joke was on the starry-eyed babe. Although Boston knew plenty of rough customers, and he attracted substantial suspicion from law enforcement, he wasn't a gangster. He was a bookmaker and a player. Over the years, he worked for Frank Rosenthal and a string of major operators from Washington, D.C., to the Strip.

He tipped big and dated women for company and accouterment, but most of his life was spent night by night out with the boys.

When legendary local mob attorney Oscar Goodman produced a gala black-tie affair at the Desert Inn a couple years ago, Boston was proud to be invited. It wasn't often a wise guy made the A list.

For the last few years Joey rarely went anywhere without his bookmaking sidekick, Marty Kane. They were the Heckle and Jeckyll of the Flamingo Road lounge scene.

When Marty died of cancer last year, Joey went pale. They were more than a couple of antique bookmakers. They were pals in a friendless racket. They cackled like hens, reminisced like a couple of old winos. They were family, Marty and Joey.

A few weeks after Kane's funeral, Joey was camped out at Cafe Michelle and had been drinking. He was polite to the reporter; something definitely was bothering him.

"It ain't the same without Marty," he said softly between sips of Johnny Walker Red. "Me, I'm a bad man. But, Marty, he was a nice fella. He was my friend."

Now they are together, wherever sharp guys can eat rich food and drink strong drinks and talk about their wins and losses and stomach upsets without fear of federal intervention.

Boston often bragged about his other best friend, Mr. Bingo, a scruffy terrier.

"Can you believe it? I'm sixty-six and I never had a dog," Joey said one night at Tony L's. He was sipping a whiskey and picking at a video poker machine. "He's a good fella. Half the time I'd like to get rid of the little bastard, but he's so damned cute."

So cute, in fact, that Joey couldn't resist bringing his pooch into the Cattleman's one night to parade him before Curly the bartender and all the barflies. Someone popped off about noticing a family resemblance, and, as proud as a father, Joey just laughed and bought cocktails.

The little dog mimicked his master and barked out a few orders, then wagged his tail. He was no tough guy, either.

Like his pal Joey, Mr. Bingo was just happy in his element. ◆

Honor among thieves brings luck to bookmaker Fat Irish

March 17, 1994

They say everyone is a little bit Irish on St. Patrick's Day.

It is fitting, then, that we take a moment to remember downtown legend Fat Irish Green, who in reality wasn't the least bit Irish but enjoyed an uncommon amount of luck in his lifetime.

It can be argued that no man, Irish or otherwise, ever enjoyed the large fellow's grand good fortune. Although records are not kept on such things, it is believed Green enjoyed the longest free roll in Las Vegas history.

Irish was fat, but he wasn't from the Emerald Isle. As legend has it, he was Jewish. A bookmaker by trade, his name was Greenberg. He was Ben Siegel's trusty assistant in the years before the infamous Bugsy built the fabulous Flamingo.

In the early 1940s, Siegel juggled the mob's race wire interests with his pursuit of points in the legal casinos of Las Vegas. He tried and failed to buy into the El Rancho Vegas on old U.S. Highway 91 (now the Strip). But he was more successful downtown, where he acquired a slice of the El Cortez and moved into the Pioneer and Golden Nugget.

Fat Irish managed Siegel's race book at the Golden Nugget. He also provided services as a bodyguard.

Siegel was successful downtown, but he envisioned a far bigger score in Billy Wilkerson's foundering Flamingo project. As history and Hollywood have recorded, building the Flamingo cost $6 million and Siegel's life.

The messy murder in Beverly Hills in 1947 left Fat Irish holding a rather substantial bag.

Perhaps suspecting trouble, Siegel gave Green a briefcase filled with the mob's money. The figure ranges from $60,000 to $600,000. He held onto the loot until contacted by the appropriate people.

Because Fat Irish acted honorably, he was rewarded. True, the fact that a hit man had just blasted Siegel's brains all over Virginia Hill's living room may have served as motivation. But honor is honor, even among thieves, and Green never worked a day the rest of his life.

Which created an interesting problem for Jackie Gaughan, who purchased the El Cortez in 1963 and discovered an overdue rent payment dating to the early '40s.

"When I bought the El Cortez from Kell Houssels Sr., I went over and said to Irish, 'I want my rent,'" Gaughan recalls. "And he said, 'I never paid any rent, and I don't have to pay any rent.'"

Gaughan regrouped and called Houssels at the Tropicana.

"I said, 'Why don't you take Irish Green to the Tropicana?' And he said, 'Sorry, he went with the deal.'"

Gaughan wrote off the debt, but years later again tried to politely evict Fat Irish. He went to the Horseshoe, where patriarch Benny Binion was well-known as a sucker for sob-stories.

"I said to Benny Binion, 'Why don't you take Irish to the Horseshoe?'" Gaughan says. "He said, 'I feed Irish for nothin'. You got to keep him at the hotel for nothin'.' Benny Binion fed him every day."

When Fat Irish died a few years ago, Gaughan received a letter of thanks from Green's sister. Enclosed was $50. It was more than her lucky brother had given Gaughan in more than two decades.

"Irish lived at the El Cortez from the day it opened until the day he died," Gaughan says. "He never paid a bill."

Green had numerous benefactors. He received a small check each month from the Flamingo and the Sands. He strolled Fremont Street like the mayor, meandering through the clubs and immediately spending whatever good gains came his way in the casinos. He was a fixture, a reminder of a time long gone.

Gaughan likes to laugh at the Siegel story, and he doesn't doubt its veracity.

"He must have gave it back because Irish sure never had any money," he says. "He was a player who played every day."

Which means he never had cash for long. Fortunately for Fat Irish, he had limitless downtown credit.

While on Fremont Street for today's Sons of Erin parade, take a moment to toast the ghost of Fat Irish Green.

In the land of the neon shamrock, no Irishman ever was luckier. ◆

New Las Vegas convinces Big Julie nothing lasts forever

July 24, 1994

So you're Julius Weintraub, the Big Julie of local legend, and your arrival in the new Las Vegas ought to be heralded by an old-timers day parade down the Strip or at least by a lounge band dedicating Sinatra tunes.

Instead you're standing in the Gambler's Book Club pitching a reprint of your biography, *Big Julie of Vegas*, enduring a few questions from gnats with notebooks and reminiscing about a time the corporate casino bosses refuse to discuss without an attorney present.

There was a day you had plenty of money and the key to the city, as it were. After all, you developed the junket business in Las Vegas and spent 20 years flying high rollers and short-pockets gamblers from New York to the Southern Nevada Suckers Convention every other Wednesday. You generated $400 million in casino revenues for your bosses at the Dunes and elsewhere. You logged more frequent-flyer miles than a gaggle of Canada geese, but today you have little more than feathers to show for it. You're almost 75, and there's no place for you in the new Las Vegas.

But you remember the city's real history. You wrote a few chapters of it, in fact.

"I spent as much time in the air as walking," Weintraub says. He's wearing a white golf shirt with a Dunes insignia, almost as if he's still representing a casino that in the end didn't do him any favors. "It was easy for me because I like people. I hated to see guys lose more than they could afford. I loved what I was doing. I loved coming to Vegas every other Wednesday, but I loved going home."

The Dunes' New York-to-Las Vegas run started in 1962, and there weren't many rules to the game. Players who qualified flew into town, gambled, often on credit, and went home with lint in their pockets. Occasionally, a few kids would slip into the crowd and take a free ride. Mountain Spa developer Jack Sommer was one; Vegas king Steve Wynn was another.

Years later in Atlantic City, Big Julie would be deemed unsuitable to work for Wynn's Golden Nugget on the Boardwalk. The casino game Weintraub had shaped had changed before his eyes. He had survived the New York jewelry business and a brutal beating by suspected Colombo crime family hoods. But the new rules overwhelmed him.

You've heard of "Guys and Dolls." Big Julie was one of the guys. In the end, casino regulators in Nevada and New Jersey decided Big Julie wasn't right for the racket he helped build into a multibillion-dollar industry.

It didn't matter that he was a standup guy whose sports-celebrity golf tournaments and various charity arm-twists had raised hundreds of thousands of dollars for cancer research and crippled children. Some time in the late '70s, he became notorious.

"I thought at one time in my life I didn't have an enemy in the world," he says. "I found out that I did."

Once Big Julie's fun book of comps was gone, a strange thing happened. Silence.

"The day you can't do a favor for anybody the phone stops ringing," he says in the quiet bookshop. He laughs, but it looks like the realization hurt him at one time.

It's just like the new Las Vegas to greet Big Julie's home-away-from-homecoming with the death of his old friend, Irving "Niggy" Devine. In the other Las Vegas, Devine was a casino operator, a meat distributor who could have spotted Meyer Lansky in a crowd. It was like old home week at the funeral service, except there weren't too many fellows left at home.

"I saw guys I haven't seen in years," Big Julie says. "I thought, 'Where have I been?' For friends and people you enjoyed being with, it was better in the old days."

Big Julie, you still carry around your 1962 sheriff's work card, just in case any law-enforcement types try to put the pinch on you and perhaps to remind you of the other Las Vegas. It's a genuine conversation piece. And maybe in your heart you hope some kid with a badge will ask you for it. It would be good for a laugh.

With kids in the casino and corporations in the front office, the city isn't the same. Why, even the Dunes disappeared while you were away.

You guys deserve something more than a kick in the pants for your time. A parade would be nice, or a plaque at least. But you know that's not going to happen. Las Vegas has changed.

You can laugh at all the money other guys made, and you remember the town that was, and that will have to suffice.

"I thought it would last forever," Big Julie says, staring into the neon memory. "I made a terrible mistake.

"Nothing lasts forever." ◆

Moneylender Jasper Speciale last of a different breed

January 2, 1992

The diner was nearly empty when the imperially slim fellow pushed open the door.

Jasper Speciale looked tired and gaunt, but he managed a smile, handshake, and few terse words. His sports shirt buttoned up tight, his mind on a steak sandwich and the business of the day, he was as always a gentleman.

Despite chronic lung problems, he managed to make the rounds and often turned up at the city's best delis and restaurants. Despite the word he had retired from the illegal bookmaking and street-corner moneylending trades, it was obvious he had no intention of spending his remaining years at a Palm Springs spa or a Florida beach. Perhaps that sporting zeal is what kept the twinkle in his brown eyes long after his lungs had soured.

Speciale's tired lungs finally gave out Saturday. The convicted loan shark, illegal bookmaker, and unique Las Vegas character died in a local hospital. He was 68 and left a fascinating street legend.

You have heard of Valley Bank. Speciale was the president of Sidewalk Savings & Loan.

Although loan sharks with hearts of gold do not exist, Speciale was a gentleman in a violent racket filled with predators. He loaned $500 to countless cabbies and poker players. At high interest, of course; that's the shylock's rub.

It didn't make him the worst guy in Las Vegas, and his personality assured his place in the annals of local lore.

Fellows possessing Speciale's old-school panache were plentiful a generation ago. Unfortunately, they have been largely replaced by glorified dope dealers and punks with pistols.

Born Gaspare Anedetto Speciale on July 13, 1923, in New York City, he was not a saint and made no such pretenses. Many of the occupations in the world of his youth were by their nature illegitimate. His pursuit of sports betting was a natural. The fact it was illegal and influenced by New York's La Cosa Nostra families constituted the cost of doing business.

At a time other kids were memorizing their multiplication tables, young Jasper was booking football games in New York schoolyards. He was eight.

By the time Speciale was a teen-ager, his bookmaking expertise was attracting attention from the cops and the wise guys.

He was arrested 19 times in New York. Bookmaking is not the street's most egregious sin. But in mob-muscled New York, those who play in the street pay the boys to prevent being hit by a bus.

Tuberculosis slowed him in youth, and chronic lung ailments shadowed him throughout his life.

So did the law.

From 1944-59, he was nicked eight times for illegal bookmaking. His candy store was known for its tasty treats and sweet odds.

After migrating to Las Vegas in the early 1960s, he operated the Tower of Pizza and later Jasper's Manhattan Florist. The food was good and the posies smelled nice, but mostly Speciale was booking bets and lending C-notes.

He eventually was charged with felonies and in 1976 was sentenced to four years for loansharking and obstructing justice.

His health steadily diminished in recent months, but you can bet your mortgage he was still working. It was in his blood.

"He only booked sports, that's all he done," a friend from Speciale's New York days said with respect. "He was honorable. He never had nothing to do with them guys."

"Them" being people connected to New York's mob families. Authorities vehemently disagree, and say Speciale had long business relationships with the Genovese and Gambino families.

None of that matters now.

Presuming he was still taking bets, someone will acquire his customers. Assuming he was still a one-man automatic teller machine, someone will collect the debts.

The beat will go on, but the street won't be the same.

His critics won't remember the Speciale whose golf tournament raised thousands for charity. They don't know about the dozen poor children he sponsored in the Dominican Republic. They won't believe his biggest collections in recent years came on Sunday morning as he escorted the baskets through the congregation at Our Lady of Las Vegas.

It didn't make Speciale's work legal, but it made him a human being with good qualities to place in the left-hand column next to his faults.

I'll let others tally the old-school sportsman's final record. ◆

UPDATE: This column was reprinted in *The Best of the Rest*, an anthology of local columnists published in 1993.

Crime and Punishment

Knead dough? Bakery boss of bosses could help raise it

October 19, 1991

In a never-ending search for fresh bagels, I stepped into the Supreme Bakery and reeled at the sight.

It wasn't cakes, cookies, or croissants. It wasn't bread, biscuits, or brioche.

It was Lucchese crime-family member John Conti.

Well, toast my Pop Tarts.

In a moment my view of the world crumbled. My mediocre career flashed before me. I decided I never would make it in the journalism racket.

How could I expect to earn a living as an occasional chronicler of organized crime when an infamous local man of honor had stopped making book and started making birthday cakes?

Who's the guy's godfather, Betty Crocker?

The news is enough to make me quit messing around with columns and join the Food section. Forget this La Cosa Nostra business; let me uncover the secrets to keeping a soufflé from sagging.

After all, if Conti was cooking bagels, and tasty ones at that, then I needed to enter another field. And I'm not the only one.

Law enforcement, which has a history of turning a relative nobody into a genuine somebody when it comes to the mob, long ago labeled Conti a man of substance on the streets of Las Vegas.

How was I to know the substance was flour?

When the authorities said Conti made a lot of bread for his family, I didn't think they meant loaves of sourdough and rye.

As usual, I misread the signs. Either that, or Conti is using the bakery for something other than pop-and-fresh purposes.

One of the busy bakers at Supreme said unequivocally Conti doesn't work there. He hangs around, perhaps he has a penchant for pastry, but he does not toil at the struggling bakery.

Would a guy who makes pie lie?

Of course not.

On a recent trek to the bakery, I encountered friendly assistants, a dozen bagels, and Conti. Although I am no expert at bakeshop organization, he sure seemed like the manager.

He didn't punch holes in doughnuts or whack stubborn bread sticks into shape, but he did have cash register privileges, surely a superior occupation to watching muffins rise. He had access to the kitchen and spoke with the hired help, but that isn't a guarantee of employment. It only made him look like the bakery's boss of all bosses.

According to the Senate's Permanent Subcommittee on Organized Crime, the 56-year-old Conti is a soldier in the Lucchese family. Not that anyone believes a word a Senate subcommittee has to say these days, but there it is.

Like other traditional organized crime groups, the Luccheses are notorious for illegal bookmaking, loan sharking, drug trafficking, prostitution, and shooting disgruntled family members in the head. Kneading pie dough is not on the list.

In an April 21, 1989, Miami newspaper article, a federal prosecutor described Conti as a loan shark, bookmaker, and drug dealer. But you know how prosecutors sometimes exaggerate. Conti hasn't been convicted of those crimes.

Conti's name entered the federal arena after he played host to fellow Lucchese family member Angelo Urgitano before the 1989 Mike Tyson-Frank Bruno fight in Las Vegas. The meeting violated a condition of Urgitano's parole, and he was forced to return to prison. Urgitano was allowed to meet with members of his personal family; his extended family was considered off-limits.

Had the judge known the so-called bad guy was an apprentice baker at heart, surely he would have relented.

Conti has several arrests in New York on gambling-related charges, but that is not a serious offense in Brooklyn. It's a condition of residency.

With all due respect to the bakery's management, it sure looks like Conti has found a new career in the pastry business.

Meanwhile, someone should inform the authorities they have been wrong about this guy.

Contrary to their faulty intelligence, all this time John Conti has been a member of La Croissant Nostra. ◆

UPDATE: Conti, now a member of the state's Black Book of persons banned from entering casinos, continues to be the subject of law enforcement scrutiny. The bakery went out of business.

Reformed thief goes straight, to the MGM security force

January 2, 1994

This weekend at the enormous MGM Grand Hotel & Theme Park, security was bolstered for Barbra Streisand's concerts.

Outside experts, antiterrorist specialists, and professional bodyguards joined the MGM's sizable staff of retired Metro intelligence unit detectives for what may have been the largest private police force in the city.

Those who attended the concerts were made to pass through airport-style metal detectors. Two former members of Israel's Mossad reportedly were hired to protect Streisand and surveil the scene.

Which is why I had to laugh when I heard the name of one of the security specialists working for the lion.

Meet Richard Stein, house dick and veteran wise guy.

At the MGM, Stein is a reformed thief who watches the thieves. He works casino security and eye-in-the-sky surveillance. It's nice work if you can get it.

But it's not easy to obtain. In the corporate gambling era, a mug with a criminal history stretching two decades often finds himself unwelcome in the casino. Instead, Stein draws a check as a member of the MGM's crack surveillance team. He watches the bad guys for money.

He ought to know what they look like.

His police record dates to 1965 in Los Angeles and includes arrests for bookmaking, forcible rape, robbery, receiving stolen property, possession of stolen bank bonds, battery on a spouse, burglary, possession of marijuana for sale, mail fraud, and obtaining money under false pretenses.

He was arrested in 1971 for burglary at the International Hotel (now the Las Vegas Hilton), which was financed by MGM billionaire Kirk Kerkorian. That's back when Stein was known as a room burglar and jewelry fence.

From hotel thief to hotel security: Who says rehabilitation is a myth?

I could further detail his exploits, but newsprint is expensive.

Talk about a one-man crime wave. His rap sheet reads like a Jim Thompson novel. Guys have been put in the state's casino Black Book for less.

But there's something else. Although Stein's last arrest came in 1985 and he has several felony convictions, his criminal life has been marked by an uncanny propensity for getting the charges against him dropped.

Stein isn't just a career street criminal.

He's also the king of the city's confidential informants. He is the sultan of snitches. His information has been effective in busting up stolen-property and credit-card rings. He also has been useful to Metro in some of its more controversial drug-trafficking and money-laundering investigations.

Not that he's played tattletale out of the goodness of his heart. He's made a small fortune turning in people who not so long ago would have qualified as his running mates.

Although his history as an informant goes back to 1969, he has made more than $121,000 just since 1988. He has drawn checks from five federal agencies: the FBI; Bureau of Alcohol, Tobacco and Firearms; U.S. Customs Service; the Secret Service; and even the office of postal inspection. But most of Stein's snitch revenue, $114,885, has come from Metro through payments and forfeitures. His biggest year was 1990, when Metro paid him $47,300.

That's almost as much as sergeants make. Come to think of it, Sergeant Stein has a certain ring to it.

In Las Vegas, playing both ends against the middle used to be a good way for a hood to lose his head. But no more. Stein is living proof it pays handsomely to work a two-way street.

An MGM security official emphatically stated that Stein is a reformed man whose experience is valuable to the resort's staff. As the Las Vegas gambling adage goes, "It takes a thief to catch a thief." Casinos have a long tradition of employing convicted card and slot cheaters to catch those still practicing the racket.

So, he's gone straight. He's highly supervised. He's good at what he does.

Funny how that is. If Stein didn't work for the MGM, its security officers would remove him from the premises. They wouldn't let him sit in the sports book, and they wouldn't let him work in room service.

As it is, the bearded 55-year-old is one of the good guys.

If this fellow is watching the bad guys, a question remains: Who is watching Richard Stein? ◆

UPDATE: Richard Stein died in 1997. Those who hated him suspected he had faked his death.

Police record adds new twist to Fabulous Vegas story

December 19, 1990

Monday morning, I read with fascination the latest install-ment of the *Review-Journal's* series neatly titled Fabulous Vegas stories.

The story detailed the activities of 31-year-old entrepreneur Eddie Munoz and his *Adult Informer*. The *Informer* is one of those free-circulation newspapers that pollute the Strip in the name of the First Amendment and a close encounter with a woman of easy inclination. Munoz called the *Informer* a referral service for outcall dance and escort services.

The Eddie Munoz I read about was a distant cousin of pub-lishers everywhere. A bit slimy, maybe, but a relative just the same. Munoz was painted in such entertaining terms that initially I was confused.

Could this fellow be the same Eddie Munoz known on the street as a bimbo-running wise guy?

With my interest piqued, I endeavored to discover whether Eddie-the-entrepreneur was Eddie-the-outcall-dance-service operator.

Wonder of wonders, the Eddies were the same person. And we printed a color photo and a story about him without mentioning his many arrests, convictions, and sordid little businesses.

Well, consider this the rest of the fabulous Eddie Munoz story.

First, Munoz's business interests are not limited to newspaper publishing. He keeps busy operating outcall entertainment services called Starlets International and Bad Girls. He also runs an answering service, vending company, and tour business.

In addition, Munoz has a history of arrests that would almost fill one of his *Informers*. His alleged transgressions range from pandering and sales of a controlled substance to battery and assault with a deadly weapon.

Although he has been convicted on gross misdemeanor drug charges, Metro detectives have been unable to nail him for pandering and living off the earnings of a prostitute.

It is a common scenario: While the working dancers often are arrested for soliciting prostitution, their criminal link to the service owner ends at the hotel room. They are sent to dance; what they do on the side is not known to the upstanding entertainment-service owner.

"I think the charges kind of speak for themselves how we feel about him," Lieutenant Bill Young of Metro vice said. "I could show you case after case where we have arrested his employees, supposedly sent out there strictly for dancing purposes, for soliciting acts of prostitution."

Of course, an article in the *Adult Informer* might lead one to think prostitution is a victimless crime between two consenting adults. In theory, it makes sense, especially in fabulous Vegas, where tradition dictates consenting adults can do almost anything. It is unlikely people who make such arguments ever have had teen-age family members fall into the business.

Most prostitutes are not women who suddenly, at age 21, decide to quit college and become working girls. Many are lured into the trade as teen-agers. By the time they're old enough to make mature decisions, they are years into the business.

But don't take my word for it.

If you can find her, ask the 13-year-old Southern California girl who recently was transported to Las Vegas allegedly to work for an outcall dance service, although not at Munoz's place. She was set up in an apartment, given a wardrobe, and supplied with false identification by one humanitarian in exchange for her devotion to the spirit of dancing.

If she is unavailable, ask the 15-year-old she was hanging around. Ask any of dozens of other teen-agers who are yanked out of the business every year by local vice cops. Many of the girls start out dancing and end up hooking.

Surely such incidents are unrelated to local entrepreneur Eddie Munoz. Although he bears no resemblance to Bob Fosse, maybe Eddie dreams of being a choreographer instead of a suspected pimp.

But, I wonder, if he is such a legitimate guy, then why do his dancers keep getting busted for soliciting prostitution?

I guess that's just another fascinating part of this Fabulous Vegas story. ◆

13-year-old runaway illustrates problem of illegal prostitution

December 20, 1990

She was a 13-year-old kid.

A runaway from Bakersfield, as immature and rebellious as most other children growing through puberty, she wound up in Las Vegas recently and was set up in an apartment with the help of a 15-year-old girlfriend and two new acquaintances, authorities allege.

She said she also received a wardrobe, false identification, a beeper, and a job as a topless dancer at a local outcall entertainment service. Her new friends helped to relocate her to Las Vegas, she said.

Who were these generous people?

Paul and Kathy Chambers, she said. Paul's personal highlights include convictions on accessory to murder, robbery, and second-degree burglary charges. Kathy is a convicted prostitute. Both have been charged with felony crimes ranging from pandering to attempting to live off the earnings of a prostitute in the wake of the recent incident. The FBI also is investigating.

When questioned by police, the 15-year-old said she worked for the Playmate Entertainment outcall dance service. The 13-year-old said she did not get the chance to go to work. Metro vice detectives found her first.

While the 13-year-old is not the youngest girl Metro's vice unit has discovered around a business notorious for its link to prostitution, such finds make even the most cynical detectives cringe with disgust.

Picking up young streetwalkers, some in their early teens, is relatively common. When kids run away from home, they get hungry. When they get hungry, they find a way to eat. Selling themselves is one of the ways. It is an old story.

Far more rare is finding one the police believe is associated with an entertainment service. Because they risk losing their county licenses and their lucrative businesses, the outcall services usually are careful to hire girls of legal age.

The 13-year-old kid was not even close, one vice detective said. Her obviously immature body and manner startled vice detectives, who are accustomed to hard stares and tough talk. She was a girl, and no amount of makeup or wardrobe could disguise it.

The scenario is not unique. She decided to run away from

home. Her slightly older friend, another runaway, told her all about her job in Las Vegas, police allege. When the 15-year-old arrived in Bakersfield accompanied by the Chambers couple, the 13-year-old suddenly had a ride out of town and into the glamorous life, authorities believe.

In time, the kid called home from Las Vegas, and the mother, using a caller identification feature on her phone, took down the number and reported it to Bakersfield authorities. Bakersfield police contacted Metro, and the vice detectives moved in and found what must have resembled a kid playing house.

"This is nothing new," Lieutenant Bill Young said. "The ages are a little unusually young, but we've arrested them in the eleven- and twelve-year-old range."

Most of the time, the girls are old enough to vote, or at least old enough to drive.

Prostitution is a Las Vegas fact. Perhaps if Southern Nevada's political leaders and upstanding residents were more realistic, then the business in Clark County would be regulated and run legally and cleanly in state-certified brothels. But that would run contrary to our clean family-oriented image, and that makes a mature treatment of the trade an unlikely occurrence.

Short of that, and despite increased pressure from police, prostitutes will continue to dot the dark streets and populate the weakly regulated entertainment services.

It is not a news story, just a fact of life. Once in a while, a child emerges from the crowd and shocks and angers even the toughest vice detectives.

She was a 13-year-old kid.

If you think local authorities plan to let this small case rest, think again ◆

Young man's hopes, dreams snuffed out in drive-by shooting

January 1, 1997

A few blocks from the heart of the Strip, Ramon Mendoza stood on the sidewalk near his son's bloodstains.

Not far from the city's dream machine, the spots on the ground and the bullet holes in the shabby apartment walls were reminders that a killing had taken place. Religious candles burned and a cross marked the spot.

The father's eyes were wet. He sipped a cup of beer poured from a quart bottle and spoke mostly in Spanish to the friends of his son, Daniel Mendoza. The 21-year-old fast-food cashier was shot to death early Saturday morning outside a McKellar Circle apartment in the heart of gang turf.

But not by a rival gang. At least, not an official one. Metropolitan Police Officer Ron Mortensen has been arrested in connection with the shooting and is being held without bail.

As I watched the father speak to his son's friends, none of whom denied their affiliation with the 18th Street gang, I wanted to freeze the moment. If only for a few minutes, I wanted the image of the grieving father to remind others that what took place Saturday in the middle of a barrio was not merely another gang-related shooting or another of a growing number of cases of local police misconduct.

It was the death of a young man who had a father, who had brothers, who had a girlfriend he planned to marry, who had friends. He associated with a gang, but living in this rough neighborhood all but makes you a gang associate. Daniel Mendoza was a young Hispanic man with a petty criminal record, a job at a Carl's Jr., and a life most people would only accept at gunpoint.

He might not have lived like you and me, but he deserved to live.

McKellar Circle feeds into Palo Verde Street, which stretches through Twain to the north and Flamingo to the south. In this neighborhood, children play in the streets and alleys. They kick soccer balls and ride bicycles like kids in better parts of town. Teen-age boys hang out around a parked car and listen to the bass-heavy music on the stereo much like teen-agers in cleaner safer places.

But this place is neither clean nor safe. It is, in fact, one of the toughest neighborhoods in the city. English is a second language for many, and the presence of police is greeted with skepticism. No one attempting to piece together the facts of the shooting expects that to change soon.

"He have his problems, but he was working," Ramon Mendoza said of his son. "He was a working guy. If you tell me it was someone else, I believe it. But not him. He give respect to everybody. He got no problems with nobody."

All that changed early Saturday morning after a blue pickup pulled up outside the McKellar Circle apartment. Six shots were fired. One struck Daniel Mendoza in the heart.

You are bound to hear differing versions of the events that led up to the shooting. Here are the words of Mendoza's friend, who said he was at the scene.

"The white boy say, 'Come here.'

"'What?'

"'Come here.'

"'What?'

"'Come here.'

"Then, boom, boom, boom, boom, boom."

Another of Daniel Mendoza's friends denied there was any kind of altercation worthy of gunfire.

"We were all cool," he said, coolly standing and smoking next to Ramon Mendoza. "The words that were exchanged were the gun going off, bro."

Ramon Mendoza added, "He shoot my son through the heart."

Another friend of the dead man made it clear that Daniel Mendoza was trying to outgrow the barrio. "He was a gang member, but lately he was trying to straighten his life. Lately, he wasn't related to no gangs. But he had friends. Everyone who knew him liked him. He had a job, man. He was working."

After speaking Spanish, Mendoza's father talked in English about what happened a day after the shooting. The cops entered the neighborhood and took pictures of all the friends, neighbors, and gang members who came by to pay tribute to Daniel Mendoza.

"I say, 'Why you don't do nothing when my son is shot?'" the father said.

By then, it was far too late.

Ramon Mendoza's son was shot through the heart. As the focus shifts to the officer accused in the killing, the son's blood is sure to be forgotten by all but those who knew and loved him.

Daniel Mendoza died where he lived, in a barrio of this dream machine with only a little hope and fewer prospects. ◆

UPDATE: Mortensen was convicted of Mendoza's murder. His partner that night, Chris Brady, was not charged.

Youth violence slithers into working-class neighborhood

February 11, 1996

Jerry Kambouris flinched and ushered his Cub Scout son into the family's home on Arlington Street.

Crime scenes are no place for children.

In the afternoon, the streets lined with aging duplexes and tract homes near Charleston and Nellis boulevards usually were dotted with kids on bicycles. It's not the worst neighborhood in the city, just another working-class outpost in an increasingly violent valley.

The yellow police line two doors away meant trouble, and Kambouris' neighbors gathered across the street to watch the cops and reporters perform the odd bolero that follows a homicide: The police roll in, the suspect is hauled off, the tape goes up, the trauma counselor stands guard, the homicide detectives take the floor, the reporters converge with dull eyes and notebooks poised. When the coroner pulls up, the bolero is near its end.

At least for the moment.

The dance is routine in Southern Nevada.

The tears flowed on Arlington Street Monday when people learned of a double homicide, but no one appeared shocked.

Kambouris paused long enough to recall his neighbors, Aida and Oswaldo Lopez Sr., who lay dead in their home. They seemed like nice working people, he said.

He also remembered their 23-year-old son, Oswaldo Jr., who is accused of knifing his parents to death and who, it turns out, has displayed his share of personal problems.

The time the young man's sidewinder got out of the house and slithered into his yard convinced Kambouris to steer clear of Ozzie Jr.

You will find no answers in this story, but consider that snake a symbol.

Other neighbors told of listening to little Ozzie threaten the kids who passed the house. They spoke softly about seeing him and his friends drinking, doing drugs, and acting tough in a drainage alley that cuts through the neighborhood.

They were appalled and saddened at the deaths. Don't think them callous, but they were not surprised.

The police couldn't do anything with the delinquents, and obviously the parents' best efforts failed as well. Ozzie Jr. phoned police and invited them over to the house, which was downright considerate of him under the circumstances.

The double homicide is bound to be lost in the crush of killings to come in Southern Nevada. It easily was eclipsed by last week's quintuple homicide in which a Las Vegas teen-ager stands accused.

And there's the 14-year-old Las Vegas girl who was killed during a shootout between rival street gangs at Pittman Elementary School. In a bit of heavy-handed irony, the gun thought to be the murder weapon was found buried in a sandbox.

Before the lives of Aida and Ozzie Sr. are relegated to small type and sketchy recollection, you should know they were from Peru but had made their home in Las Vegas for many years. She worked as a housekeeper and he waited on and bused tables.

They didn't make big money, but they were prudent. They bought a duplex, lived in one half and rented out the other. Ozzie Sr. bought a bicycle for Christmas and was riding it to stay in shape. Theresa Richardson, who lives around the corner from Arlington Street, knew them for 13 years.

"They were super-nice people. They were hard-working," Richardson said. "They gave that kid everything. There was nothing that kid wanted. I know drugs has a lot to do with it. Those kids don't value life. They don't care."

A decade ago, Richardson watched after little Ozzie when his parents were at work.

"I said, 'Please listen to your parents. Please do what they ask you to do.' But he wouldn't listen," she said. "He wouldn't go to school. He quit school. I know he was heavy on drugs."

She appeared to realize what was wrong with the young man, but she wouldn't pretend to know how to fix him.

Youth violence is nothing new to America. It's been around since the time of Billy the Kid and before. During Prohibition, some of the nation's most notorious gangsters were little more than teen-agers.

In a society that celebrates violence in its pop culture and gorges on it in the media, the dance of death at the hands of young people shows no signs of ending.

Blame it on a breakdown in the family. Blame TV violence, Hollywood immorality, the death of God, or even lead-based paint. Blame too much parenting, or not enough. Blame it on too many hugs, or too few.

Then take your children inside and hope that the sidewinder poisoning society slithers by your door. ◆

Ghosts of Runyan past mix with Goodman present at roast

February 20, 1991

Amid the hundreds of guys and dolls, mouthpieces and news hounds, good fellas and square apples who crowded into the shadows of the Desert Inn Terrace Room, one imperially slim apparition seemed familiar.

It was Damon Runyon.

The writer's dark eyes darted around the room. His ears, more keen than any FBI wiretap, picked up bits of dialogue. Runyon sat with Benjamin Siegel, Gus Greenbaum, John Rosselli, and Moe Dalitz. He nodded to others floating in the crowd: Anthony Spilotro, Nick Civella, and Morris Shenker among them.

As surely as any of the hundreds of living beings attending attorney Oscar Goodman's roast Sunday night, the ghosts of Las Vegas past were present in all their sartorial splendor. The celebration of Goodman's 25th year in defense, specializing in organized crime, was a throwback to what often is called the golden age of Las Vegas. In other words, as the old-timers like to say, back when the mob ran the town.

A generation ago, a tuxedo and an invitation made a guy legitimate at a party. Doing something as politically incorrect as trading one-liners with a mob associate was not cause for a federal investigation. Those days have gone the way of spats and top hats in clean, cold, and corporate Las Vegas. In case you haven't heard, we have outgrown our Runyonesque deeze-and-doze roots.

We are legitimate.

We are legitimate.

We are legitimate.

That is what was most intriguing about Sunday night's congregation. Hosted by Salvador Dali, the party was thoroughly legitimate. Upstanding judges mixed with high-powered attorneys, resort executives, lowly reporters, and a few brave politicians.

And there were the wise guys. Plenty of partners and associates of organized crime were present. Most were gentlemen. A few obviously flunked out of charm school.

Runyon laughed and took copious notes.

Where else but at such a party in Las Vegas, USA, could a videotape of Goodman's associates range from judges Bill Jansen and John McGroarty to television's Mike Wallace and Dick Cavett to drug trafficker Jimmy Chagra and Patriarca family member Vincent "The Animal" Ferrara?

If Fellini directed a '90s version of "Guys and Dolls," it would look like the Goodman party.

The Spilotro and Civella families, thinned by murder and incarceration, were represented. Jimmy Chagra's brother and daughters were present; Chagra is serving life in prison.

Contrast that with the appearance of Golden Nugget Inc. Chairman Steve Wynn, the epitome of the new and professional Las Vegas.

But it was a night best suited for Runyon's romantic street characters and ironic plot twists.

After all, people can joke about mob assassinations, drug trafficking, and casino skimming, but the reality is something less than humorous.

As you will recall, most of Runyon's Las Vegas pals died violently. A bullet through the eye, a slashed throat, a one-way submarine excursion in a 55-gallon oil drum, the demise of some of the city's forefathers is nothing if not sensational. While their grisly murders preclude our ceaseless call for respect from having anything but a tinny sound, they conjure a dark magic that visitors find immensely seductive.

As mob lawyers, politicians, and entertainers skewered the man of the hour with sarcasm and embraced him with praise, I thought how much Goodman is like Las Vegas. He may be the quintessential Las Vegan.

With a giant illustration of Mount Rushmore-plus-Goodman hanging in the background, the mob mouthpiece cried out for justice for all people and for fairness from a media he plays like a ragtime piano. He lashed out at wicked gaming authorities and excoriated gutless politicians who were afraid to honor him in person on his special night.

It all made soul-stirring sense.

It was vintage Oscar.

His legal mind should have earned him wide respect years ago, but his decision to represent society's notorious citizens has scented him like the zookeeper charged with care of the skunks. No matter how hard he works or how well he scrubs, the pungence of his associations will remain. Someone always will smell something funny.

Most of the time, Goodman keeps his sense of humor. That is one of his most endearing qualities.

"If I'm a mouthpiece, that's what I'm supposed to be," Goodman said once in a "60 Minutes" interview with Mike Wallace.

Later, he zealously insisted the Mafia does not exist.

Runyon laughed at that one, too. ◆

Update: Oscar Goodman continues to practice law in Las Vegas and was the subject of a 1998 documentary, *Mob Law*.

The mob, the law, and Oscar Goodman's Rolls-Royce

February 25, 1993

The party's over for Philadelphia mob boss Nicodemo Scarfo, but attorney Oscar Goodman is stuck with the hangover.

Goodman's headache comes in the form of a 1973 Rolls-Royce Silver Shadow, a motorcar he asserts he received as partial payment for picking up the tab for a short-lived mob victory party in 1988.

When Scarfo and his organization were acquitted of the murder of Sal Testa in Philadelphia, a champagne celebration broke out at the Four Seasons Hotel. Goodman won acquittal for Scarfo's nephew, Philip Leonetti, and promised reporters a party that would not soon be forgotten.

He was right. Boy, was he right.

The bubbly cost $100 a bottle, the Louis XIII cognac went for $50 a sip, and the Cosa Nostra cheapskates stuck Goodman with a $16,000 tab. He charged it, then received an offer he couldn't refuse:

Scarfo's Rolls-Royce in trade for the party bill. Spruced up, it would be worth as much as $19,000.

With Scarfo destined to die either in or out of prison, perhaps Goodman sensed it would be best to settle up as soon as possible.

The Silver Shadow's bullet holes were almost quaint. The FBI bugs were real conversation pieces. Goodman doled out another $4,000 to restore the car to top condition and imagined himself riding in style through the streets of Las Vegas.

But the auto fantasy, like Goodman's victory and the Scarfo mob's freedom, was fleeting. The mouthpiece never got behind the wheel.

The FBI, not known as party animals since the gay days of J. Edgar Hoover, unceremoniously seized the car. Today, the vehicle is as out of action as Scarfo after being forfeited as the alleged proceeds of the drug trade.

Goodman is back in court, this time as a friend of the defendant in a federal forfeiture case known as the United States of America v. One 1973 Rolls-Royce.

To prosecutors, the case is a simple forfeiture matter. Scarfo bought the Rolls with drug profits and used it to transport drug money.

To Goodman, it's the principle that counts.

(Easy for him to say. Win or lose, he still has his Mercedes.)

"I think it's a very important issue here, and I'm going to the mat on it," Goodman said. "They should not be able to take something you're rightfully entitled to."

Although he doesn't expect many people to sympathize with a millionaire mob lawyer's struggle for a Rolls-Royce, Goodman said the same principle applies to middle-class people who, for example, come into ownership of homes previously used as drug houses. The forfeiture law must be corralled.

Although at the time the framers of the Constitution frowned on buying products made in England, Goodman is sure they would identify with his plight.

"That's the reason we left England—to escape tyranny. The founders decided there could not be seizures of property without due process of law," he said. "That's what has happened here. The government can seize property, bankrupt people, put them out of business, cause them domestic strife, cause them worry to the point of ulcers, and the person is completely innocent."

On Wednesday, the U.S. Supreme Court ruled 6-3 that the government may not seize property purchased with drug proceeds if a third party receiving the largess was ignorant of its source.

The government, no doubt, believes the longtime mob attorney is well aware Scarfo didn't buy the Silver Shadow with S&H Green Stamps.

Goodman remains adamant: He suspected members of the Scarfo mob were killers, arsonists, and unrepentant whist and rummy cheaters.

Who would dream they would do something as deceitful as drug trafficking?

"In every Mafia induction ceremony I have ever heard of, the one thing that is always prohibited—the one thing they're told they can never do—is drugs," Goodman said. "The credo supposedly is no drugs."

He's right.

The fact that credo went out with spats is another matter.

Including airfare and court costs, Goodman-the-party-caterer is now out about $28,000. The incarcerated Rolls-Royce can be viewed through the fence at the Vilsmeier Auction Company in Montgomeryville.

Its unofficial owner can be seen researching cures for hangovers and plotting one luxury car's liberation. ◆

Old-world wife paying the full fare for serious mistakes

August 9, 1995

The gray-haired defendant clad in jailhouse blues didn't look like much of a gangster.

Height: 5-foot-5. Weight: 115 pounds. Physical infirmities: glaucoma in the right eye, 75 percent hearing loss. Prior arrests: 45-year-old misdemeanor charges, no convictions.

Still, Jeanne Manarite wore shackles into her resentencing hearing Monday afternoon in U.S. District Judge Lloyd George's court. Rules are rules, and Manarite was convicted in 1993 of violating five of them in connection with a federal sting operation aimed at Las Vegas-based organized mob figures. She originally was sentenced to 46 months for her role in a chip-cashing scam at the Maxim Hotel and a boat burglary in Marina Del Rey, California. Her convictions range from money laundering to transporting stolen property.

The case was remanded by the 9th U.S. Circuit Court of Appeals for resentencing on a technicality, and on Monday Jeanne Manarite hoped to hear that, after more than 30 months in prison, she was being released.

Presuming her hearing aid was working, all she learned was bad news. Her original sentence was reinstated. A new set of sentencing guidelines become effective November 1, with a possibility of a reduction in her sentence, and that now becomes the target date for her next appeal.

In the interim, she will return to the Federal Correctional Center at Phoenix, where she works in the kitchen.

The life of a big-time gangster isn't all it's cracked up to be, but then not even the most cynical federal investigator believes Jeanne Manarite is the second coming of Scarface. She is the wife of a member of La Cosa Nostra. It's not as glamorous as Hollywood would have you believe.

The main mob figure in Jeanne Manarite's life is Genovese crime family member Sam Manarite. They have been married for better and, mostly, worse for 54 years. Papa Manarite has spent 22 of the past 26 years in the penitentiary. Now they are full-time pen pals.

"We had an opportunity for them to say, 'enough's enough,' but they didn't. My hope was to bring her home," Manarite's son, Dominick Manarite, said after watching his mother taken away in chains. "She's gone through the system as a lady, not a troublemaker. She has accepted her sentence not with a smile and not with arrogance. She knows that what she got involved with was wrong. But to understand it you'd have to understand my father. He's a different kind of guy. He comes from a different world that doesn't exist anymore."

In his world, Sam Manarite was known as a head-thumping loanshark. For his role in the chip scam and burglary, Manarite received 10 years. Only a lucky break when the sentencing guidelines change will put the 76-year-old multiple offender back on the street. A diabetic, he suffers from a bad heart and worse arteries. He also has a terminal case of playing the sucker for a government that feeds off his inability to quit committing dinosaur criminal acts in Las Vegas, a city in which his shock of white hair and menacing glare are well-known to law enforcement.

Jeanne Manarite is the guy's wife. Thanks to her husband, she walked smack into a sting operation. She did the crimes. There isn't time enough left in her life for her to explain all the reasons why.

"She was as involved as anyone in the case, if not more so," Assistant U.S. Attorney Jane Shoemaker said.

True enough. But what courtroom observers saw on Monday was not merely some mobbed-up Ma Barker character practicing the lost art of *omerta*, but an old-world wife paying the full fare for her mistakes. Some felonious, others matrimonial.

"I just feel I've served enough time," she said simply.

If you were expecting tears or a plea for forgiveness on bended knee, forget about it.

By the time the judges finish tallying the sentencing guidelines and balancing the double-jeopardy issue, Jeanne Manarite will be eligible for parole.

After enduring more than half a century of marriage to Springfield Sam, double-tough Jeanne Manarite can do the remainder of her 46 months standing on her head.

Whether making her do so constitutes justice is another matter. ◆

Grandfatherly mobster can only hide mean streak for so long

July 19, 1998

With his shock of white hair, slight build, and deep tan, Sam Manarite could be your dear old grandfather or the retired guy next door who spends his mornings weeding his petunia patch.

Except that Manarite wears standard-issue jailhouse togs and sits across the table in a small research room at the North Las Vegas Detention Center.

But, I'm telling you, he could pass for somebody's granddad.

It's when he speaks that Manarite, the mob soldier who's now over 80 and has spent more than one-fourth of his life in prison, sometimes betrays his darker nature.

I've met a few men with rougher reputations than Springfield Sam, but even fewer who could charm you with their casual style. Sam appears so tan and fit that you'd swear he's been vacationing in Florida instead of rotting in the penitentiary, but that's what I'm talking about. Springfield Sam is that smooth, and I appreciate that.

Born in Springfield, Massachusetts, and raised on the streets, Manarite is known as a Genovese crime family soldier. He has kicked around from Boston to Hialeah, Los Angeles to Las Vegas. His arrests range from gambling to murder with a heavy emphasis on loansharking and other activities related to street-corner usury.

In his prime he had a reputation as a man capable of murder, one who would collect a loan with a knitted eyebrow if possible, a golf club if necessary.

His handicap has been getting caught. He always gets caught, because he's always committing crimes.

It's what he does. That, and sit in prison.

But I like him the way I am intrigued by the tigers in the zoo. A Bengal tiger is such a fascinating creature that it's possible to forget it is not just an overgrown house cat, but a carnivore capable of crushing your skull without a second thought.

Even if he does resemble a grandfatherly figure, Sam has that other reputation.

So what's on your mind, Grandpa?

"I got roughed up," Sam says in a sotto voice. We are alone in the room. "One of the marshals did it."

As Sam is a federal prisoner, he means one of the U.S. marshals assigned to escort him from the North Las Vegas facility to federal court and, on occasion, to the holding cell in the Foley Federal Building.

As he tells the tale, it was one marshal in particular who just happens to be the husband of the Strike Force prosecutor who sent a good portion of the Manarite family to prison for Sam's last desperate caper. Sam's wife, Jeanne, wound up doing 40 months for her role in a burglary operation. She was Sam's lookout.

Sam pleaded for her freedom, but it was too late. Jeanne is free now, and last I heard was in poor health but living in San Diego.

Sam remains bitter. He also remains in jail for at least one more year.

I listen as he dramatically recounts the harm he was done, and I notice that Sam's face shows no sign of a beating. But perhaps it was the rubber hose treatment, or maybe a big bruiser jabbed him with a baton to the ribs. These things can happen to prisoners, even to ones who look more like Grandpa Walton than Scarface Al.

The battering might not show, but Sam says it has given him headaches. Sam is not without his medical maladies. As an octogenarian, he has been carved on more than the Christmas goose. He had heart surgery, a gall bladder removed, a third of his stomach taken out, a lung removed. He has had eye surgery, blood clots, and brain scans.

All at government expense. After all, he is our guest.

With so many parts taken out, it sounds like Sam is staging an escape one piece at a time. Very slowly. So as not to attract suspicion.

More than his bad heart and ailing stomach, Sam suffers from a chronic case of extended incarceration. But a verifiable example of a marshal mugging a prisoner, one who had his hands bound at his sides, would be a worthy story.

Don't forget, Sam is old enough to be someone's grandpa.

But in the middle of his dramatic rendering of events, Sam's dark eyes flash.

"I told him to uncuff me, but he wouldn't," Sam says, malice suddenly streaking his voice. "If I could've got close enough to him, I'd have bit his nose off."

Why, Grandpa, what big teeth you have.

Suddenly, the spell is broken.

Just when I am ready to believe that Sam Manarite—despite his 50-year criminal record—is the victim of injustice behind bars, he goes and blows the play.

Grandpa becomes Hannibal Lecter.

Sorry, Sam. Better luck next time. ◆

Midnight Idol wined, dined with Guido What's-His-Name

September 9, 1991

Guido Penosi.

A made member of the Gambino crime family. Convicted of narcotics and tax violations. Described as a fancy Hollywood cocaine and heroin dealer, which means he pushed the stuff from the backseat of a limousine instead of a Sunset Strip side-walk.

In the mid-1980s, federal law enforcement called Penosi the Gambino family's West Coast overseer. He is nicknamed "the Bull" because of his size and toughness, and, perhaps, because "the Blob" was taken.

Big, fat, scary. Penosi is the sort of fellow who gives the average person the willies. If he's not careful, someone will make a movie about his romantic life.

In addition to being a large hood, Guido was a large Wayne Newton fan.

Whenever Newton's decade-old libel suit against NBC is discussed, I don't wonder about the accuracy of the four broadcasts that linked his 1980 purchase of the Aladdin to the Gambino family.

I wonder about Guido.

Although it remains unclear whether NBC's news reports were true, it is officially known they weren't libelous. The U.S. Supreme Court confirmed that Monday, when it let stand a 1990 federal appeals court decision overturning Newton's 1986 multimillion-dollar libel victory.

All that is finished.

Guido remains.

Newton said in court he met Penosi in 1963 at New York's famed Copacabana Club, which in those days averaged about one hood per table. Newton was a smooth-faced teen-ager, and Penosi was a fan who waved $100 bills at the kid while making special musical requests.

Newton said he refused the money but accepted the friendship. In retrospect, maybe he should have taken the money.

Through the years, Newton kept in touch with Guido. Not close enough to learn his last name, but close enough to spend quality time. He dined at Guido's Florida home. He accepted Guido's expensive gifts.

After a caller threatened the life of his daughter in 1980, Newton accepted Guido's help, too.

Presumably, by this time Newton knew Guido's last name.

"I would have called the devil himself to save my daughter's life," an emotional Newton said during his 1986 trial.

By dialing his friend Guido, he came close to doing just that.

Penosi directed Newton to Frank Piccolo, who was the Gambino family's Connecticut rackets boss. Newton didn't know that, of course. He only knew that after he told Penosi's friend about the death threats, the threats ceased.

Now, a cynic may wonder why Newton didn't call the FBI instead of Guido What's-His-Name. I say you can't argue with results.

Penosi and Piccolo were accused in 1981 of conspiring to extort money from Newton and singer Lola Falana. It seems some people believed those death threats against Newton were ploys to win his favor with a long-range goal of making money from the Midnight Idol.

Penosi was acquitted. Piccolo's defense rested in September 1981 in Bridgeport, Connecticut, when he was filled with more holes than a dime-store fife. These things happen to mobsters, not that Newton knew he was one, of course.

After all, he knew Guido for nearly 20 years before learning his last name and never dreamed the big fat guy was a mobster.

In fact, Newton has spent much of his adult life in Las Vegas, but maintained in court he had never met a mobster.

It should be remembered that Newton is an upstanding Las Vegas citizen. He is the perennial Entertainer of the Year in the Entertainment Capital of the World. He gives to charity. Why, he even raises Arabian horses.

He does not have the best memory in the world, but, then again, that didn't keep Ronald Reagan from the presidency.

Still, if Wayne Newton knew Guido What's-His-Name for two decades and failed to figure something was amiss, then perhaps it's best he didn't own the Aladdin for long.

Come to think of it, maybe the Midnight Idol should stop going out after dark altogether. ◆

Fans need not fret over Midnight Idol's financial troubles

February 11, 1993

Wayne Newton's admirers shed an ocean of tears when he announced in August he was filing personal bankruptcy.

Life does mean things to some beautiful people, and it had been downright cruel to the Wayner.

The mass of Midwesterners who adore the Midnight Idol from his jet black coif to his big silver buckle had to have been heartsick at his predicament. They worship this man, dare it be said, the way some people love Elvis.

And they were ready to collapse when they heard the bad news.

Newton was $20 million in debt with little relief in sight.

No matter that finding ways to spend the $250,000-a-week salary he earned at the Las Vegas Hilton would prove a full-time job for most people. Newton managed to blow that much and millions more before pulling the bill-paying pin and filing for Chapter 11 bankruptcy reorganization.

Listed among his creditors are the Northeastern Bank of Pennsylvania, $8.3 million; General Electric Credit, $1.2 million; the Internal Revenue Service, $341,000; and various legal firms, $300,000.

What a crowd.

Talk about a tough room to work.

His fans figured it had to put Newton under the kind of intense stress that sends common folks to the Heart Attack Hotel.

Bankruptcy is a terrible thing. Just ask the average middle-class credit-card junkie with three kids and the latest appliances.

His credit is ruined, his future is bleak. He has nightmares of being chased by wolf-faced bill collectors and IRS auditors with their eyes on his kids' piggy banks.

For seven years the bankrupt worker struggles to pay the rent and provide for his family. Private health care is out of the question. Flying to Venus is more likely than owning a new car.

Between the liens, levies, and stigma of middle-class bankruptcy, the lowly worker doesn't have a chance.

Given such realities, just imagine what bankruptcy might do to Newton's legendary voice.

Well, those nuts about Newton need not fret. He isn't dining on Arabian horse flesh, and he hasn't moved into the Casa de Motel 6.

His fans will be pleased to know Newton's financial distress hasn't prevented him from feeding his family with enough left over for his, ahem, South African black-footed penguins.

Although Newton has sold some of his celebrated Arabians, he still maintains a substantial personal stable. Apparently, the equestrian life runs in the family.

During recent federal bankruptcy proceedings in Reno, Newton successfully argued to U.S. Bankruptcy Court Judge James Thompson that it was appropriate to pay $1,000 a week for riding lessons for his daughter, who has four horses.

The animal husbandry doesn't end there.

Newton also keeps an extensive collection of exotic birds and even genuine South African black-footed penguins at his Casa de Shenandoah mansion. The menagerie ranges from a Japanese chicken to a tawny eagle, from a Mandarin duck to a Chilean flamingo.

Suffice it to say the penguins, eagles, and flamingos do not feed themselves. And Newton cannot be expected to give up his singing career to play Jim Fowler to a bunch of birds. He also doesn't do lawns.

Newton's sprawling Southern Nevada ranch features 17 acres of manicured pasture, but you won't find the Midnight Idol perspiring in the noon-day sun. He employs six gardeners, and Thompson agreed Newton needs every one.

Although Newton's fans will understand, it makes some working stiffs wonder why the judge, an obvious admirer, bothers to go to all the trouble of donning a robe and sitting on the big bench.

Why not just display his Newton Forever T-shirt and join the frothing fans in the front row?

It's obvious why last year Newton felt comfortable commenting, "I'm really keeping everything I want to keep. It isn't a matter of losing my home or the plane."

After all, it's only bankruptcy.

It's not something serious like Vegas Throat. With his economic philosophy, the Midnight Idol would make a fine congressman.

How those mean old creditors can possibly justify harassing this man is beyond comprehension.

Isn't it enough that he is forced to sing "Danke Schoen" night after night? ◆

Blitzstein may limp back into prison for parole violations

February 13, 1992

With the day's lunch money burning a hole in my britches, I approached the First Street entrance of Binion's Horseshoe for another in a series of attempts to turn a turkey on rye into a double sawbuck at the casino race book.

Alas, I never made it to the ticket window.

Outside the lobby, Las Vegas street character Dominic Spinale approached. After an exchange of pleasantries, he moved toward his Mercedes parked at the curb. His passenger was hard to miss.

Herb Blitzstein.

Longtime Chicago mob guy, Anthony Spilotro buddy, convicted felon, and paroled federal prisoner residing at a downtown halfway house. He was the "Fat Herbie" newspaper readers came to know during popular *R-J* columnist Ned Day's heyday in the early 1980s.

Spilotro and Day are dead now, and Blitzstein isn't feeling too good himself.

Hanging around an old pal could violate Blitzstein's parole, and Spinale qualified as one. They were acquainted from the days when Blitzstein reputedly was a Spilotro street lieutenant. Spinale did a little time for participating in an interstate book-making ring involving New England's Patriarca crime family. He wasn't Public Enemy Number 1, but he was poison for Blitzstein.

A sentimentalist at heart, I figured Blitzstein didn't need additional grief. Beyond his mob history and criminal convictions, he was a 57-year-old scuffler who had survived a pair of heart operations, gangrene, and prison food. Surely he could survive a ride with Spinale.

As they drove away, I wondered how long Blitzstein would last on the street before being slapped with a parole violation.

As it turns out, I didn't have to wonder long.

Metro announced Wednesday it has recommended Blitzstein's parole be revoked for failing to steer clear of his former associates only a few months after gaining half his freedom. Although he has just three months remaining on his eight-year sentence for a 1987 conviction on wire fraud and tax charges, he likely will spend it in the slammer at taxpayer expense.

Or, maybe in a hospital at taxpayer expense.

You see, Herbie is in a helluva shape. If he were a horse, you would shoot him.

His heart has endured seven bypasses. His right foot has been partially amputated. He doesn't have enough little piggies left to go to market, eat roast beef, or walk two blocks without experiencing excruciating pain.

Without a ride, all he can do is stay home. Or, in his case, halfway home. That is his excuse for catching a lift with Spinale.

"If I say hello to a guy and he gives me a ride to the doctor, what is that?" Blitzstein asked. "He was never an associate of mine. All my associates are dead. He's just a guy I know here. He's a friend."

That was enough for the cops to suggest Blitzstein be shipped from his First Street halfway house to more structured accommodations. The federal correctional facility in Boron, California, for example.

Blitzstein made no excuses for his past, but said he is being picked on by the police because of his history with Spilotro. He also said he has been harassed since taking a day job with John Momot at the attorney's downtown office.

"My name is Blitzstein. They want to send me back to prison," he said. "I can't do anything. I can't go anywhere. I don't know anything. I just want to be left alone."

In 1989, Blitzstein failed to gain an early prison release for medical reasons. His parole was rejected earlier because of his organized crime connections.

That's what makes Blitzstein's predicament and apparent violation so pathetic. It is self-inflicted.

With his bum heart and rotten leg, he said he probably won't live to retirement age.

"I'm a medical time bomb," Blitzstein said. He paused, considered his life's lot, and laughed a little. "One thing I can tell you. I wish I would have listened to my mother and become a lawyer."

It is a toss-up whether the world needs a gimpy old hood more than another attorney.

Then Blitzstein returned to his attack on the mean-spirited police. He insisted his only desire is to finish his sentence and leave Las Vegas for good.

His days of running, or even walking, the streets may be through, but as he spoke I wondered about the odds of Herb Blitzstein staying out of prison long enough to die a free man.

Given his latest misstep, it looks like a long shot at best. ◆

Herb Blitzstein died violently in town that was in his blood

January 8, 1997

Herb Blitzstein liked to talk about leaving Las Vegas, about building a bankroll and escaping the heat on the street.

He would move somewhere new, somewhere his face and

reputation weren't so notorious. Go some place the mention of his name didn't make the local cops' mouths foam. Maybe he'd return to Chicago, his hometown. Strictly for a fresh start, you understand.

It's a story he liked to tell me when we ran into each other on the street. I would ask him how he was feeling, and he'd talk about his heart. I would ask him what he was up to, and his line never varied.

"I'm retired," he'd say. "I got nothing going. I can't do anything. I can't go anywhere. Those days are over."

We both knew he was right about those days, just as we both knew the tale of his retirement was just a story.

Herb Blitzstein knew he would never leave Las Vegas, just as he knew he would never really quit the street life. In his way, Blitzstein loved Las Vegas. The town was in his blood, and the memories of his heyday as the right-hand man of Chicago mob tough Anthony Spilotro were in his head.

Blitzstein's blood flowed Tuesday. He was shot in the head by someone who was well-acquainted with his daily routine.

More than a decade after Spilotro's grisly demise, Blitzstein died violently. The town that was in his blood finally had seen it spilled.

It didn't surprise the local investigators who tailed him for two decades. He was a mob guy and mob guys die that way. Here's how they think it happened:

When Blitzstein missed his morning appointment Tuesday, his pal Joe started to worry. For months they hadn't been out of each other's sight for more than a few hours. Running mates is what they were. Co-conspirators, some would say.

After seven heart bypasses and a couple of toes amputated, Blitzstein no longer moved as fast as he did in the days he walked point for Spilotro, but he was seldom late for their daily briefing at the Any Auto Repair on East Fremont Street or some out-of-the-way coffee shop.

At 63, with multiple felonies and a notorious past, Blitzstein was on his way into Nevada's casino Black Book and headed for more trouble as word circulated the streets that he was back in business. He always denied it whenever I asked him, but I didn't expect a signed confession from a life-long scuffler.

When Blitzstein didn't answer his phone, Joe drove to Herb's two-bedroom Mount Vernon Avenue townhouse on the southeast side. Joe opened the front door with his key. Blitzstein was slumped over a chair, and at first his friend thought the aging mob guy had suffered a heart attack. He called 911, but before the ambulance arrived he discovered the truth: Blitzstein had been shot in the back of the head with a small-caliber handgun. The bullet entered through the base of the skull, informed sources say.

It wasn't a movie, wasn't some outtake from Scorsese's *Casino*, the revisionist look at the violent life and death of Spilotro that Blitzstein cursed daily. Whoever did the work probably surprised Blitzstein as he was walking from his garage through the door leading to his kitchen and living room.

The homicide has the markings of a mob hit. Outside the police barrier, Metro homicide investigator Wayne Petersen wouldn't speculate on a motive.

"With Mr. Blitzstein's colorful past, there are lots of different avenues to explore and lots of different people we need to talk to," he said.

Blitzstein's friend and defense attorney, John Momot, arrived only minutes after the police. Momot, who had survived his share of close calls as counsel for organized crime associates, was shaken by the news that his friend of two decades had been murdered. His client even planned to fight his recent nomination for the Black Book.

"We were litigating this," Momot said. Reflecting, he added, "We've been litigating since the moment I met him."

Blitzstein's son, Rick, was at the scene along with two family friends. The son remained on the street outside the townhouse for hours and watched as the coroner took away his father's body.

FBI agents Walt Stowe and John Plunkett reviewed the crime scene, as did investigators with Metro's Intelligence Services Bureau.

The investigation is just beginning, but the cause of death is pretty clear. In his dark way, Herb Blitzstein loved Las Vegas. But the place had changed, and he couldn't leave it.

The town was in his blood, you know. ◆

Slain mobster's pal chooses one unconventional tribute

February 6, 1997

When Slick heard his pal Herb Blitzstein had been killed in the traditional manner, he found himself at a loss for what to do next.

He couldn't just order flowers. With rare exceptions, wise guys do not buy their associates roses. It's bad for the image.

In days gone by, Slick might have packed a bag and hid out for a few weeks. Being the friend of a dead mob guy can be hazardous to one's health. But this is 1997, and he fought the urge to slide down into Southern California's card-room sub-culture.

Nor did he start packing a pistol and keeping his back to the wall of the topless bars and late-night lounges he frequents. Guns are messy, and authorities frown on men of his pedigree possessing handguns.

He didn't decide to go on a bender in Blitzstein's honor, either. Slick doesn't drink like he used to, and he is unwelcome most places dice are pitched.

Instead of running, gunning, or gambling, Slick thought about his pal, Herb. He was a generous man in a pinch, a fellow who spread around money when he had it, and enjoyed being known as a George guy. You know, a big tipper.

Slick and Herb had become real friends over the years. They were as close as wiseguys ever get. Both had survived Anthony Spilotro's dangerous friendship, but Herb Blitzstein still had gone the way of most lifelong street criminals.

Slick was at a loss, all right. So much so that he decided to do something sure to elicit laughter from polite society. He went to church and prayed. He does that regularly these days.

He genuflected, then had something of an epiphany right there in the pew. He suddenly knew what he would do for his pal.

Slick would ask the parish priest for a favor. But would the father dedicate a Mass to a lost soul not even of the Catholic persuasion?

It was a long shot.

Jewish by birth, Blitzstein was a practicing hedonist. When he should have been studying the Torah, Herb found himself memorizing the *Racing Form*. Herb was a lot of things, you understand, but he was not a hypocrite.

Make that an over-the-rainbow long shot.

It wasn't as if Slick had a lot of markers with the religious community. He probably considered himself lucky to be able to enter the house of worship without wearing a disguise.

But one does not argue with epiphanies. So Slick approached the priest and cautiously uttered his request.

To his credit, the good father did not drop the chalice or mumble a word about the odds of Blitzstein's soul winning any races to the Pearly Gates. Instead, he nodded and agreed to do his best.

As Slick listened, he prayed, too. Not for any miracles, mind you, but for a little understanding. Slick knew that there but for the grace of God he might have gone the way of Herb Blitzstein.

"What am I going to do, send flowers?" Slick asks. "He wasn't religious or anything like that, but flowers just die away.

"So I asked the priest, and he said prayers for his soul. I said, 'A friend of mine was murdered the night before. He wasn't a Christian and he wasn't a believer.' The priest said, 'God is merciful.' When I went in, I heard him dedicate the Mass, but, you know, he didn't mention any names."

Perhaps the priest knew some of his square parishioners had delicate hearts. But Slick was comforted by the words, and he figured it was the best he could do for his friend under the circumstances.

"Herbie didn't care about making money anymore," Slick says. "He was satisfied with less. He just wanted to be comfortable and didn't want to be harassed. He wasn't the tough guy the press made him out to be. He was a soft touch, a very very soft touch."

A soft touch with some very very tough business associates.

"I know him better than anybody. My guess is it was a robbery," Slick says. "They probably wanted to kill him rather than rob him and have Herb know it was them. So they clipped him and took all his stuff."

They left behind a few friends, and Slick is one of them. But Slick's not a tough guy, just a gambler and sports bettor with a bad reputation. All he can do these days is pray for a few winning horses and a peaceful retirement.

Now you know how Herb Blitzstein came to have a Mass read on his behalf.

Word is, Slick slipped a little something extra in the collection plate that day at the church on his friend's behalf.

Herb Blitzstein would have appreciated knowing he was a George guy to the very end. ◆

Singing Mafia soldier's act has knocked 'em dead for years

February 5, 1998

Ladies and gentlemen, put your hands together and give a warm Las Vegas welcome to the incomparable Bobby Milano.

Of all the men indicted in the FBI's Operation Button-down sweep of organized crime in Southern Nevada, Milano's portfolio is easily the most entertaining.

Talk about a multi-talented performer.

Bobby Milano is a singer, actor, and mafia soldier. Let's see

Engelbert Humperdinck top that.

As of Monday, the Buffalo, New York, native also was one of the 25 men accused of mob activity in Las Vegas, which includes the January 1997 murder-for-hire case of local money-lender Herbie Blitzstein. Milano is charged with racketeering conspiracy and possession of counterfeit Visa International traveler's checks.

Who knows, maybe he will use the old they-didn't-take-American-Express defense. Hey, it could happen.

At 62, Bobby Milano is living a dream, some say a fantasy. Milano has been in the entertainment business many years. In the early 1980s, law enforcement noticed his presence in the organized crime business as well. In 1988, he pleaded guilty in a Los Angeles federal court to extortion conspiracy charges and was sentenced to a year in prison.

Born Charles Joseph Caci, Milano is the younger brother of 73-year-old Palm Springs-based mob capo Vincent Dominic "Jimmy" Caci. Everyone knows tough guys don't dance. Well, Jimmy Caci doesn't sing, either.

His younger brother is different.

Milano has sung many times for friends at Mr. Kelly's in Palm Springs, packed in the sporting crowd at Tracton's on Ventura Boulevard in Encino. In Las Vegas, he played to pals and fans at the Tropicana. His most requested ballad is "King or Slave."

When this guy sings for his supper, you better listen.

The real question is, does everybody duck when he announces his greatest hit?

Milano has numerous movie and commercial credits, including appearances in *The Untouchables* and *The Gangster Chronicles*. Before someone utters the words "typecasting," it should be noted he also has cut commercials for automobiles and fast food.

With Bobby Milano's portfolio, he could play himself in a movie. That is, if he's available.

Alas, there's the problem.

With confidential informants and undercover FBI agents crawling all over the case and hundreds of surveillance and wiretap tapes collected, it's hard to imagine any of the defendants being available for a job, whether it be of the acting or bank variety.

His status as a made member of the Peter John Milano crime family says plenty about the caliber of the traditional mob in the late 1990s.

As a rising star in the L.A. mob in 1980, Craig Anthony Fiato met Bobby Milano between sets at Tracton's. Three years later, Fiato would wear a wire for the FBI and help put away Milano and more than three dozen other criminals for offenses ranging from extortion to murder conspiracy.

If those allegations sound familiar, it is because not much has changed for the Milano crew. The nature of the crimes alleged in the recent indictment indicate the old mob hasn't changed its method of operation much.

"These guys are like old dogs who can't learn new tricks," Fiato said in a recent interview. "They're living in a dream world. They'll never smarten up. You know why?

"They don't know how to do anything else."

But that night at Tracton's, with Mafia titan Mike Rizzitello at the table, Milano was a singer. He was a mob aficionado; his brother was the real gangster.

"Bobby Milano was a fan," Fiato said. "He's always been a fan. But that's the way it is with Pete Milano's crew. Bobby rode his brother's coattails.

"Later, when Mike and I heard Bobby had been made, Mike said, 'Can you imagine they made this singer?' That's what attrition has done to them. Bookmakers and singers become made guys. It's a joke. I didn't take it seriously. If he's a singer, he doesn't have the tools necessary to do the real work."

By "real work," Fiato of course meant commit acts of violence.

"The only thing Bobby could hold in his hand was a microphone, never a gun," Fiato said. "The only way Bobby Milano could kill anybody was to sing them to death."

Now he's one slip from singing "Jailhouse Rock" and "Folsom Prison Blues."

While a gentle nature generates little respect on the street, it is sure to come as a relief to Bobby Milano's fans. They love the way he knocks 'em dead, but don't want to be called as material witnesses. ◆

Las Vegas businessman seeks revenge in wife's slaying

December 21, 1990

As Dave Tipton sat in his small office at All-Around Video, a sentimental pastiche of a family's home movies played on a television monitor.

It was someone else's family, someone else's children, parents, and grandparents caught laughing and grinning into the camera as Gladys Knight soulfully sang "The Way We Were."

Our conversation began with the unprompted methodical description of the slaying of his wife Bobbie Jean, family maid Marie Bullock, and delivery driver James Myers at the hands of Steve Homick on December 11, 1985, at Tipton's home on Oquendo Road. He detailed the grisly scene as calmly as someone might explain how to change a car tire.

Tipton discovered the bodies and the blood when he returned home that afternoon. After five years, his mourning has been replaced by an intense hatred for Steve Homick.

Since then, Tipton has moved, remarried, and started a new business repairing and processing videotapes. He knows nothing but time will separate him from the nightmare, and not even time can change the terrible truth.

Homick, on trial in federal court on racketeering and murder-for-hire charges, was convicted of the Tipton killings at the state level and was sentenced to death. He is appealing that decision, and at a minimum is five years from paying for his crimes.

"He's having a ball right now. He's having a good time,"

Tipton said. "The courtroom is better than a twelve-by-twelve cell. This is a man who smirked down at the victims' families."

Homick, a longtime Las Vegan, has been implicated in six slayings and myriad lesser crimes ranging from robbery to drug trafficking. A former Los Angeles police officer and minor league baseball pitcher, he was after Bobbie Jean Tipton's jewelry when he entered their home that December morning. Bullock had just arrived for work. Myers was checking on a meat delivery.

After forcing Tipton to open a safe, Homick killed all three with a pistol. Two defenseless women, one tragically unlucky deliveryman.

"Even if he got a million out of the jewelry, it's not worth three lives," Tipton said. "And he enjoyed it."

In the years since the killings, Tipton has pored over grand jury testimony and court documents. He attended the state trial and was called as a witness in the federal trial. He can quote the testimony of Homick's associates and has memorized the medical examiner's report. He knows almost as well as some of the investigators what took place that day.

"I've never seen a death penalty case as clear as this one," Tipton said, a transcript of the 464-page grand jury proceedings nearby. "I think he's as evil as Hitler, the Son of Sam, and Richard Speck. He's the devil."

But Homick is a long way from the gallows.

The very nature of his evil will keep him alive for a while. It takes years for six slayings performed at three separate times to be processed legally. The killings of Gerald and Vera Woodman in Southern California, the torture slaying of Raymond Godfrey in Las Vegas, the federal racketeering trial in Nevada and the time-consuming appeals processes will keep Homick from his ultimate end much of the 1990s. That fact continues to eat away at Tipton.

"It must make sense to them," he said of the multi-party federal indictment issued after Homick had been sentenced to die in Nevada. "It doesn't to me. It seems like it's a never-ending thing."

Federal prosecutors allege Homick headed a murderous

organized-crime ring. Although Homick has the highest profile of those implicated, the federal charges encompass many crimes and criminals.

Only one haunts Tipton.

"I'm a good person. I bust my hump for a living. I have no ax to grind with life," Tipton said. "I'd say this guy's ruined the lives of twenty-five or thirty people. This is the Holocaust for me. It's the worst thing that could happen.

"I could push the button with no remorse."

In time, that won't be necessary. ◆

Steven Homick, a murderous hail fellow well met

January 24, 1991

"Somebody bothers you, you let me know. I'll take care of him for you."

—Steven Homick, to friends and acquaintances

Many people who have come in contact with Steven Homick agree on one thing: He seemed like a nice friendly fellow. A little strange around the edges, perhaps, but harmless all-in-all.

Athletic, outgoing, generous at the bar, always willing to do a friend a favor, Homick portrayed himself as a sort of overgrown Eagle Scout or a protective big brother. He was a Las Vegas kind of guy, a hail fellow well met.

He was only too happy to do a good deed for a pal. An attorney pal, a cop pal, a hotel pal. Of course, there might come a time when he would need something. But that's what friends are for, isn't it?

First impressions, however, aren't always accurate impressions. As many people now know, the pleasant outgoing Homick is a killer.

As Homick's racketeering and continuing criminal enterprise trial in U.S. District Court comes to a close, I continue to wonder about his strange life in Las Vegas.

The 50-year-old Homick is a former minor league baseball player, an ex-Los Angeles cop, a veteran casino worker, a skilled carpenter, a one-time security guard. He was a jack-of-all-trades, but that was just one aspect of his multifaceted character.

He also was a knee-busting bill collector, a burglar, cocaine trafficker, jewel thief, and sadistic contract murderer. He was a bona fide wise guy who ran a crew of loyal hoods.

Over the years, Homick managed to gain entrée into varied and exclusive enclaves of local society. He met many of his influential contacts at the Las Vegas Sporting House, where politicians, casino executives, cops, and creeps work out in close proximity. Homick was a good athlete and was highly proficient at handball and racquetball. He also had plenty of time to chat with his good friends.

In time, his circle of acquaintances grew. Homick knew casino executives, police detectives, high-profile attorneys, hardline prosecutors, and local judges. He also knew arsonists, murderers, and mobsters.

How did he do it?

Acquaintances of Homick describe him as a colorful character who had a working knowledge of law and law enforcement. He also had a fair understanding of the darker side of Las Vegas. Combine this knowledge with his gift of gab, and a strange propensity to speak in parables and riddles, and Homick appeared fascinating but harmless. He talked like a wise guy, but he acted like a nice guy.

He was the sort of fellow who, if born in a different time, might have lived on the pages of an O. Henry or Damon Runyon short story. He is the kind of man who still can get along without attracting too much attention in Las Vegas.

But Homick, of course, was neither harmless nor selfless. Sooner or later, the day came when Homick wanted favors from his good friends. He went from harmless character to manipulative con artist.

He would do favors for you so that he in turn could make use of you some day in some way, one acquaintance of Homick said. Others echoed that impression.

While Homick's federal trial nears completion, he still faces a double-murder rap in Los Angeles. In 1989, he was sentenced to die for a 1985 triple murder and robbery in Las Vegas.

A funny thing happened on the way to the guilty verdict in the 1989 trial. During the drawn-out proceedings, someone rigged a locked door leading from the courtroom so it would not close properly. The door alarm was deactivated.

If a defendant could get through the door and lock it, then he could make his way to the street and freedom with relative ease. By accident, a court official discovered the problem. Metro's SWAT team was called out the next day, and the long trial ended without incident.

Homick was found guilty of killing two women and a deliveryman. He shot each three times with a .22-caliber pistol, one as she opened a floor safe, a second as she prayed, and the third as he attempted to collect a bill for a meat company.

Strange, Steven Homick seemed like such a nice guy. ◆

You Are My Sunshine

The joy, and pain, of the holiday season

December 25, 1994

Excitement and mystery surround the traditional holiday orgy of gift-giving, but I feign disinterest. Are my presents among those shimmering under the tree? I would rather not know. In fact, I'll let some other jolly soul open those gifts. Since the Christmas I had ants in my pants, opening presents hasn't been the same.

It started harmlessly enough with an 11-year-old's fascination with the myriad mysteries beneath the tinsel and the bulbs. The possibilities were endless, and I began contemplating them in early September.

By December, I was a bug-eyed little spastic: One part parental interrogator, one part international spy.

"So, overall, taking into account all the variables, and speaking in general terms, what are the chances I could get a m-m-m-mini-bike?"

I could barely speak the words. Poised on the cusp of adolescence, a mini-bike meant motorized freedom and high-speed rides through the forbidding Baja-like desert that stretched out just beyond our neighborhood. Mostly, it meant a chance to look much older than 11.

Yes, a mini-bike. I would trade all the Hot Wheels, slot cars, Rock 'em Sock 'em Robots and Wes Parker autograph model first baseman's mitts for one mini-bike. Preferably a Cat mini-bike with knobby tires, cushioned seat, and a full three-horsepower Briggs & Stratton engine.

Oh, the power and the glory.

Father's response never varied: Omerta. The code of silence commonly used by Mafia dons and fathers around the holidays. Seated in his living room chair, my father would groan and give me that brow-knitted, iron-jawed stare.

Trouble.

But nothing I couldn't handle.

Pop was no squealer, but I was not without resources. In an attempt to find the precise identity of the gifts I would receive,

I made hourly searches of the home and vicinity.

Under the bed, check. Closets, check. Attic, check. Trunk of the Impala, check. Backyard storage shed, check.

Damn.

The standard tearing of the corner of the gifts was no use. Knowing I could not be trusted, my parents commonly switched boxes and used high-tensile wrapping tape of the kind favored by UPS shippers and experienced kidnappers. I dulled knives trying to slash open those boxes.

With the days waning, I resorted to the final traditionally accepted desperate measure: shake the hell out of the packages until those mystery gifts confess their true identity.

For me, rattling the presents was an annual tradition, but it was one that infuriated my mother. No child of hers was going to spoil the mystery of the packages, even if she had to choke every little hellion in the brood to keep the promise.

With mere hours remaining, the suspense grew too great. While the others were diverted by television, I belly-crawled to the tree. Once the coast was clear, I shook the packages. A little at first, then until my brain ached.

Five minutes into the wrestling match, I struck paydirt. The telltale rattling betrayed the contents: Surely it was something mechanical. A good sign. Presuming I had not shattered it beyond repair, I had a quality gift item on my hands.

On Christmas morning, the truth revealed itself in my mother's laughter.

"Because you're always shaking your presents, I decided to mix walnuts and Christmas candy in with your gift," she said.

Tricked by my own mother. How could she?

Worse yet, I received the weakest gift any 11-year-old boy could imagine: clothes. Pants, shirts, socks, and underwear. Clothes, for crying out loud.

Then came the worst news: "Now run and try them on. I want to see how they fit."

My spirit broken, I moped to the bedroom and pulled on the corduroys. Stiff as cardboard, they whooshed sarcastically when I walked and chided me all the way back to the living room. Suckersuckersuckersucker.

"Those make you look so handsome," she said. But by then I was beginning to fidget. These pants were more than uncomfortable; they were biting the spite out of me.

I caromed around the living room like a Superball. The family first mistook my agony for my usual fits of mania, then took notice when I stripped off the pants and yelped like a coyote.

The Christmas candy mother had used as a decoy had attracted a colony of red ants, which had taken up residence in my new corduroys.

The family roared as I hopped around in my underwear. Extremities covered with ant bites, I vowed never to shake another Christmas package.

The welts were just beginning to show when my father, suddenly smiling, wheeled in the mini-bike from the garage. I wiped my tears and shouted again. The Baja beckoned.

I rode standing up for weeks. ◆

One night at the ballpark can bring back thrills of youth

April 19, 1992

It was another night at the ballpark. I escaped the Las Vegas Stars press box and took a chair outside on the top deck in the warm summer wind a story above the murmuring crowd.

The illuminated grass was soothing, and the intoxicating smell of peanuts and hot dogs wafted into the night. The organ played in the distance, and the fans whispered and roared below.

Suddenly, a pop foul.

Off the first-base side, above the lights and down on the top deck. The notepad flew, the scorebook did too. Sports writing was only an excuse to get into the game free, anyway.

I was a big leaguer, a little leaguer, a tongue-wagging retriever.

I was six years old going like 60. Lost in the chase was the realization I was alone on the upper deck. After nearly taking a header over the rail and into the parking lot, I corralled the baseball.

It was a genuine Pacific Coast League foul, officially free for the grabbing and, as I clutched it, legally mine all mine.

I gripped six different pitches and smelled the horsehide. I love baseball, and the slightest fragments of the game send me dreaming of the rare moments I played like more than a hopeless hack.

My reverie was interrupted.

"Hey, mister," a little voice said.

I shook it off, watched the next pitch, admired my prize.

"Hey, mister."

I leaned over the rail, stared down at a scrawny kid. His cap tilted back, he was maybe eight years old.

"Hey, mister," the kid said. "Do you want that ball? Are you using it? Do you want to keep it?"

Did I want to keep it?

No, kid, I thought. I want to toss it into the trash like a Butterfinger wrapper. Of course I want to keep it. I want to stare at the wonder of the stitching, grip curves and knucklers, sliders and forkballs, and let no one touch it.

Ever.

It's my ball, you little beggar. It ties me to the game. One Tuesday in '75 I was a pretty good player. I played Little League, high school, and college baseball, you know. I tripled once.

But I didn't say any of that.

"Do you want that ball?"

An hour seemed to pass as I contemplated the question's infinite philosophical ramifications, and hoped the kid would be distracted.

I peeked down, his eyes stared up.

"No, I guess not," I said.

I let it drop over the side like a fish too small for keeping. My heart followed it all the way to the ground. The kid scooped up the ball and was gone.

For all I know, the kid had a million of them.

Now he has mine.

I spent several summers writing baseball stories at Cashman Field, hanging around the dugout and growing comfortable with the idea I wouldn't get closer to the big leagues than the bleacher seats. The memories range from the kid and dozens like him to eye-popping home runs launched by future major league stars Kevin McReynolds, Danny Tartabull, and Jose Canseco.

It's hard to believe the Stars' franchise is in its 10th season. It has provided a soothing sense of community to a relentlessly transient town. Las Vegas would be a colder place without its minor league team.

Volumes have been written about the game's impact on the heart and the nation. Baseball is a piece of living nostalgia. It puts us in touch with our youth and our parents' and grandparents' youth. Baseball is a memory machine.

Minor-league baseball has replaced its big brother when it comes to generating genuine emotion.

It is difficult for most of us to feel empathy for a multimillionaire who whines when he breaks a fingernail. After all, we play hurt.

It's much easier to relate to the tribulations of a struggling minor leaguer fighting long odds for a chance at the spotlight. After all, we minor leaguers far outnumber the other guys.

For that reason, bush-league ball is easy to be corny about. Like now, for instance.

The minor leagues are about hard work and hope and Horatio Alger. There really is something thrilling about the grass; it really is a field of dreams. It conjures the kid in everyone and makes us feel there was a moment when we, too, took a big league swing.

Did I ever tell you about the time I tripled? ◆

Motorists' prayer: Comeoncomeoncomeon comeoncomeon

April 15, 1994

When a dog from hell began barking from inside the radiator of my gasping '84 Mazda, I guessed something was amiss.

When more satanic smoke billowed from under the hood than out the tailpipe, even I was alarmed.

After only 133,457 miles, on Wednesday night the pockmarked pickup became demon possessed. Linda Blair didn't groan like this motorized malcontent.

Its shattered grill grinned like a gargoyle with missing teeth. Its shocks were marshmallows, and the radio hadn't rock 'n' rolled since Santana had a hit. As the cowboys say, the truck was rode hard and put away wet. But it had been reliable and didn't even complain when I forgot to check the oil during the Bush presidency.

I took the barking as an omen and gunned it into the parking lot of an AM/PM market.

Water, I thought. The little fella needs water.

Or oil, maybe. A quart of oil.

Or, more likely, the last rites.

I narrowed the possibilities. Either I had sucked Stephen King's St. Bernard into the radiator, or the engine was gut shot.

Problem is, I am not mechanically inclined. Any contraption more complex than a can-opener leaves me stumped, usually with scuffed knuckles and a smudge of grease on my forehead. And that's just with kitchen appliances.

Being a man, I am not allowed to let on that I am befuddled when a piece of rye bread gets lodged in a toaster. It also is forbidden to admit I can't tell a differential from a dashboard Jesus.

So I tried water, oil, epithets, chanting. Nothing worked.

Come on, I thought. Come on. Start one more time. Turn over just once more after all these years. Didn't I get your engine rebuilt and buy a new battery? Didn't I put up with stares from other drivers? Didn't I spend the past eight years avoiding parking attendants out of embarrassment? Didn't I just drop a month's pay into your stinking, rust-riddled hide? I cranked the ignition the way a mean auntie twists a kid's ear. Come on.

Comeoncomeoncomeoncomeon.

Damn.

Comeoncomeoncomeoncomeon.

Damn.

While I was busy ruining the starter, a fog moved in and consumed the parking lot and self-serve islands. The hound howled from under the hood.

The truck cab filled with noxious white smoke. Suddenly, I was trapped in a Cheech & Chong skit getting a petrochemical contact high.

Dizzy and desperate, I strained my publicly educated brain to recall a few lessons from junior-high shop class.

It was no use. I had spent an entire semester attempting to master the mysteries of the wood lathe. I planned to craft a Christmas-candy bowl for my mother, but rapidly whittled my way down to a lamp, then a table leg, then a Japanese martial arts weapon. I wound up with a C in the class, but Bruce Lee would have been proud of my nunchakus. Mom liked them, too.

Unless the engine needed a good lathing, I was in trouble.

Comeoncomeoncomeoncomeon.

Damn.

Comeoncomeoncomeoncomeoncomeonyourottenheap oftoxicgarbage.

Damn.

I thought about God and how I had strayed from the Church at age eight, how if I'd been a better Catholic I might not have this trouble. I wondered if God accepted foxhole conversions in convenience-store parking lots. I wondered if Mr. Goodwrench answered prayer.

Comeoncomeoncomeoncomeon.

The engine belched like a frat house after a beer bust, then caught one last time. It trembled and grumbled and coughed and rumbled. I was back in business, ready to roll on down the highway, as long as I hurried.

With the heat needle pointing north, I headed south. The cloud obscured the window. I laughed like a maniac as the store customers took cover. I was a one-man L.A. basin, a seething smog monster in a four-cylinder chariot rattling down Interstate 666.

I revved the engine, slammed it into first, and traveled just less than a quarter mile before the Mazda expired like a baritone bowser in the *R-J* parking lot.

The beast was still growling and smoldering when I called for a ride. But the dog's day was done. From the smell, well done.

It was my turn to bay the moon, scan the classifieds, and wonder why they don't make them like they used to. ◆

Memories of friend linger while lives follow different paths

November 12, 1995

The call came from the front desk. The operator's voice was nervous. Someone to see me.

As it often does, the past arrived without an appointment or a change of clothes.

When I heard the visitor's name, I immediately thought of my basketball days, wondered where all the years had gone and how this insane world can travel through space at 66,600 mph and manage to force two guys with nothing in common but grade school to bump into each other. I knew, too, that the reminiscence was going to cost a few bucks.

My friend had changed. He was still tall and muscular and sleek enough to breeze to the basket, but his clothes were ragged,

his complexion was bad, and his eyes were searching.
Prison is never kind, but the street is far meaner. He was on
parole, working off his community service, desperate for a job.
"I was doing fine. I was working. You know I was working," he said. "You know, but I slipped. I messed up. I know I
messed up."
He said he had given his life to God, and I decided to believe him.
As we talked, I saw myself as that skinny white boy packed
off to C.V.T. Gilbert Elementary on a bus bound for the glory to
be found in a society brimming with friendship and racial equal-
ity.
Friendship was the easy part. Grade-school insecurities
motivated students to bond quickly. That, and basketball on the
asphalt courts.
I was a 10-year-old cursed with big feet that moved with all
the alacrity of oak blocks. I lived in daily fear of being the last
mope selected for the lunchtime game.
Most of the time, my friend picked me even when it was not
to his advantage. We were friends, and friendship forgives a
world of athletic sins.
No one questioned that he was the king of the court. His
jump shots made the chain net sing. With his little brother buzzing like a gnat around him, repeating schoolyard insults and
fetching stray bank shots, we knew he would shoot his way to
stardom.
Drug use was an ugly uncle in his family, but he appeared
destined for better things. If anyone in his family would rise
above, it would be him.
I reached my level of hardcourt incompetence in junior high,
but my friend was a high school standout. His long-range jumper
was good enough to take him to college, where staying eligible
proved more difficult than any common defender.
Back home, he worked as a dealer at a Strip casino and
played city-league basketball, filling junior-high gyms with his
rainbow jumpers three nights a week. He hung out at three-
point range and played just enough defense to embarrass his

man a few times a game.

He moved easily up and down the courts of our youth, but the day had changed. He had changed, too.

His older brother was a notorious junkie who snatched so many purses he qualified for a 10-year prison stretch. His younger brother, who had idolized my friend, was killed in a gang shootout.

My friend did not escape the street unscathed. Like his older and younger brother, he had picked up a drug habit. It didn't run his life at first, but soon enough the hoops stopped. Then he blew his good job.

He hit me up for money a couple of times. I didn't buy the tales of his car trouble and family friend in need, but I knew those stories weren't meant for me. They were for him.

Then the contacts stopped. He disappeared. I thought about him sometimes when I passed the casino where he once worked, but I filed away the childhood memories and basketball days.

Then came the call and the past came back like a highlight film with a tragic ending.

As we talked I noticed that his hair had gone gray and he had lost the confidence of youth.

"I just got to get a job, John," he said. "I can't live like this."

He said he needed some money for a haircut and shave, and so I slipped him a few bucks and tried not to remember whether I had heard the story before.

Mostly I tried to be encouraging, fumbled a few useless words, and watched him walk toward Bonanza Road.

Friendship was the easy part. Although we were from the same planet and even the same neighborhood, we ended up in different worlds.

Now he's on parole after serving more than a year in prison. He's back on the streets he used to run so effortlessly, the streets that took one brother's life and sent another to the penitentiary.

He swears he has seen the light and wants me to believe him. And so I do.

Those basketball days are long gone, but I remember the time he picked me when no one else would. ◆

Old friend survives it all and now is ready to live again

June 20, 1997

"I was afraid it would turn out this way."
—Old Lodge Skins in *Little Big Man*

My friend and I cackled as we recalled the scene in which the ancient Cheyenne sage took in the changing landscape of his life and pronounced, "It is a good day to die," and then did not. The sight of the infinitely sincere Chief Dan George lying there waiting for the end to come, then feeling the first drop of rain on his cheek, made us bust up every time.

We laughed at the story and ate our sandwiches the other day during our last lunch together. He drank his black coffee, I sipped an iced tea. We reminisced about all the things that haven't killed him in the 73 years that have passed since he was born on a wheat farm outside Grand Forks, North Dakota. He knows the last few years of his life have mimicked Old Lodge Skins' own.

A broad-shouldered, thick-headed Norwegian kid, he broke wild horses and nearly his neck in Eastern Washington, was shot twice in Europe during World War II, registered enough bar brawls to rate a mention in *The Boxing Encyclopedia* and managed to survive every one.

He wrote for newspapers for a living, tapped out novels for his sanity, loved his Sam more than anything on Earth.

By way of telling you about their life together he says, "My only claim to fame is I was thrown into a saloon by the cops once."

It was a crowded night at the Roll Inn in Renton, Washington, and he and Sam sat sipping their drinks. Suffice it to say he came to the rescue of a lady in distress, started a bar-clearing fistfight, and wound up on the street, only to be pardoned by the police when the true culprits were sorted out. Chivalry could get your nose broken, but it counted for something 40 years ago.

Like a farm boy who had read Sir Walter Scott and Louis

L'Amour, my friend was always rushing to someone's rescue whether they needed it or not. Sam understood.

It's part of what she loved about him.

"She always said the only reason she married me is she always wondered what was going to happen next and didn't want to miss anything," he says. "We were married 32 years."

Sam died seven years ago. Of all the things that have nearly killed my friend, her death came closest.

"I still miss her, you know," he says, peering into the mist of their lives together back in Western Washington.

But, contrary to what the pop songs promise, people don't really die of broken hearts. And so my friend kept breathing, kept passing the days, praying for rain in the desert.

While other men in their 60s were taking up golf and dying slow deaths in front of their TV sets, he played hockey against jocks a third his age. Got knocked flat and returned the favor.

When time permitted, he rode his horses, a handsome Morgan and a wild-eyed Arabian. Like a prisoner, he marked the days and cared for his animals.

Not that those days were bereft of laughter. There were Friday nights listening to Dixieland jazz at Pogo's Tavern and afternoons at his hideout near the Gilcrease Ranch, where a visitor would find the door unlocked, a cold beer in the refrigerator, and the big Morgan standing in the kitchen. Life goes down easier with humor, and we had our share of good times.

Two years ago, he started getting weak and immediately put his affairs in order. He tearfully gave his horses to a good home, kept his dogs and his son near him for company. He knew he was going to die and was more concerned for his pets than himself.

Doctors diagnosed him with lung cancer, gave him six months to live. He took the terrible treatment and waited.

"For some reason, that just aroused the spirit of competition in me," he says.

He still carries a six-inch metal shunt in his chest, has experienced enough chemotherapy and radiation for a dozen lifetimes, knows the next checkup could bring bad news. Somehow, he emerged with a clean bill of health.

"Except for my brain, which was always suspect," he says.

We laughed together and ate our sandwiches and knew we probably wouldn't see each other again. Seattle is a long way from the desert. As we shook hands and said our good-byes, I was filled with the pride of our friendship.

My friend is going home to live and not die, where the Northwest rain will often hit his cheek, and the memories of his Sam will be close enough to touch. ◆

Plane-crashing, hurricane-riding uncle drank life to the lees

June 25, 1998

Jerry Curtis, my wandering uncle, had the uncanny knack of making friends wherever his many adventures took him.

But he was not above dropping in unannounced.

Take the time Jerry and his wife, Marian, flew his single-engine Cessna across Mexico and down through Central America. Over Costa Rica, Jerry experienced engine trouble. He crash-landed in the jungle, his plane hanging precariously from a banana tree.

He disassembled the craft piece by piece and hired natives to float the parts via canoe down a piranha-infested river. Once the plane was fit to fly, he resumed his journey. The natives, well-fed and well-paid, were sorry to see him leave.

Jerry's life was jammed with such stories. Picture Hemingway without the writerly pretensions and you have an accurate snapshot of my uncle. With his graying beard and confident swagger, he was at home on horseback, in the air, or on the bridge of his 36-foot Grand Banks.

My own father was mostly about work. Uncle Jerry worked hard, but knew how to play. He lived wildly and well for most of his 70 years. He battled cancer with the tenacity of a bare-knuckle fighter and died on Friday. He was my mother's twin. This is a vignette of how he lived. It is not the whole story, for his adventures would fill many volumes, not that he had time to write them. He was too busy living.

Jerry had his own sense of time that defied anything crafted by a Swiss watchmaker. Leave with him for a morning drive, and expect to be gone three days. Along the way, you'd be sure to break down somewhere English was not spoken, befriend a local, be invited to a fiesta, drink too much tequila or his favorite Jack Daniel's, and return home sunburned but safe 15 minutes before the family called out a search party.

Most men have hobbies. Jerry had passions that he fell for like a sailor on shore leave. He spent decades exploring Mexico, built and lost his fortune in the ceramic tile business three or four times, flew the props off his airplanes, was a gentleman cattle rancher at Williams Canyon outside Anaheim and the Kingston Ranch at the west end of Sandy Valley. Like his father before him, Jerry was in constant motion and always primed for the next adventure.

He was a pretty good pilot, actually, but he was tough on the machinery. He always insisted on pushing planes and his nerve to the limit. He would land on power-line roads and dry lake beds, knew every rutted strip in Baja, and chased sunsets from here to Guatemala.

One other thing. He crashed every plane he ever owned.

"And some that didn't belong to him," elder daughter Lynda Fleming says. "Dad loved living on the edge: Not quite so close that someone would throttle him, but close enough to feel the fingers around his neck. Growing up, we were the only teenagers who looked forward to spending weekends with their parents because we were always going some place exciting."

The best trips were the mapless journeys that included big fish, ample whiskey, and the echo of laughter.

When doctors diagnosed Jerry with cancer, he sold the Kingston Ranch and bought the Grand Banks. Instead of sailing off into a Mexican sunset, he found himself pitching and rolling in a hurricane. Wracked with pain, he stood at the helm for 10 hours and rode out the storm. He wasn't as afraid as he was excited.

That boat was a lot like my uncle: Too broad in the beam to call a thing of beauty, but hell for stout and without an ounce of quit.

He ran on empty most of his life and occasionally paid the price, but he was never far from a friend. He made them as he went along and leaves behind daughters, Lynda Fleming and Diane Mannschreck; son, Thomas Curtis; stepdaughter, Karen Vogt; stepson, Eric Grijalva; and little sister, Nancy Mathis. Even Jerry's former wife, Gwenn Curtis, remained his friend.

His family and friends will return to Kingston Ranch at 9 a.m. Saturday. There will be laughter, a few tears, and a wealth of stories.

"Dad could always live just beyond his means," Lynda says. "Whether he was making fifty dollars a week or fifty thousand a week, if he had it, he spent it. But he taught us all a lesson: If there's something that you want to do, you had better do it. You may not get a second chance."

He drank life to the lees, my uncle did, and made the most of every sunrise.

What most people call the experience of a lifetime was just another day in Jerry Curtis' wonderful life. ◆

Father's life a portrait of courage, principles, and caring

March 10, 1996

In a world ruled by celebrity, my father was anything but famous.

If you didn't know him well, you might believe he was just a simple working man whose words and deeds did not often make the news.

This story surely would have embarrassed him, but I have

to try to tell you a little about his life and let you in on a secret.

My father was a prince in painter's clothing, a selfless man in a self-centered world. As if to illustrate the fact, his name was Prince Lyle Smith Jr., but everyone called him Smitty or plain P.L.

His heart was anything but ordinary. It was strong as any marathoner's and beat only for his wife and six children. It stopped beating on Wednesday night after those keeping vigil had fallen safely asleep. He was 68.

Born in the desert, my father began working in a mining mill when he was 12. He took time off from work to join the Navy in World War II. When the war ended, he returned to the desert and the job.

Work defined my father's life. He worked too hard, cared too much, and died too soon. But presenting the fruits of his labors was one way he showed his love for his family. Teaching us to see with our hearts was another.

His craft was painting, his art the outdoors.

He could mix any color in the spectrum by sight, refinish the most care-worn furniture into something beautiful.

When we were children in Henderson, he made us bicycles out of junk parts and painted them as bright as anything from Sears & Roebuck. The Smiths might lack for money, but my father wanted to make sure his children always rode with their heads up.

He was not an educated man, but he believed in the rights of working people and tried to help. He was raised around Okies and walked with the ghost of Tom Joad.

That's how he became active in Painters Union Local 159. He recognized that organized labor was far from ideal, but he also believed the alternative was unacceptable for many.

His old friends will remember all the groceries he bought, all the Christmas presents he delivered, all the funerals he paid for, all the caskets he helped carry. My father, of course, never mentioned it.

He was at home in nature and moved through wild places with uncommon grace. He knew the names of plants, could call burros, songbirds, mule deer, and bighorn sheep. If I told you he could catch jackrabbits bare-handed would you believe me? Once near Pioche I saw him catch a red-tailed hawk that itself had just hunted a quail and had forgotten our presence. He let the nervous bird go, and we laughed as it flapped out of the county.

As a boy in Keeler, California, near Owens Lake, he spent days at a time in the desert with only his .22 and canteen. When he wasn't working, he lived like royalty in the Sierra Nevada. He fished in the creeks and lakes, carved whistles from willow branches, built fences for the Civilian Conservation Corps.

My father was an accomplished survivalist with no political agenda. He was that rare naturalist who felt no need to preach about conservation while in the wild for the same reason the devout do not chatter in church.

Although not a religious man, my father saw God in every sunrise and heard a sermon on every desert breeze.

He was not made for the city. Henderson was about our speed, but we moved to Las Vegas in 1968.

My father loved to jitterbug and drink whiskey, but for years he danced too little and drank too much. The day he stopped drinking was a proud moment for our family. He pretended not to notice, but he was proud, too.

When doctors told him he had throat cancer and lung disease a few months ago, no tears came to my father's eyes. He did not ask God for a miracle or wonder about the cruel vagaries of fate. He was a man and, by his definition, men did not show weakness in front of their families.

When he saw the worry cloud our eyes, he smiled and comforted us.

"It's no big thing," he said, his voice full of rasp. "But if I'd known this was going to happen, I would have quit smoking instead of drinking."

We laughed because he laughed, and that was the whole point. He knew the road he was on and approached his life's final hours the way he faced everything else. With quiet courage, and an eye on his family.

The secret is out now. My father was a prince disguised as a common painter. If only the world were so common and so kind.

Our family will hear his soothing voice on every desert breeze. ◆

Across the cyberspace universe, two sons find a father

April 27, 1997

I have this recurring dream. Sitting before the computer, my hands float over the keyboard. I press the right sequence of letters and numbers, somehow reach through cyberspace and begin to hear a distant voice. The voice of my father.

I type faster, and his baritone grows stronger. In moments, I am closer still as the keys blur and the codes send me through corridors stretching beyond the World Wide Web into something like real space.

In the dream, I hear my father's voice so clearly, but I always wake up before seeing more than his shadow trailing into the night. I never get to ask him questions about his life.

It has been more than a year since my father died of cancer, but after the dream his voice resonates in the predawn air as if he had just left the bedroom.

I recalled the dream recently after sitting and listening to Dave Lanson's story of finding his own father through the computer. Not the voice of a ghost, but a ghost come to life.

In 1964, Les Lanson left his wife, Mary Jo, and sons, Jim and Dave, in the Chicago suburb of Northlake. At the time, Jim was in high school. Dave was just four.

When the couple divorced, the father faded from his boys' lives. There would be no Cubs games, no playing catch, no holidays. It's not a unique story, but Les Lanson left his sons full of questions only he could answer.

Jim went into the Air Force. Dave finished school, entered

the Navy, and eventually became a copy editor at the *Review-Journal.*

Mary Jo worked much of the rest of her life to provide for her broken family. The father's name was rarely mentioned.

"At one time we had a Beaver Cleaver-type family," Dave says. "That changed when my dad left. My mom worked two and three jobs raising us in a single-parent home before it became the norm in society. I thought about him over the years. At times I felt cheated, but that's the way it was. My mom never bad-mouthed him. He was just gone."

Last summer, a year after Mary Jo died, Jim Lanson began wondering whatever became of his father. He logged onto the Internet, patched into a vast listing of the nation's published telephone numbers, and punched in his father's name.

As simple as that, a name, address, and phone number popped up. Les Lanson lived in Pasadena, Texas.

Then came the hard part. Talking on the phone to a total stranger.

"When I called, his wife answered," Dave says. "I said, 'Is this the Lester J. Lanson residence?' When she said it was, I said, 'I think I might be his son.'"

A 72-year-old retired repairman took the phone, and the connection was made. The conversation was difficult. Les Lanson's voiced cracked with emotion, but they agreed to talk again soon.

They spoke again at Christmas. After more conversations, they agreed to meet in the San Francisco Bay area for a family reunion of sorts. Nearly a lifetime had passed.

Last month, Les, Jim, and Dave spent three days together. Dave learned a few things about his father, including their shared talent for illustrating.

"I guess I got that from him," he says. "When I saw him, I knew that he had settled down and become a family man. He became everything I wish he would have been earlier."

Seeing his father brought back a flood of memories. Dave recalled pretending to shave while his father shaved and prepared for work. He remembered the face 30 years younger in a black-and-white world that no longer existed.

After nearly three decades, the sons of Les Lanson aren't bitter.

"We both kind of decided to put it in the past," Dave says. "I guess I'm more thankful that I have a parent who is still alive."

When Dave calls, he hears his father's voice across the miles and the lost years. But like he says, that's in the past. There's still some time left, and they plan to get together again, either in Texas or Las Vegas.

"I'd like to go there and visit," Dave says. "I'd like to go to a ball game with him. It's the old cliché, father-son thing."

They have plenty of catching up to do.

Will cyberspace open passageways leading to the past, then beckon us to follow?

The answer is clear for Dave Lanson and the thousands of people who reconnect with friends and family members each year through the computer.

As for me, the question is answered where the dream meets the day.

A father's voice is fleeting, but worth pursuing. ◆

Bachelors face choice: down the aisle or into the ground

October 18, 1990

News Item: Being single can be deadly, according to a national study that says unmarried, middle-aged men are twice as likely to die as those who have spouses.

It's official. The bachelor's life is hazardous to your health.

Apparently, it took card-carrying university professionals to discover that a guy who lives on a diet of beer and cotto salami sandwiches risks an early demise.

Forget stripping homosexual photographers of their national endowment grants. Let's find the agency that funded this study and reduce it to rubble.

But perhaps I'm too insensitive. While nothing states the obvious like a university study, upon further inquiry the survey appears to have plenty of merit.

According to the University of California at San Francisco study, 23 percent of men age 45 to 54 who lived without a spouse died within 10 years. Only 11 percent of married men checked out in that time, apparently of boredom. That truly is an astounding difference.

Perhaps wedded males live longer because being married soothes their spirits, the study suggests. The heart is a delicate thing and needs a woman's touch. Married men lead more stable lives. They eat more reasonably, drink to less excess, and get more rest.

Or, perhaps unmarried men age 45 to 54 die because they tend to chase unmarried women age 18 to 25. After all, the heart is a delicate thing.

Despite its shortcomings, the study codifies what women have known throughout history:

Men are basically miserable creatures whose chief interests are limited to the bedroom, the refrigerator, and the six-pack. As they age, the bedroom is replaced by the television or, in the case of the upper-middle-class male, the golf course.

An exception to the Miserable Male rule is the phenomenon known as the Sensitive Male, or the Phil Donahue Male. Beware the Sensitive Male. He's not only miserable; he's a liar, too.

Some men are just too miserable to live with women. If a man is too miserable to live with a woman, then he may be too miserable to live, period.

Why are men this way?

Men defy Darwin's evolutionary expositions. They simply have not evolved since Cave Man Days. Oh, they've changed their underwear and put on a clean shirt. But they haven't evolved.

In their funny way, women continue to evolve. Why, just look at Madonna and Martina Navratilova.

But men?

Ugh.

After millions of years of fine-tuning our temples in the Evolution Fitness Center, we still get a kick out of seeing how loud we can belch. Men find all sorts of bodily functions fascinating.

Overall, women are cleaner, smarter, and a helluva lot better-looking than men.

Married men attempt to evolve, but only under duress and the threat of losing one of the big three—sex, food, or beer. It's either pretend to be more advanced or face the consequences of living with a human air-raid siren, also known as the whining spouse. And that's enough to kill at least 11 percent of married males age 45 to 54.

Motivated by the same primal urges that rule their single counterparts, married men learn to pick up their socks, replace the toilet seat to its full upright and locked position, and belch in the garage.

Bachelors, conversely, need not put on such airs. Until a woman comes over to their apartment, of course. Then they fall right into line.

Away from woman's watchful eye, bachelors don't eat right, don't sleep right, drink too much, and don't pick up after themselves.

In a rare moment, the single man will admit this universal truth: Man does not live on furry bread products and Velveeta alone. You gotta have beer to wash it down.

Bachelors know long-term exposure to fermenting socks is carcinogenic, but it's a risk they take.

Bachelors know milk as thick as Play-Doh is still functional. Just spoon it on to your cereal as part of your balanced breakfast.

In all, bachelors know they are going to die young. But, by God, just try to save them and see what you get—myriad miserable males.

As a bachelor since my early years, I feel pretty good. But in

a sensitive moment, I know that university study is accurate.
If men don't get married they will die.
Smiling. ◆

Selective deafness: 'til deaf do us part

August 9, 1991

A couple of friends recently were married.

Moments after the rice hit the pavement, I began to worry about their chances at staying that way. After all, statistics show one in every two marriages ends in divorce. The other usually ends in gunfire.

Fortunately, the newlyweds returned from their honeymoon still talking. I lost my bet, but something inside was gratified.

In celebration, I offered a passel of advice on how to remain happily married. They immediately ignored the offer and since have changed their phone number.

You may ask the same question they uttered: "You're single, live alone, and are not particularly bright. What the hell do you know about marriage?"

Well, I've never shot myself in the foot, either, but I'll bet it's not as pleasant as it looks. The fact is, I write about a lot of acts in which I've had only limited participation: murder, community service, the educational process. The list goes on and on.

After years of exhaustive research, I've arrived at a sound theory on the root causes of matrimonial harmony.

Stretching back to the dawn of time, women have endured all manner of abuses from their biblical soulmates and biological cellmates. For the most part, this phenomenon can be traced to the fact that, while Cro-Magnon man may have been as dumb as dirt, he did not allow Cro-Magnon woman anywhere near the wooden clubs and stone axes. If he had, today men would be wearing the high heels and push-up bras. This

ancient need to keep weapons away from women has mani-
fested in the male urge to carry golf clubs, but that is another
story.

Anyway, woman somehow has managed to endure man's
endearing qualities without doing the one-way, lemmings-to-
the-sea migration. By endearing, I mean the really cute things
unique to men: like the in-depth discussion of bodily functions
and their impact on global warming. Neat earthy stuff like that.

The fact is, the female memory is faulty. Research indicates
male hearing is equally flawed. Overall, the combination is nothing short of a miracle. Between poor memory and poorer hearing, some marriages survive decades.

That men don't hear as well as women is not because they
spend eight hours a day using jackhammers. From lawyers to
laborers, the effect is the same.

Scientists have found that the degree of auditory dysfunc-
tion is directly related to the number of years the male has been
married. This is a fact, and you can look it up in my new book,
"'Til Deaf Do Us Part: The Miracle of Male Hearing Loss."

Forget what you've heard about nasty canal wax and un-
sightly ear hair. Those explanations fall short of the truth now
revealed. The miracle emerges slowly but progresses with each
anniversary. The longer a couple stays married, the more
strained the male's hearing becomes.

This is one secret to a happy marriage.

My father, for instance, has been married to my mother off
and on for more than 40 years. They get along as well as most
couples their age and experience.

You know, like Ali and Frazier.

When it comes to my mother's occasional psychotic rantings,
my father is as deaf as the proverbial post. The louder she gets,
the less he hears. By the time she pulls out a bullhorn for emphasis, he is blissfully and absolutely deaf.

You could crash cymbals inches from his head and he would
fail to hear them.

Cymbals, nothing. You could crash Buicks.

His face goes through a few contortions, but otherwise he

shows no outward signs of discomfort. His eyebrows knit, his eyes cross slightly, and he gets up to pour another cup of coffee.

Male deafness.

It's one of nature's wonders.

In time, the conversation cools. As the talk becomes calmer, his hearing slowly returns. By the time the subject has changed to something tame, like politics in the Middle East, he can almost hear the phone ring.

Sure, he has that slight facial tick, but that can be blamed on the caffeine.

In the interest of science, I have endeavored to unravel the mysteries of marital bliss from my mother's unique perspective. The secret she has learned no doubt would be beneficial to others, or so I surmised.

But, for the life of her, she can't remember any. ◆

UPDATE: Then it was my turn. Patricia Goldberg and I married May 21, 1994.

A great day finally arrives for Amelia's appreciative parents

February 2, 1997

If you didn't know better, you might think it's just another day at Family Court.

The half-bored bailiff senses something in the air, something like spring. A trip to Family Court does not normally generate smiles and salutations. But today is different. The bailiff greets my wife, Tricia, and me with a grin and can't help smiling at our Amelia wrapped in my arms. Everyone loves my little girl. She is a sweet, 20-pound bundle of pure sunshine.

Today, Amelia becomes ours forever.

Today, a judge will decide that our 10-month-old adopted daughter is officially and irrevocably ours. Ours in name, ours in law. Ours forever. Ours like the moon and stars.

She had been ours in spirit from the moment we met her birth mother, a bright, beautiful young woman who immediately knew that we were the right people to care for the life she accidentally had made. But when it comes to adoption, 10 months is like 100 years. A lot can happen, and most of it's bad.

What others could not know was the agonizing longing childless couples go through as they travel through the years hearing the voices of other people's children. Others could not appreciate the surgeries Tricia had endured and the painful questions that remain unanswered when couples fail to produce offspring.

We knew we were taking a chance when we decided to adopt, but no one enters into the process without feeling a fair amount of desperation. The potential for heartbreak was nothing compared to the prospect of a gray life without a child. I know plenty of couples who are delighted not to have kids, and that's good for them, but some people are meant to have children.

In late November, we sat in Judge Steve Jones' courtroom and listened as two dozen couples were divorced in rapid succession. Families were dissolved in an instant, and Tricia and I held hands and were awed by the awful matter-of-factness of it all.

Then it was our turn. We had come to have the rights of the biological parents terminated and entered the court fretting over everything that might go wrong. Instead, everything went right. The judge looked only a little puzzled when the couple sitting before him began crying like children.

Then we waited until our attorney, John Hunt, decided it was time to move forward. Our state caseworker, Barbara Draper, had finished her background check, and we counted the hours as we raised the baby in our home.

Today is the day.

We arrive early for court. We remember the baby but forget the cameras we set aside at home to capture this moment. As if in a thousand years we might forget.

Other couples are there. We share smiles and nods of understanding, but we keep to ourselves. So close to our goal, no one is too confident. It is as if we might accidentally break the delicate bond that tethers us to our children.

Amelia has smiles for everyone. And a message for me. "Dada," she says, resting in my arms. "Dada, dada, dada." It is the greatest word I've ever heard.

Now it's time to see the judge.

In his chambers, Judge Gary Redmon calmly greets us. Recalling those divorce actions and all the calls I've received from parents clawing and scratching for possession of their children, I do not envy the judge his job. At Family Court, this is one of the few instances in which a judge makes a decision guaranteed to please everyone in the room.

The adoption process, a culmination of months of hoping for the best and worrying about the worst, is over in a few moments. The judge congratulates us, smiles at Amelia, comments on how beautiful she is. We beam as proud parents will.

Through eyes blurry with tears, I make out the part of the document that reads, "Now, therefore, it is ordered, adjudged and decreed that the said minor child is hereby declared to be adopted by Petitioners, Patricia Smith and John L. Smith, that said minor child shall henceforth be regarded and treated as Petitioner's natural child and have all the lawful rights as their own child, including the rights of support, protection and inheritance..."

I hold the adoption decree like a deed to the future itself. Years of anguish melt away in the warmth of this moment. Amelia is ours for good, ours forever, ours like the moon and stars.

"Mama," our girl says, reaching out her small hand to touch Tricia's cheek.

"Yes," my wife says, her eyes wet with joy. "It's me, mama." ◆

Charismatic bear holds one big part of a little girl's heart

August 3, 1997

It started in the middle of the night with a sharp stabbing pain in my ribs. I rolled over, awoke with an anguished cry in the dark.

Cardiac?

Gall bladder?

Bad tuna casserole?

Nothing so tame.

It was Piglet. Hard plastic and sharp as a Ninja throwing star. One of the Bear's buddies.

We're talking Pooh, Winnie T.

I took it as a sign, uttered something unprintable, and hurled the offending swine into the night. Piglet landed ears up. I know this because I stepped on it on the way to the bathroom.

It was then my wife, Tricia, and I realized that our sweet, wonderful, priceless daughter, Amelia, had been abducted by the worldwide Pooh Cult.

Forget Scientology. This Pooh guy is everywhere. With chapters in every store in America, he's the Reverend Sun Yung Pooh.

He is such a tubby-little-cubby-all-stuffed-with-fluff type of fellow that he's sure to deceive casual observers. "Bear of very little brain," indeed. He fooled me at first, but no more.

Pooh crept into my daughter's life subtly, the way they all do, the little masher. First it was a harmless stuffed Pooh with a musical honey pot. Kind of sweet, you know? Then it was the official Pooh cup, spoon, and bowl set. And the Pooh bib, of course. Those I could live with.

But add to that the Poohjamas, bed sheets, and Pooh house with wicked plastic friends (batteries not included), and even I began to spot a pattern. Our little girl was showing the early signs of addiction: All Pooh, all the time.

"The first step is to admit you are powerless to control this Pooh," I told Amelia.

"Oh, bother," her eyes said.

"It's a phase," my wife said. "She'll grow out of it."

"I don't know," I replied. "It's Pooh today, head-banging rock music tomorrow. By the end of the week she'll want credit cards and the keys to the Sentra."

For us the turning point came when we made the mistake of letting her watch the cult's indoctrination video, "Winnie the Pooh and the Honey Tree."

"Harmless viewing," family members said. "She'll love it," so-called friends assured us.

One sitting and our little girl was lost to us. At least temporarily. She stared transfixed, hanging on every syllable and song. When the end credits appeared on the screen, she began to chant, "Pooh, Pooh, Pooh." This Pooh is her Mick Jagger, her Sandy Koufax, her Mahatma Gandhi.

My wife and I stared at each other, baffled by the silly seduction that takes place time after time in the Hundred-Acre Wood. Amelia only became more enamored with each viewing.

"Pooh, Pooh, Pooh," she cried. "Pooh, Pooh, Pooh."

In our home, we dare not speak the name.

One rhetorical misstep and her mantra echoes through the house. She halts her freestyle Crayola wall mural, which I must say shows genuine artistic promise, and marches like a midget zombie toward the television.

"Pooh, Pooh, Pooh," she calls.

Papa? He's passé. Mama? A mere memory.

Pooh has taken control.

So for us, it's icksnay on the oohpay. We have developed code words for Mr. You Know Who. He is "The Bear," "Ursa Cartoonae," and the "Tubby Little Cubby Pain in the Patoot."

Recently, the Pooh problem grew acute when my wife brought home a potty chair.

Now, Amelia is an apprentice potty trainer with real potential. Her trouble is semantical, I suspect. After all, when we say "poo," she hears "Pooh" and immediately goes into a trance that would impress the Mummy.

Her mantra never wavers: "Pooh, Pooh, Pooh."

"No, honey," I said. "Not Pooh. Poo. Put poo in the toilet."

Amelia looked askance, shrugged, and ambled off across the room.

She returned a minute later with her stuffed Winnie under one arm, grinned at me, and jammed the willy-nilly silly old bear head-first into the potty.

That's my girl.

When I tuck her in at night, struck silent by her sweet perfection, I know I am a father of very little brain who frets over the smallest things. The twinge I feel is her presence in my heart. I say a prayer for her, for our family.

My wife and I spent years hoping for a child. Now that we have Amelia, we must prepare, day by day, to give her back to the world. That thought humbles me, and I am overwhelmed by the assignment. But I know it's better to just live and do your best than sweat the possibilities.

Eventually, I know this Pooh thing will pass.

To be honest, it's that subversive Barney who really has me worried. ◆

Daughter's sunshiny smiles make Father's Day a formality

June 21, 1998

I stand in the doorway after a day bad enough to depress Dostoyevsky, feeling lower than the welcome mat I'm standing on, and then I see you.

Two feet high with a head full of blond curls, you hear the door open and take off like a runaway pony across the living room. You call my name, and I swear I am 10 years younger and nothing on Earth matters more than this moment.

You throw your arms around my knees and nearly knock me to the floor, for I have become feather-light and dizzy. I am a palooka of putty in your hands. I hug you tight, smell your hair like hyacinth, hear you giggle at my tickle, and am warmed by your smile.

The soundtrack to this reverie never varies.

"You are my sunshine, my only sunshine," I hear as the bad day melts away.

Right now I am not the half-wit wordsmith, but the king of the whole wonderful world. I have won the lottery and an Olympic gold medal, the Triple Crown, and the World Series. All we lack is confetti for our ticker-tape parade for two.

Daughter Amelia, you are my sunshine, my heart's needle, my Emmy, Oscar, and Nobel Prize.

Until you came along, Father's Day was something my dad enjoyed. But now I have learned his secret: Every day is Father's Day when your daughter smiles at you.

It's funny, really, but I didn't know what I was missing all these years. I go along, stumbling through life, thinking I'm doing something important.

Then you came along.

Now you're two. Terribly, wonderfully, irrepressibly two.

Your mother and I can't remember how we got along without you. Or, frankly, what a quiet, debris-free meal at home felt like.

It wouldn't be supper without a cherry tomato bounding across the dinner table like a ball through the infield. I make the backhand stab, flip to Mom's napkin and complete the double play. Occasionally, a morsel reaches the floor, where Sparky gobbles it up like a canine Ozzie Smith.

But that's my girl. In a league of her own.

Nothing is the same since you joined the team. Not meals, not sleep, not the furniture or the wardrobe.

Every shirt I own is stained. Fortunately, I'm a journalist so no one notices. I wear each mark the way a general wears his medals.

Swinging in the park is fun again. Digging in the sand is an adventure rivaling anything involving Indiana Jones. A few scoops and we have created mountains and kingdoms and socks full of grit.

Lying on our backs gawking at the clouds, I can feel myself

attached to the planet. And I know why.

The reason fidgets next to me like a tangle of kittens and string. You are Einstein's theory personified: Energy equals you. As if to illustrate the point, you gather your footing and take off giggling across the grass. Your laughter is a song and the daylight dances in your hair.

"You are my sunshine, my only sunshine..."

At home, you help your mother in the kitchen like a whirlwind assists a pile of leaves. It takes an hour to recover, but Mom, who does so much work and gets so little credit, never complains. Not even when she discovers days-old cookie dough and enough crackers to feed all the birds in town wedged into the couch cushions.

Yardwork is the best it's ever been now that you're my assistant. You've pulled the heads off the tulips and given the bouquet to Mom.

It's all right. I say tulips are overrated. They'll return next year.

Watering is a celebration, the Mardi Gras with a garden hose. Occasionally, the grass gets wet. The purple perennials get drunk as sailors as a sea washes over them.

You save the best dousing for yourself. When I'm not looking, you drench yourself and laugh at my expression as the water fills your shoes.

You, my daughter, are 100 percent: In all our time together, you've never missed a puddle.

My father once told me that his children and his wife were the joys in his life. At the end of the day, he said, they were all that mattered. Smug as a vicar, I nodded my head but had no clue as to what he was saying.

Now I do.

So forget the bad ties. Forget the barbecue gadgets, power tools, and greeting cards. For Father's Day, I don't want tickets to the ballgame or a bottle of scotch.

The greatest gift a man could ever receive greets me at the door each night with a hug strong enough to make the world a better place and a laugh that makes time stand still.

You are my sunshine, sweet Amelia.
Every day is Father's Day now that I have you. ◆

About Huntington Press

Huntington Press is a Las Vegas-based book publisher. To receive a copy of the Huntington Press catalog, call 1-800-244-2224 or write to the address below.

Huntington Press
3687 South Procyon Avenue
Las Vegas, Nevada 89103
(702) 252-0655 • fax: (702) 252-0675
email: books@huntingtonpress.com